SIGNS OF THE STARS

FREDRICK DAVIES
SIGNS OF THE STARS

PRENTICE HALL PRESS ★ NEW YORK

Photo Credits

Bob Guccione (page 153), courtesy of Bob Guccione. Diana Ross (page 5), photo by Barry Landau. All other photographs provided by the following: Memory Shop, Movie Star News, Star Power News Service, Travel and Theatre Shoppe, Wide World Photos.

Copyright © 1987 by Fredrick Davies
All rights reserved, including the right of reproduction
in whole or in part in any form.

Published by Prentice Hall Press
A Division of Simon & Schuster, Inc.
Gulf + Western Building
One Gulf + Western Plaza
New York, NY 10023

PRENTICE HALL PRESS is a trademark of Simon & Schuster, Inc.

Library of Congress Cataloging-in-Publication Data

Davies, Fredrick.
Signs of the stars.

Includes index.
1. Horoscopes. 2. Celebrities. I. Title.
BF1728.2.C44D38 1987   133.5'48   86-43175
ISBN 0-13-842808-5

Manufactured in the United States of America

10 9 8 7 6 5 4 3 2 1

First Edition

I DEDICATE THIS BOOK TO:

Cappy Badrutt Hand (Cancer), who—through her great inner and outer beauty and her thorough understanding of astrology—opened up to me the intimate world of the rich and famous in Paris, London, New York, Beverly Hills, and St. Moritz.

Carroll Righter (Aquarius), my inspired astrological teacher and dear friend, whose great wisdom, knowledge, and sense of humor have guided many of Hollywood's major stars through their careers.

Rolla Nordic (Sagittarius), the Queen of the Tarot, whose profound knowledge and teachings triggered the sleeping psychic spirit within me.

Casper Baker Gary (Aries), my longtime friend and business partner, whose immeasurable knowledge of historical, political, and show business facts helped me in my research.

Morna Murphy Martell (Pisces), who directed and coauthored with me the play *The Great Truman Capote* and has always, over the years, kept me in touch with my show business roots.

Ivy Rosina Davies (Gemini), my mother, who always encouraged and never inhibited my childhood dreams and fantasies, and Ernest Davies (Taurus), my late father, a Fleet Street printer and former publisher, who at the time of my birth was printing a book on astrology and who bought me my first printing press when I was 10.

And to my brother, Malcolm John Davies, and my aunt, Evelyn Harvey (both Capricorns), who have always been supportive, enthusiastic, helpful, and loving in looking after my personal and professional life, while I have traveled around the world.

SPECIAL THANKS TO:

My agents Gene Winick of McIntosh and Otis, Inc., and Suzanne Lorenzo for their professional expertise and 100 percent enthusiasm.

Mark Ricci of the Memory Shop, Kazuko Hillyer of the Travel and Theatre Shoppe, The British Information Services (NYC), Buckingham Palace Press Office, Earl Blackwell's Celebrity Service, publicist Barry Landau of Barrington Landau Public Relations, Star Power News Service, Associated Press Wide World Photo Library, and the Hollywood Reporter, for photographs and biographical research.

Joey Adams, Cindy Adams of the *New York Post,* Candy Jones, Regis Philbin, Kathie Lee Johnson Gifford, Liz Smith of the *Daily News,* Oprah Winfrey, Bernice Perry, Michael D. Beinner, Jacqueline Richardson, Marriet Olguin, Ralph Martell, Lee Merrin, Bruce Merrin, Mary Arnold, Debbie Arnold, Joanne Carson, Chuck Holden, Craig Blair, Lewis Anton, Barbara Abbott, Christine Davies, Tammy Kennedy Wolfe, Tony Morris, Gloria Colbert, Jeanie Sims Antony Clavet, Leo Shull, and so many others who have created this astrological world for me.

And most important, my editor, Sarah Montague, who added her own touch of class to the book, assuring that the rich and the famous also remained chic.

Contents

Introduction   xi

ARIES

Child of the Zodiac (March 21–April 19)   1

Whiz Kids and Human Dynamos (March 21–March 31)   3
    Elton John, Dr. Frank Field, Warren Beatty, *Diana Ross*

Dynamic Entertainers (April 1–April 10)   7
    Marlon Brando, Eddie Murphy, *Debbie Reynolds*

Philanthropic Magicians (April 11–April 19)   12
    Peter Ustinov, Olivia Hussey, Tim Curry, *Robert Stigwood*

TAURUS

Banker of the Zodiac (April 20–May 21)   17

Financial Architects and Comptrollers (April 20–April 30)   19
    Ryan O'Neal, Queen Elizabeth II, Jack Nicholson, *Shirley MacLaine*

Philosophical Street Singers (May 1–May 10)   23
    Paige Rense, Lady Rothermere, Donovan, *Candice Bergen*

Disco Spinners and Weavers (May 11–May 21)   27
    Michael Fish, Stevie Wonder, *Cher*

GEMINI

Orator of the Zodiac (May 22–June 21)   33

Champagne Conversationalists (May 22–May 30)   36
    Barbara Parkins, Bruce Weitz, Beverly Sills, Allan Carr, Bob Hope, *Joan Collins*

Beautiful Nightingales (May 31–June 10)   42
    Tom Jones, Joan Rivers, Michael J. Fox, *Brooke Shields*

Scientific Heralds (June 11–June 21)   46
    Grace Jones, Donald Trump, *Paul McCartney*

CONTENTS
viii

CANCER

Mother of the Zodiac (June 22–July 22) — **51**

Lamplighters of Darkness (June 22–July 1) — **53**
  Meryl Streep; *Diana, Princess of Wales*

Prophets of the Times (July 2–July 11) — **58**
  Merv Griffin, Arthur Ashe, *Sylvester Stallone*

Inspirational Faith Healers (July 12–July 22) — **62**
  Bill Cosby, Phyllis Diller, Diahann Carroll, *Diana Rigg*

LEO

Royal Sign of the Zodiac (July 23–August 22) — **67**

Sun Kings and Queens (July 23–August 1) — **70**
  Mick Jagger, Susan George, Geoffrey Holder, Tom Wilson, Giancarlo Giannini, *Jacqueline Kennedy Onassis*

Glorious Travelers and Philosophers (August 2–August 11) — **76**
  Neil Armstrong, Lucille Ball, *Dustin Hoffman*

Triumphant Warriors (August 12–August 22) — **80**
  Princess Anne, Madonna and Sean Penn, Robert De Niro, *Robert Redford*

VIRGO

Teacher of the Zodiac (August 23–September 22) — **85**

Traveling Professors (August 23–September 1) — **87**
  Sir Richard Attenborough, Richard Gere, Michael Jackson, *Lily Tomlin*

Disciplined Workers and Timekeepers (September 2–September 11) — **92**
  Valerie Perrine, Arnold Palmer, *Raquel Welch*

Artistic Analysts (September 12–September 22) — **96**
  Greta Garbo, Twiggy (Lesley Hornby), Larry Hagman, *Lauren Bacall*

LIBRA

Artisan of the Zodiac (September 23–October 22) — **101**

Cultural Mediators (September 23–October 1) — **104**
  Bruce Springsteen, Christopher Reeve, President Jimmy Carter, *Olivia Newton John*

Friendly Reporters (October 2–October 11) — **109**
  Susan Sarandon, Sigourney Weaver, Luciano Pavarotti, *Rona Barrett*

Romantic Gumshoes (October 12–October 22) — **115**
  Roger Moore, Angela Lansbury, Johnny Carson, *Carrie Fisher*

CONTENTS

SCORPIO

Detective of the Zodiac (October 23–November 22) — **121**

Patriotic Sorcerers (October 23–November 2) — **124**
  Helen Reddy, Henry Winkler, Dan Rather, *Burt Lancaster*

Seductive Vigilantes and Watchdogs (November 3–November 12) — **129**
  Charles Bronson, Kate Capshaw, *Sally Field*

Inquisitive Humanitarians (November 13–November 22) — **133**
  Charles, Prince of Wales; Dick Cavett; Ted Turner; *Goldie Hawn*

SAGITTARIUS

Philosopher of the Zodiac (November 23–December 22) — **139**

Gambling Politicians (November 23–December 2) — **142**
  David Merrick, Caroline Kennedy Schlossberg, Richard Pryor, *Woody Allen*

Humorous Missionaries (December 3–December 12) — **147**
  Ellen Burstyn, Teri Garr, *Frank Sinatra*

Fighters and Lovers (December 13–December 22) — **151**
  Don Johnson, Liv Ullman, Jane Fonda, *Bob Guccione*

CAPRICORN

Disciplinarian of the Zodiac (December 23–January 19) — **155**

Humble Organizers (December 23–January 1) — **158**
  Régine, John Denver, *Mary Tyler Moore*

Stubborn Politicians (January 2–January 10) — **162**
  Joey Adams, David Bowie, *Jose Ferrer*

Idealistic Revolutionaries (January 11–January 19) — **166**
  Robert Stack, Patricia Neal, *Muhammad Ali*

AQUARIUS

Humanitarian of the Zodiac (January 20–February 18) — **173**

Universal Reformers (January 20–January 29) — **175**
  Mikhail Baryshnikov, Tom Selleck, *Eartha Kitt*

Metaphysical Pioneers (January 30–February 9) — **179**
  President Ronald Reagan, Carroll Righter, *Mia Farrow*

Radiant Humanitarians and Trendsetters (February 10–February 18) — **184**
  Marisa Berenson, Yoko Ono, Matt Dillon, *John Travolta*

CONTENTS
x

PISCES

Conscience of the Zodiac (February 19–March 20) **189**

Romantic Martyrs and Inspirational Poets (February 19–February 29) **193**
  Prince Andrew, Duke of York; Gloria Vanderbilt; *Elizabeth Taylor*

Home Entertainers (March 1–March 10) **196**
  Harry Belafonte, Glenda Jackson, *Lynn Redgrave*

Born-Again Mystics (March 11–March 20) **200**
  George Plimpton, Rupert Murdoch, *Liza Minnelli*

Interpreting a Horoscope Chart **205**

Introduction

ASTROLOGER TO THE RICH AND FAMOUS

The "rich and famous" are special people, neither better nor worse than the average, but because they live in the limelight they glow with an aura that attracts others to them. Many of them are born during the New Moon or Full Moon, a certain sign of potential stardom or luck in life; but others have very ordinary, nondescript horoscope charts that give no hint of their star status. If there is one common denominator that almost all luminaries share, it is the ability to make the most of every aspect of their horoscope charts and of the ups and downs in their lives. They are the people who push where their planetary strengths lie and disregard their weaknesses or fight to overcome them should they prove to be major obstacles in the climb up the ladder of success. Although luck favors these people in many instances, their success results more from the fact that they are in tune with themselves than from their merely trusting to fate, and this is something anyone can learn.

Instead of allowing other people to change them or criticize their personalities, talents, or wealth, they show others that they really love themselves first, with all their flaws, and from that point they seduce other people to love them too. No matter how eccentric, flamboyant, bad tempered, or violent some of them appear to be in public, they still attract their fans and supporters. Others—who appear to be sweet, charitable, and willing to do anything to please their loved ones, fans, and the public—are still very strong willed when it comes to directing their lives. They know where they are going—sink or swim—and by being proud of themselves and understanding their own idiosyncrasies, they are able to pursue their goals resolutely. Energy of this kind creates its own special tide, and stars usually carry family, friends, and business associates—like ducklings possessively chasing a duck—in their wake.

Some celebrities have made a practice of using their tempers to attract publicity. Frank Sinatra and Sean Penn seem to enjoy their attacks on journalists and photographers; they can use that side of themselves to get the attention they feel they need or show their contempt for those in whose hands they might become putty without some control over input. Certain celebrities, like Greta Garbo and Howard Hughes, have deliberately become hermits, which only added more mystique to their magic.

To be successful, let alone famous, it helps to have a one-track mind, whether it reflects a determination to be Number One on the Hit Parade, like Michael Jackson or Lionel Richie; to own the Empire State Building, like Harry Helmsley—one of the greatest real-estate czars in the United States; to paint an award-winning landscape; to write a best-selling novel; or perhaps just to make a million dollars. *Knowing what you want* is the first step to becoming rich or famous.

Being rich doesn't ensure becoming famous, nor does fame guarantee riches—some people are simply famous personalities. But the two groups rely very much on one another. As in the days of Pope Julius II—who financed Michelangelo's painting of the Sistine Chapel—modern artists, musicians, actors, and writers seek the rich to sponsor their creative works, and so have Broadway angels been responsible for the making of many great performers, composers, and lyricists.

Similarly, in many cases, the well born and wealthy, whose lives could easily become a boring social round, or businesspeople, who could easily be obliterated by financial details, surround themselves with the creative people who are currently making headlines in fashion, movies, music, or publishing. Not that their everyday money-making activities should be considered mundane—after all, there is a certain amount of thrill seeking involved in making a few million dollars on the foreign exchange, selling a family estate, or winning a legal battle over a legacy. But somehow it doesn't mean as much as creating a "work of art," and if one doesn't have the talent to do that oneself but does have the money, then one helps to influence the trends by buying paintings and sculpture, by financing theatrical or musical presentations, or by inviting certain rising stars to well-publicized parties.

I will admit that there is an excitement to life when famous people seek you out, invite you to their homes, and include you in their dinner parties and other social events. The former "beautiful people"—a term that tends to imply fast and trendy—who have now matured into the more-established "rich and famous" group really *are* beautiful, and their life-styles are exciting and elegant beyond belief. However, I have never let my awe and admiration of any star stand in the way of an honest reading or horoscope chart. I have made predictions about many stars that they might not have agreed with at the time, but they have later admitted that what I saw in their horoscope charts was correct.

I am not a doomsday prophet; I also do not consider myself a gossip, and my clients appreciate the fact that their private lives are kept secret by me.

The secrets I reveal in this book are those that I deem not unkind to tell and that I hope will help guide the lives and fortunes of those born under the same astrological signs as the famous individuals concerned.

The stories will inspire, give support, and entertain. But the deep, dark secrets I have shared on many a warm afternoon on a patio in Beverly Hills or on those cold winter nights overlooking Manhattan from a wraparound penthouse on Park Avenue—they will have to stay locked in my files, known only to myself and the stars involved.

My life now revolves in circles of twelve, according to the twelve signs of the zodiac, so I will talk of my experiences with the stars in terms of these magical "star signs." There are my Aries people: energetic, impulsive, and compassionate; the Taurus crowd: loyal, gentle, and self-reliant; my wonderful Geminis: witty, affectionate, and idealistic; the Cancer people: nurturing, homeloving, and tenacious; my dazzling Leos: flamboyant, loving, and entertaining; my Virgo brothers and sisters: analytical, modest, and scholarly; the Libra beauties: agreeable, refined, and diplomatic; my dynamic Scorpios: ambitious, secretive, and philanthropic; the optimistic Sagittarians: humorous, outspoken, and freedom loving; those steady Capricorns: determined, dignified, and helpful; my Aquarian friends: curious, creative, and intuitive; and, last but never least, my beloved Pisceans: inspirational, honest, and hard working.

I dedicate my book to all those star signs and star persons who haunt my days and dazzle my nights.

YOU AND THE STARS

No two people are alike, and no two people born under the same zodiac sign are alike. Moreover, each of the twelve signs of the zodiac can be divided into three groups, each with a definite personality of its own.

As each sign covers approximately thirty days, each of these groups encompasses a decanate, or a ten-day period of approximately ten degrees of the zodiac circle, and I have given each of these groupings a special name describing its basic nature and character.

Most of us have heard of the "three faces of Eve," who—in the same physical body—expressed three totally different personalities that had very little in common except the bond of her real self. It is often like that in astrological readings of people who, though born under the same sign and possessing some physical similarities, reveal that they are very different from each other in many ways. The gap can be especially great between people born early and late in a sign, but though people born close together may have manifest similarities, they, too, can be very disparate.

Sun sign astrology, which has made horoscopes fashionable in the popular press and magazines throughout the world, has given the unfortunate impression that the total population of the world can be pigeonholed into twelve neat groups and that these twelve groups will behave, work, and love in the same predictable manner.

To really understand an individual's character and potential in life, one must examine the total horoscope (the map of the sky) as seen at the exact moment and exact location of his or her birth. The planets take 25,000 years to return to an exact combination and location, so everyone born varies from day to day, year to year—even minute to minute—and has a very different chart and a totally different life-style. A good example is twins born within minutes of each other; while some researchers have shown that there are many "coincidences"—similar accidents on the same day, marriages or promotions on the same date, and illnesses and talents—others have demonstrated that socioeconomic factors, accidents, and their own natures will lead other sets of twins to lead totally different lives—one perhaps developing the more positive and successful traits of a sign and the other showing only its negative or difficult traits.

In the case of the celebrated and successful, the different degrees of the zodiac can determine the nature of their ambitions and the paths they choose to fulfill them, as well as aspects of their personalities and personal lives that impinge on their public luster.

Examining a total chart involves several steps. The first is determining the correct sign of the zodiac; then comes considering the placement of the Sun, Moon, Mercury, Venus, Mars, Jupiter, Saturn, Uranus, Neptune, and Pluto and the Ascendant, the Nodes, and the Part of Fortune, as well as the angles of the houses and the mathematical variations possible for each. Last, one considers which of the three decanates the sun falls in, in order to make the greatest possible distinction of character.

Each zodiac sign is divided into three astrological groups reflecting the range of that sign's temperament and talents.

For each division I have given a celebrity chart and discussed in detail that person's life and character—character attributes and flaws, work and how it has brought fame and fortune, and love and sexual attitudes—all the things that make up not only the famous but the rest of us as well. In addition, each section refers to other stars who share that designation and its traits. By comparing yourself to those who share your sign and decanates, discovering the many ways in which your chart coincides with theirs, and seeing what they did to maximize their potential, you, too, can gain tips on how to become "rich and famous." For many of these stars, success meant hard work and life was not always easy, but most say that it was their trials and tribulations—the very obstacles and restrictions they encountered—that made them determined not to let fate play tricks on them. They took their lives and "fates" into their own hands and created their own destinies. I have shared those destinies through this book—now it's your turn.

Note: In most cases, the birth data for each star will consist of date, year, time, and place. Partial birth data is given when complete information was either unavailable or confidential.

ARIES
Child of the Zodiac

SUN IN ARIES, RULED BY MARS
March 21 – April 19

There's no disguising the fiery and aggressive enthusiasm of Aries—ruled by the exciting and warlike planet Mars, fighting life's battles, and giving energy to less vital signs of the zodiac. The dominating qualities of this martial god give dynamism, vitality, and childlike wonder and faith to every ideal and project that those born under this sign lend their attention to (even for a moment), yet this same power can cause untold anxiety, nervousness, and worry. In a flash, a positive, controlled group of precision workers can turn into a bloodied, battle-worn army embarked on a course of action that can only end in annihilation.

On the plus side, Aries people are contagiously enthusiastic and witty. Their conversation will keep the most restless child or adult enthralled for hours.

Aries are always busy; they wear out their less dynamic colleagues, and while they may woo everyone with their humor and imaginative schemes, watch out for the days when their belligerent and quick tempers are on the loose. Yet their anger is short lived, and they forgive and forget just as quickly. They have no patience whatsoever, and their karmic lesson is to learn that—like the seeds planted by the farmer when the Sun is in Aries (in April in the northern hemisphere)—it takes time for the ideas to grow and develop into the glorious blossoms envisaged months previously. Their impatience always makes Aries create mountains out of molehills—probably the biggest obstacle to an otherwise cheerful and optimistic sign.

Passion and unpredictability—they are both found in Aries, male and female. In love they like to be the boss, and their powerful and forceful love natures can turn their partners into quivering, submissive maidens or knights, loving every dominated minute and floating on Cloud Nine.

While Aries love their romantic partners to be subordinate to them, they hate them to appear weak, and the more they fight back the more turned on and in love Aries will be. Because of this, a long relationship with an Aries will have many ups and downs, with untold numbers of physical fights and verbal attacks, all ending in the most passionate embraces and sexual encounters. Their partners must be warned not to take any physical aggressiveness too personally! When truly in love Aries can be gentle and sensitive, but somehow their sexuality is brought to a fever pitch through conflict, either of the mind or the body, bringing both partners to a climax of such magnitude that it makes any suffering worthwhile.

Aries is the first sign of the Zodiac, the house that rules the actual personality and disposition of an individual—the mind, the soul—that unique part of a person that is identified by a certain spirit. It is the leader of the other twelve signs, yet it is still their child, with the traits of a clever military strategist encouraged by the naïveté and innocence of a newborn babe.

It is hard to imagine any Aries allowing themselves to become prisoners to a job or profession. Out of boredom, many change jobs so often that their résumés may run for pages, yet each and every job they tackle reaches an exciting level of success before monotony takes over. Aries love the military life, uniforms, weapons, and training that includes hand-to-hand combat (it is not surprising to find detectives and police among them). Experts in physical fitness and the martial arts, some become teachers of sports, fencing, karate, or wrestling or executives who escape at lunchtime to the local health club for an hour of exercise instead of two hours of gourmet eating. Because they can successfully manipulate the pawns in life's chess game, they are in their element when they are in the top position, but they also encourage energy and ambition in their employees. Aries are successful in the arts, especially as agents or managers of rock groups, actors, and fine artists. There is tremendous excitement for them in the wheeling and dealing, in setting their minds and strategies against the bargaining of the other party.

Aries can never be defeated, no matter how many obstacles, disappointments, rejections, thefts, and losses; they have the ability and strength to come back knowing that eventually they will win.

Whiz Kids and Human Dynamos

ARIES DECANATE, RULED BY MARS
March 21–March 31

This is Aries in its purest form, with double the amount of energy and vitality and the planet Mars working overtime. Manic to extremes in everything they do, these Aries are clever hustlers on the streets of life or military planners around the table in a bunker at the front of the battle zone.

No challenge is too great or insignificant, no obstacle insurmountable, and no goal unattainable, for here is brilliant, decisive, and fearless leadership.

These Aries have strength of character, commitment to goals, and physical prowess, making them winners in every competition. In social or business spheres, as soon as such Aries enter a room and are introduced, they are in control. They see the whole group as possible adversaries, in opposition to their plans and ideas, putting them on the offensive. They are prone to become more and more outspoken, frank instead of tactful, and, lacking diplomacy, to dash in where angels fear to tread. Nothing would suit these Aries better than to launch a verbal battle or punch an opponent on the nose. Aries are as fiercely territorial at home as they are aggressive abroad, and they rise quickly and decisively to any challenge of their dominion. (Not for nothing did dynamic Diana Ross call her group The Supremes.)

These impatient dynamos always want immediate answers to their questions, creating an impression of urgency about every project. If they don't get an immediate response, they are likely to go on their happy ways seeking other goals. They are so restless and impatient that if they do not have success immediately they just cannot wait. However, once they do commit to something, they can do in days, with great style and panache, what might take others months of work and worry.

With admiration and disbelief, outsiders watch these Aries perform seemingly superhuman physical and professional feats as, using their primitive instincts, they conquer the impossible.

These driven Aries can suffer from stress and poor eating habits, and they are really accident prone but stalwart enough to ignore pain and inconvenience through physical handicap. As the sign rules the head, most problems stem from the various senses—weak eyesight, poor hearing, and the health hazards associated with the nose, ears, eyes, mouth, and skin.

But being in shape is part of the manic healthy attitude of Aries, and therefore their bodies are far stronger than their minds and their brains can get exhausted sooner than their bodies.

Romantically, once these Aries have been caught, they are sexually inexhaustible, with all the power and energy of a fast-moving locomotive and the endurance of a tank. They enjoy giving and receiving a little pain, but underneath they are a very sensitive sign. Aries can perform proficiently in every area of their lives at the drop of a hat (or any other article of clothing). And the location doesn't have to be chic or sophisticated; the more down-to-earth and back-to-nature the environment, the more basic and animalistic they will be.

SIGNS OF THE STARS

ELTON JOHN

This Aries "Pinball Wizard" (his role in *Tommy*) started playing the piano when he was three. Elton John is a performer with great feeling, energy, and amazing show business flair. When I met him at the opening of *Grease* in New York, he gave me his birthdate and added, "I've never been able to understand myself; perhaps astrology will help."

Elton was born in Pinner, Middlesex, England, on March 25, 1947, at 2:00 A.M. His name at birth was Reginald Dwight, which he used professionally for twenty years, but it wasn't until he was inspired to change his name to Elton John that his fortunes changed for the better. Like all Aries he loves to wear hats and glasses—probably a result of the Easter bonnet influence (Easter is usually celebrated during the time of Aries). And the head and eyes are ruled by this sign, thus the sparkling "specs" and flamboyant plumage.

Naturally, with Sagittarius as his Ascendant, he would be attracted to sports and is the owner of an English soccer team. After years of loving his freedom, another Aries-Sagittarius trait, he suddenly shocked his fans by marrying sound engineer Renata Blauel. Perhaps she has helped him to understand his own very complicated personality, responsible for such great talent.

DR. FRANK FIELD

Who else but an Aries could make the daily weather segment of the news into a "star turn," become a media superstar, and be able to negotiate or demand a salary usually given only to movie stars? Dr. Frank Field, of course, born March 30, 1923, in New York City, at 10:30 P.M.—an Aries with his Moon in Virgo, the sign of the schoolteacher, and his Ascendant that powerful twenty-nine degrees of Scorpio.

I did Frank's horoscope onstage in New York. With his Moon at the top of his chart in the tenth house of career, exactly next to his North Node, the point of destiny, there was no doubt that great success lay ahead. Also, since the Moon affects the tides, weather, water, and people, it wasn't surprising that he could bring his knowledge as a meteorologist to the public in such an informative and entertaining way.

Independent, impulsive, and self-confident, he has been able to change networks, do commercials, and keep teaching the viewers about weather conditions as if he were the "wizard" controlling the elements himself.

WARREN BEATTY

Another dynamic Aries, brother of formidable Taurus Shirley MacLaine, is actor Warren Beatty, who changed the spelling of his name to bring better luck to his career, adding a second *t*. He is billed as the star, director, and producer of many of his movies.

Born on March 30, 1937, in Richmond, Virginia, at 6:30 P.M., he is an Aries with his Moon in sexy Scorpio, and his Ascendant is Libra, the sign of beauty. It is no surprise that with all that sex appeal he is so hyperactive in his pursuit of romance with beautiful women, particularly many of Hollywood's leading ladies.

He won an Oscar as best director for his movie *Reds,* which he also produced and for which he wrote the script. Among his most exciting roles was Clyde in *Bonnie and Clyde*—Aries ruled by the planet Mars, god of War, just loved those shootout scenes!

DIANA ROSS

Born: March 26, 1944, at 11:46 P.M. in Detroit, Michigan

Attending the glittering royal premiere in London of the movie *Lady Sings the Blues* in which Diana, an Aries, played the legendary blues singer Billie Holiday, also an Aries (born April 7, 1915), I was amazed that the audience treated Diana with such awe and respect. On that exciting and electric evening, the guests stood up and cheered, gave her a standing ovation, and waited uncharacteristically, with almost religious reverence, as this modern-day legend exited the theater following the royal party.

Diana was raised with her five sisters and brother in a ghetto housing project, where poverty crowded them three in a bed. Reflecting on her life, Diana said, "I learned a lot of things since those early days. One of the most important things is, whatever you do, make yourself happy—because how you feel is the way you go. The image you have of yourself is important."

At first this striking beauty had wanted to be a model and fashion designer, and finally her dreams were publicly recognized when she designed the clothes she wore as a model in *Mahogany,* one of the biggest-grossing hits of 1976, and one that produced another platinum record for this glittering star.

With such a strong horoscope chart, there was no way that Diana could fail. Being a dynamic Aries, with all that drive and energy, she was willing to do everything and eventually became not only a star but a producer, a designer, and the owner of her own film company: "You can't just sit back and expect people to do things for you. You've got to get up and do it yourself. If you think you'll succeed, you will be successful."

Her Ascendant is Scorpio, which is even more powerful, determined, and ambitious than her Aries; and her Moon in Taurus gives her a streak of stubbornness but strong loyalty to both her lovers and her fans. It is the Taurus Moon that gave her her singing talents (Taurus rules the throat and is especially good for singers and speakers) as well as her creative skills in fashion.

With Venus, the planet of love, and her Sun located in the fourth house of real estate, it was astrologically appropriate when she dropped her longtime lover, Berry Gordy, Jr., the Motown record mogul, to marry real-estate man Robert E. Silberstein. But with Uranus, the planet of sudden happenings, in her seventh house of marriage—along with Saturn, the planet that means restrictions and limitations, particularly with men—this apparent dream marriage ended abruptly in divorce.

This tendency to thrust away from seemingly ideal situations may have also been the reason why, after so many years of Number One hits with the Supremes, she took off on her own to become the superstar she was determined to be. In 1973 she became *Cue* magazine's "Entertainer of the Year," was given the Golden Globe Award for her acting, and was nominated for an Academy Award as best actress for *Lady Sings the Blues.*

Family is vitally important to her, and having Venus located in the house of family makes her a devoted and inspiring mother. She is concerned about the welfare of her own three children and all children everywhere. She dreamed of building a playground in New

SIGNS OF THE STARS

York's Central Park. That dream is now a reality. In 1983 Diana gave a free outdoor concert. Though it was postponed by thunder and rain that drenched the 350,000 loyal fans who showed up for the first performance, in true Aries spirit Diana returned the next day. Even though this cost her thousands of extra dollars and she lost money on the television and record productions of the event, she proudly presented Mayor Ed Koch with a check for a quarter of a million dollars—to build that park she dreamed of.

Diana is a true whiz kid and a human dynamo, and, as star of *The Wiz*, with her protégé Michael Jackson, she recreated Judy Garland's role of Dorothy in *The Wizard of Oz*. In the musical, she sings, ". . . believe in yourself." Follow her advice and you won't go far wrong.

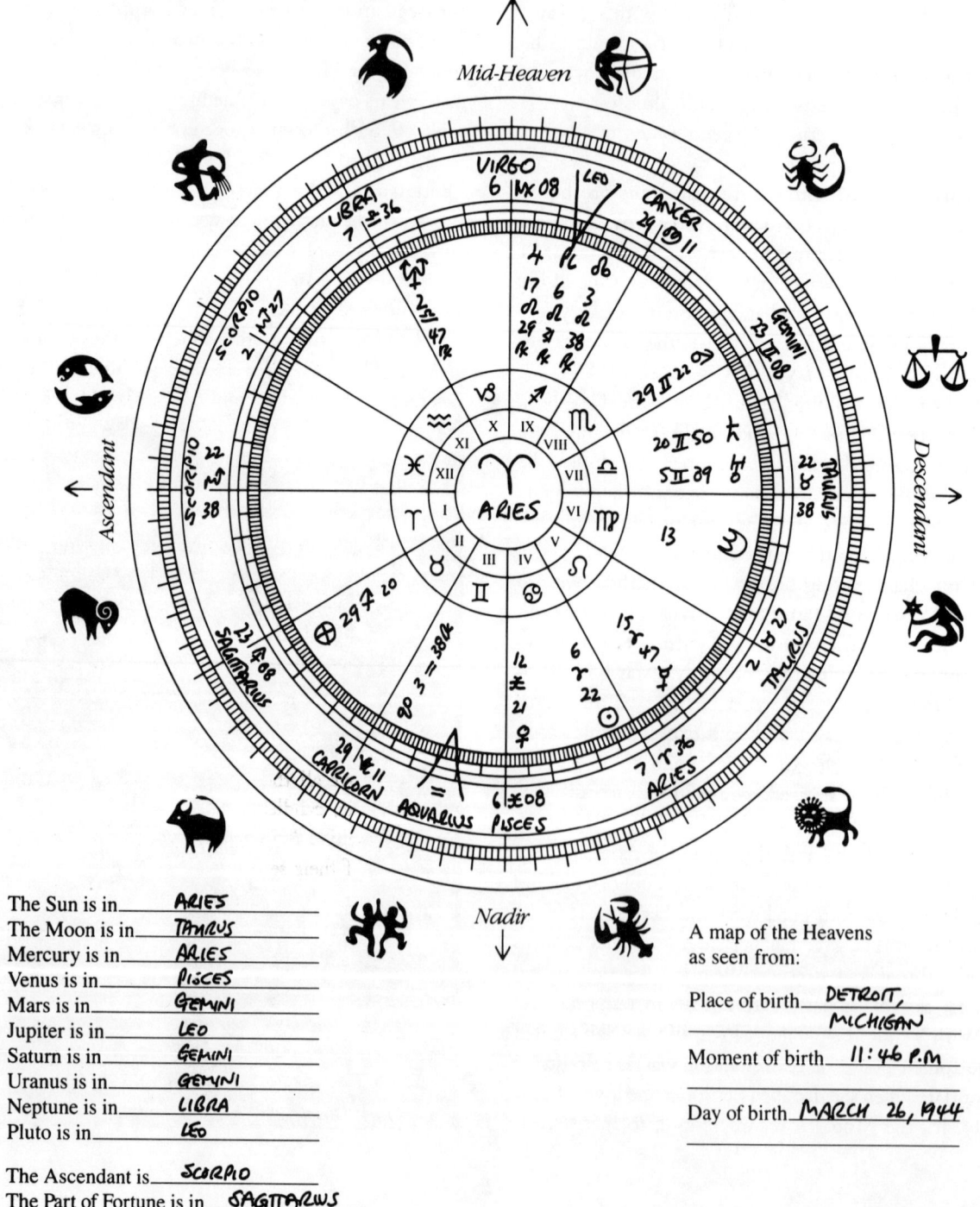

The Sun is in _ARIES_
The Moon is in _TAURUS_
Mercury is in _ARIES_
Venus is in _PISCES_
Mars is in _GEMINI_
Jupiter is in _LEO_
Saturn is in _GEMINI_
Uranus is in _GEMINI_
Neptune is in _LIBRA_
Pluto is in _LEO_

The Ascendant is _SCORPIO_
The Part of Fortune is in _SAGITTARIUS_

A map of the Heavens as seen from:

Place of birth _DETROIT, MICHIGAN_

Moment of birth _11:46 P.M_

Day of birth _MARCH 26, 1944_

Dynamic Entertainers

LEO DECANATE, RULED BY THE SUN
April 1–April 10

These Aries have the energy of the planet Mars and the radiance of the Sun, together giving warmth and comfort to all. But they also have a touch of Leo about them and feel they need to be treated with special care and reverence. Most of all, they want the spotlight and have the drive to succeed in any field of show business and public endeavor. Give them an audience and, like Debbie Reynolds, they will glow with stardom and bring magic to the job or project they are promoting.

Rockettes at Radio City Music Hall in New York, martial arts demonstrators, the champion skeet shooter at an international meet, the hunter whose latest catch makes Page One of the local newspaper—all must have a birthdate around this time. Things that they touch cannot help but become a great success, publicitywise at least, for they are organizers as well as creators.

Even as young children these Aries always wanted to go on stage and could always be counted on to entertain guests, from two or three to 300. They are in their true element while showing off but want to see the smiles and hear the applause. "Dynamic entertainers" on the social scene, too, they will treat people to lavish outings and sumptuous meals.

There is no such thing as a quiet person born around this time—inside they are boiling with enthusiasm. Given the right time and the right place, they will wave the flags, bang the drums, and welcome the heroes back from war (when they are not themselves those heroes), the victorious local football team back home, and march on City Hall if things displease them about taxes, and how pets are being treated in the neighborhood.

It is important for these Aries to be happy in love, or depression can set in and then they cannot take control of the situation. These Aries need happy love lives and fun, although they are not so boisterous as those born in the first ten days of the sign. These need dignity, a sense of humor, and a romantic setting that will help them give the love they are bursting to pour on their loved ones.

They love all the rituals of lovemaking—wining, dining, music, candlelit dinners—yet underneath they are still primitive Aries who can shock with the powerful nature of their sexual demands.

These Aries look for fashionable marriages, and they have composed many a Hollywood scrapbook. They always keep a romantic touch to the marriage, long after the wedding photos have started to turn yellow around the edges in their antique silver frames. At every lamppost, under the bridge, or by the bus stop, they will kiss their loved ones good night and tell them how much they love them, almost seducing them.

MARLON BRANDO

Marlon Brando changed the style of acting and has influenced the performances of many of the stars of Broadway and in Hollywood. He is a graduate of the once-controversial Method school of acting, and, in 1947, gave a performance as Stanley Kowalski in *Streetcar Named Desire* that became a classic. His almost inaudible way of speaking in some of his movies gave a very intense and strangely dynamic magic to every role.

He was born April 3, 1924, in Omaha, Nebraska, at 10:37 P.M. at the time of the New Moon, so both his Sun and his Moon are in Aries, and his Ascendant is that critical twenty-nine degrees of Scorpio (President Ronald Reagan, Jackie Onassis, and Dr. Frank Field, among many others, have it as their Ascendant). It was this influence that made him an outspoken political activist. He marched with civil rights demonstrators and workers in Alabama in 1963, and he refused his Academy Award in 1972 as best actor in *The Godfather* "because of the treatment of the American Indian in motion pictures."

Jupiter in Sagittarius, the sign of the filmmaker, in his first house gave him luck right from the beginning—from his early success on Broadway and his first Oscar in 1954 for *On the Waterfront* to his memorable performance in *Apocalypse Now* in 1979. But his dynamic personality off the screen as well as on it made him one of the most controversial actors of our time.

EDDIE MURPHY

It seems that he has always been a star, yet it was only in 1980 that he got such a great reception from the viewers and TV critics for his appearances on "Saturday Night Live." And then he was only nineteen years old.

Three years later he was signing a multimillion dollar film deal in Hollywood, becoming one of the biggest box office attractions in the world. He is a dynamic entertainer.

Born in Brooklyn, New York, on April 3, 1961, he is an Aries with his Moon in sexy Scorpio, and somehow he is able to get away with some of the most outrageous, questionable material because of the fun he has while performing. His Mercury in Pisces made him a natural for the movies, and his great imagination and astute powers of observation make his impressions of other stars the work of a "genius."

DEBBIE REYNOLDS

Born: April 1, 1932, at 5:49 P.M. in El Paso, Texas

I first met Debbie Reynolds in Las Vegas, the perfect setting for this vital and radiant star. The resounding bell ringing of jackpot winners keeps the adrenaline pounding every minute of the day and night. There is never a pause, never a dull moment. For those who don't want to gamble, there is still the vicarious excitement of watching others enjoying their wins and sympathizing with them when they lose. These Aries are the best entertainers in the world in the most glorious theatrical settings money can buy.

Aries Debbie was in rehearsal for one of her precision nightclub shows at the Desert Inn, but she looked as fresh as a daisy. Like the general of a winning army, she used her charm, inspiration, and leadership qualities to get the best out of her team.

Like all Aries, she is happiest when working hard. If there is one special asset that has made her a star, it is that capacity for effort. She works every day of her life. Aries are as energetic and tireless in their private lives as in their careers, and Debbie brought up her children by Eddie Fisher, Carrie and Todd, virtually without missing a beat in her professional life. Being natural leaders, like Debbie, Aries love to manage their own lives and to produce their own "show."

I had actually flown to Vegas with her daughter Carrie, prior to her great success as Princess Leia in *Star Wars,* and during a break in rehearsal Carrie introduced me to Debbie. "Freddie has been sent to do your horoscope, Mother," said Carrie. "He's a present from Joan Hackett." Debbie was all smiles and seemed delighted to meet me. She and Joan had been friends since Joan arrived in Hollywood in 1966 to star in *The Group.* "I can give you half an hour between shows," she beamed, clearly unaware that a horoscope takes many hours of study and exploration. I beamed back. "I'm here for the weekend," I explained. Without a moment's hesitation or pause, she immediately responded laughingly—"Then in that case I'd better put you up in my suite"—spontaneous, gracious, and generous in true Aries spirit.

The Debbie Reynolds Show was exciting from beginning to end. There was hardly time for Debbie to take a breath, and I didn't want to blink in case I missed something. Her wonderful impressions of Mae West, Zsa Zsa Gabor, Barbra Streisand, and many other stars brought the house down, but her use of wigs throughout the entire show was another endorsement of her Aries sign and behavior. Aries rules the head, and they love hats and wigs. Also, Aries' favorite color is red, and her entire cast as well as herself were dressed in bright scarlet, sequined top hat and tails for a finale that got a standing ovation.

SIGNS OF THE STARS

It was so appropriate that Debbie starred in the movie *The Unsinkable Molly Brown*, the true story of one of the survivors of the ill-fated "unsinkable" *Titanic*, which sank on its maiden voyage after hitting an iceberg. (Incidentally, this happened on April 15, 1912, during the period when the Sun is in the sign of Aries.) Debbie is truly unsinkable—with her energy and vitality it would take a ton of bricks to keep her down.

Recently I attended Debbie's show at the Westbury Music Fair on Long Island, New York, and during a quiet dinner at the hotel after the show with our mutual friend publicist Barry Landau, she commented on how she has kept active and busy, unlike many of her fellow stars. "It's so important to keep up the legend of the great stars," she said. "Whenever we hear that one of the greats is having a hard time keeping up their standard

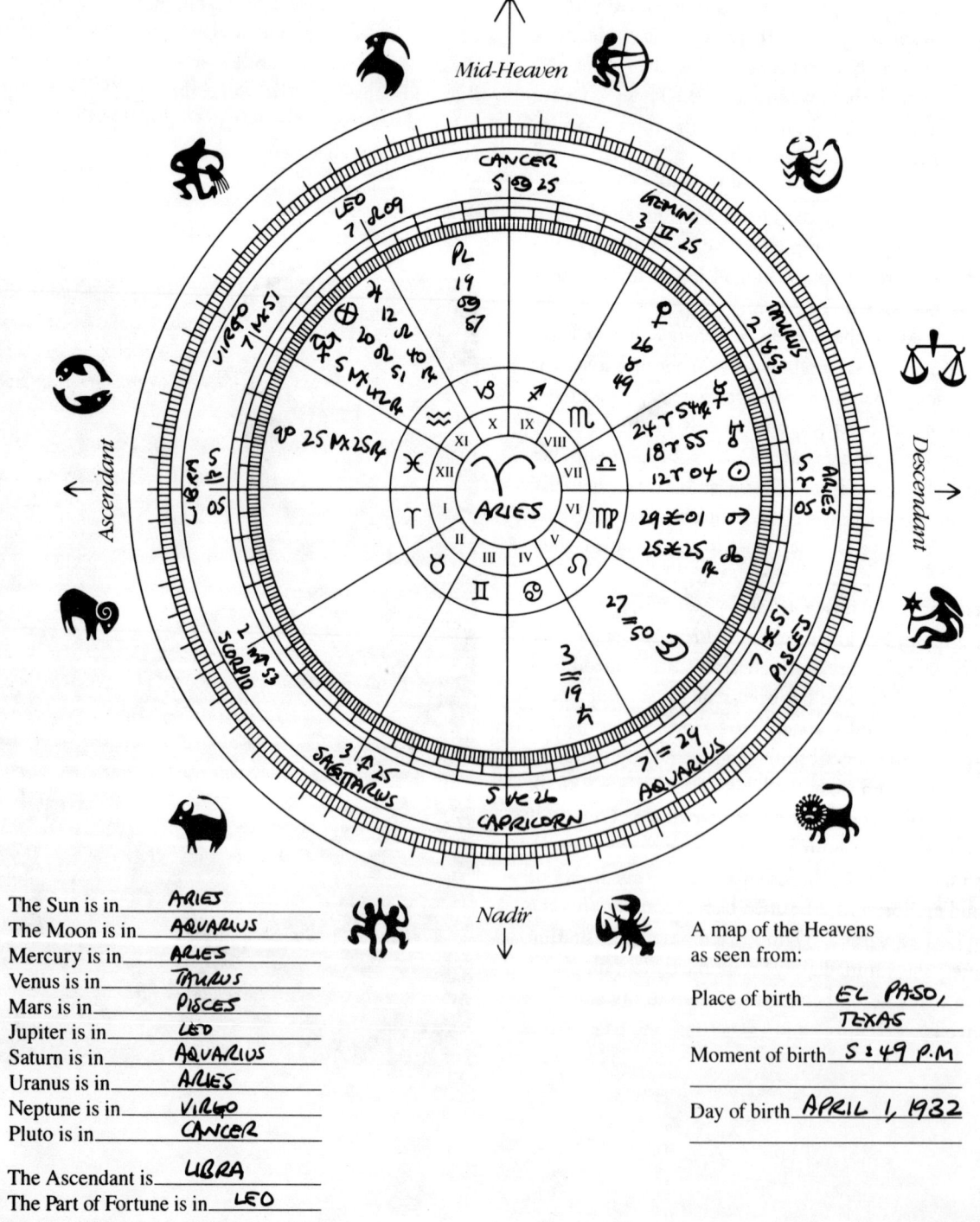

The Sun is in ARIES
The Moon is in AQUARIUS
Mercury is in ARIES
Venus is in TAURUS
Mars is in PISCES
Jupiter is in LEO
Saturn is in AQUARIUS
Uranus is in ARIES
Neptune is in VIRGO
Pluto is in CANCER

The Ascendant is LIBRA
The Part of Fortune is in LEO

A map of the Heavens as seen from:

Place of birth EL PASO, TEXAS
Moment of birth 5:49 P.M
Day of birth APRIL 1, 1932

of living, paying their bills and running their large homes, we [the other legends] get together to help. . . . You've got to keep legends alive!" This generosity is typical of Aries—the true spirits of the Red Cross of the zodiac—all knights and dames coming to the rescue whenever they can.

With a horoscope chart like Debbie's, life can never be dull, and no matter how exhausted and overworked she may become, she will never retire. She is an incredibly potent mixture of her sun sign Aries, her Moon sign Aquarius, and her Ascendant (or rising sign) Libra.

It is her Libra rising that gives her that ageless quality. She still looks facially and physically as she did in *Tammy and the Bachelor* in 1957. Combined with the energetic Aries influence, the busier and more active she is, the longer she will keep her youthful looks. The Moon, located in Aquarius, gives her that wonderful comedy timing and talent for impersonation. The Moon also represents the home, all wholesome family matters, and America, and Debbie has brought much joy and happiness into the homes of millions through her television appearances, her movie reruns, as well as her new home video of aerobic exercises, *Do It Debbie's Way*.

Mars, the planet of action, is in the sign of Pisces, which rules the feet, in the sixth house of work, and this is the key to Debbie's dance performances, in which energy and precision are fascinatingly combined.

Luckily for Debbie, the planet Venus—usually associated with love but which also rules the finances of our lives—is well placed in Taurus in the eighth house of income (one that includes gifts, legacies, inheritances, and other means of building up one's fortune). Thus Debbie has been able to earn money from a multitude of activities—singing, speaking, producing, managing, investing, and handling her own business affairs—and has been able to weather the financial crises of others in her family. For example, when her second husband, shoe tycoon Harry Karl, lost his fortune, he also lost $15 million of hers, and even after he went bankrupt she was still responsible for $2 million of his debts. For a while, it seemed as if she had lost everything, but "unsinkable" Debbie was never down. Debbie says, "If you have faith and a sense of humor, you can survive anything."

Pluto, the planet of big business—associated with the great movie empires of Hollywood's heyday, the casino syndicates of Las Vegas, and the enormous recording world—sits high in Debbie's chart in the tenth house of career, ambition, and fame. Given this, there was no way that Debbie could miss the enormous rewards destiny was to bestow upon her. It is as if her life had been mapped out for her by protective angels in both the show business and the ethereal senses of the word.

But, Aries-like, Debbie prefers to handle her empire herself, strategically plotting and planning every show, from casting to promotion, as if it were a battle. In this effort, as in her personal life, she has many well-wishers and friends, and Jupiter, the planet of good fortune, and her Part of Fortune are both located close together in Leo, the sign of show business, and in the eleventh house of influential friends.

Uranus, the planet of change, in the seventh house of marriage, has brought Debbie three marriages, the first to Eddie Fisher. When Eddie ran off with Elizabeth Taylor after the death of Liz's husband Mike Todd, Debbie married Harry Karl. Divorced in 1976, six years later Debbie married Richard Hamlett, who lives in Virginia and Miami Beach, Florida. Uranus has given Debbie many changes in marriage, and this usually indicates change of name through marriage. But Debbie chose to do this professionally. Born Mary Frances Reynolds, she chose Debbie—a name that, combined with her horoscope chart, rocketed her to stardom.

Philanthropic Magicians

SAGITTARIUS DECANATE, RULED BY JUPITER
April 11–April 19

These Aries are the most generous people in the world, selfless yet egocentric, leaders who not only take their troops into battle but help carry the wounded and disabled to a place of safety regardless of the danger to themselves. Their Mars-influenced warlike temperaments as well as the jovial, philanthropic disposition of Jupiter gives them the skill and planning strategy of great military leaders. They want to organize everyone around them and channel them into the professions that will best show off their talents. Like world-class conceptualizer Robert Stigwood, they make great producers, and they will not stop at funding their protégés until they either reach stardom or the purse of gold finally runs out, which strangely enough it never seems to do.

Quick-talking evangelists on street corners, marchers to prevent the demolition of an opera house or concert hall, church leaders who give up their comfortable suburban lives to work with deprived people in slum areas or in remote villages of Africa, chairpersons of national charities who spend long hours raising money for various causes and end up augmenting the funds in order to achieve the desired result, neighbors who come to the rescue of others who are suddenly taken sick or are in trouble, even looking after the children and pets and asking nothing in return—all these and many more like them are blessed with this Mars and Jupiter combination.

Their sense of humor shines through the hardest chores, and no matter how much work is piled on them or they take on themselves, they successfully finish with a flourish. Like knights of old, they always seem at the ready, armor burnished, prepared for another battle; modern-day Don Quixotes, they ever seek the "impossible dream."

Their love of gambling, combined with their reckless nature, makes them easy prey for tricksters and con artists. If there's a risk attached, they jump in feet first, head first, any way at all, but they are into the fray body and soul without weighing the risks or consequences. Money runs through their fingers like mercury; they just cannot hold onto it, but they have the tremendous faith that there is plenty around and more will arrive when necessary. Eventually, though, even these Aries have to say no to continual pressure from fundraisers and civic-minded entrepreneurs.

They cannot sit still for one minute; skilled in all the martial arts, they have the agility and grace of dancers and the determination and strength of prizefighters. Yet to look at them—slim, youthful, and eyes full of innocent wonder—it would seem impossible for them to loose the volcanic eruptions that boil deep down inside till they are forced to let fly at the nearest person (or the punching bag at the local gymnasium).

A vigorous sex life, bolstered by romance, will keep these Aries emotionally serene and balance the frustrations and worries that Aries usually feel. They can even see the humor in the sport of making love, and their prowess and skill livens up their loved ones' erogenous combat zones. They make sex almost a religion, but once they have found their true love (having made many philosophical converts on the way) they will continue to experiment with love's adventures and variations with their soul mates.

Long-term romance is difficult with them because they must never think that they are ensnared in a trap. Life's normal structures and restrictions—school, home, family, office, and other social disciplines—make them rebellious. They are best when they and their love interest are pursuing some common ideal on life's battlefield.

ARIES

PETER USTINOV

One of the most amazing men I have ever met, and probably the most talented and versatile in the theatrical world, is actor Peter Ustinov. Nowadays it is common to be a "jack of all trades," a Renaissance man, in the world of show business. Many superstars are now producing and directing as well as starring in their own movies. But Peter has always done it all.

We celebrated the Fourth of July in London several years ago, and I was fascinated by his wealth of personal anecdotes and stories about his life. He was an actor at the age of seventeen, a star at eighteen, and by the time he was nineteen he had turned playwright and, a year later, producer. And all at a time when it was customary to pigeonhole artists and actors.

Peter was born in London, on April 16, 1921, at 11:30 A.M. and is an Aries with his Moon in Leo (the showman) and his Ascendant Cancer. This Cancerian influence makes his home a vital part of his life; he has married three times, has four children, and now lives in Paris and Geneva. His nurturing disposition has made him a driving force with UNICEF and UNESCO. He is truly a "philanthropic magician."

OLIVIA HUSSEY

I traveled with Olivia to South Fallsburg, New York, to have a private meeting with her beloved guru, Swama Muktananda, whom she affectionately called "Baba." He was born May 16, 1910.

Olivia and I had been friends for many years, since her days in London just after her memorable performance as Juliet in Franco Zeffirelli's *Romeo and Juliet* when she was seventeen.

The audience with Baba was very enlightening. I asked him, "What is the purpose of human life?"

He replied, "Happiness. Some people find it, some don't."

Olivia Hussey was born on April 17, 1951, at 6:40 A.M. in Buenos Aires, Argentina. Her parents were British. Like the city, she is a "good Aries," with her Moon in Leo, which attracted her to acting, and her Ascendant also Aries, giving her tremendous energy and drive. She actually commutes between California and Japan—where her husband Akira Fuse (Sagittarius, December 18, 1947) is a major singing star—and looks after her sons Alex and Max at the same time as she shoots her latest television show or movie.

Giving a great deal of her spare time to her spiritual devotions and to philanthropic charitable deeds, Olivia is a magician in the lives of everyone who comes in contact with her, whether friends or fans.

TIM CURRY

I had the honor of being the first person to interview Tim on television when he appeared on my "Fredrick Davies Star Power Show" in New York.

Though he is an Aries, born at noon on April 19, 1946, in Cheshire, England, he seemed much more reserved than I would have expected. Possibly this trait may be a result of his birthday being on the cusp (the dividing line) of Aries and Taurus so that he showed some of the quieter characteristics of Taurus, the bull. In fact, I thought he was very shy at first meeting.

But as soon as he starts to perform onstage or in the movies, he becomes a true, flamboyant, outrageous combination of his Aries sun sign, his Sagittarius Moon (film), and his Ascendant, the show business sign of Leo. He has developed a cult following from London to Los Angeles for his bigger-than-life stage and screen performances as "Frank'N Furter," an infamous multisexual transvestite bully, in the legendary *Rocky Horror Picture Show*.

He followed it on Broadway with a much more controlled, intellectual portrayal of the poet-publicist of the Dada movement, Tristan Tzara, in the play *Travesties*.

In between shows, he withdraws into himself to study, and read, but he is always ready to take on a challenging role to bring magic to his audiences.

ROBERT STIGWOOD

Born: April 16, 1934, at 3:10 A.M. in Adelaide, South Australia

Like many of the stars and artists he encourages, Robert Stigwood—the most successful show business mogul in the world—is basically shy, but underneath that gentle, big-brotherly exterior, he is a tough, well-organized, and brilliant businessman. He is "a showbiz whiz with the Midas touch."

Robert was born in Adelaide, South Australia, on April 16, 1934, at 3:10 A.M. and is astrologically and professionally a perfect example of "a philanthropic magician." After making several big hit movies and records, he announced to his already well-paid staff that he was going to give his eighty-odd employees a share in the profits of his movies. As a result most are now rich and successful. A galvanic fantast, this producer of *Jesus Christ Superstar, Saturday Night Fever, Grease, Sgt. Pepper's Lonely Hearts Club Band, Moment to Moment, The Fan, Grease 2,* and many other films has brought magic and fantasy to young and old alike.

Like many pioneers, Stigwood came from a comfortable family life. His father was an electrical engineer in Australia, and Robert was educated at a private college. But when he decided to seek fame and fortune in London, his family stopped his allowance, and he arrived with literally only a handful of change. "They thought it would be good for me."

Like many Aries, Robert started off as an agent; then he moved into record producing and was blessed with five big hits the first year. In eleven short years he was able to build his show business empire starring young and talented artists that include the Bee Gees, Eric Clapton, John Travolta, Lily Tomlin, Olivia Newton John, and Peter Frampton.

Mercury, the planet of communication, is Stigwood's rising planet and is especially good for an agent or producer, as it promotes flexibility and quick-wittedness. These skills enabled him to negotiate, among other deals, the sale of U.S. rights to two hit British television shows, "Till Death Do Us Part" and "Steptoe and Son," which became the bases for "All In the Family" and "Sanford and Son."

The planet of illusion, Neptune, is located in his sixth house of work, and he was destined from birth to work in the movie industry.

Films were part of my involvement with Robert. For his film *Tommy* I was asked to cast a chart and determine with him and his staff the most propitious date for the premiere. We chose March 18, but something did not seem quite right. The morning of the premiere I went over the horoscope chart minutely. Then it struck me. The time we had chosen for the opening was 7:30 P.M., and I realized that there was a bad astrological occurrence at that time, which wouldn't lift until 8:00 P.M.

I called for a messenger and quickly sent over the new chart for the opening to Stigwood's Central Park West office. I attached a blazing rhinestone-studded star to it so that he couldn't miss it.

He didn't. Stars had flown in from all over the world for his opening. The theater was full, and everyone was waiting; you could sense the nervousness in the audience as the minutes ticked by. Would Robert dare keep his celebrity guests waiting thirty minutes? Yes. At two minutes to eight the curtains opened, the lights dimmed, and on the stroke of eight, the film's title showed on the screen. There was thunderous applause.

Later that evening, while Robert was celebrating the film's success at an after-theater party held in the subway station at Fifty-seventh Street and Sixth Avenue, he told the *New York Post* that he had held up the curtain because I had told him to wait. The paper noted that the bright spark he personally added to the evening was the conspicuous blazing star he wore on his tuxedo lapel. It was nice to have launched two in one evening!

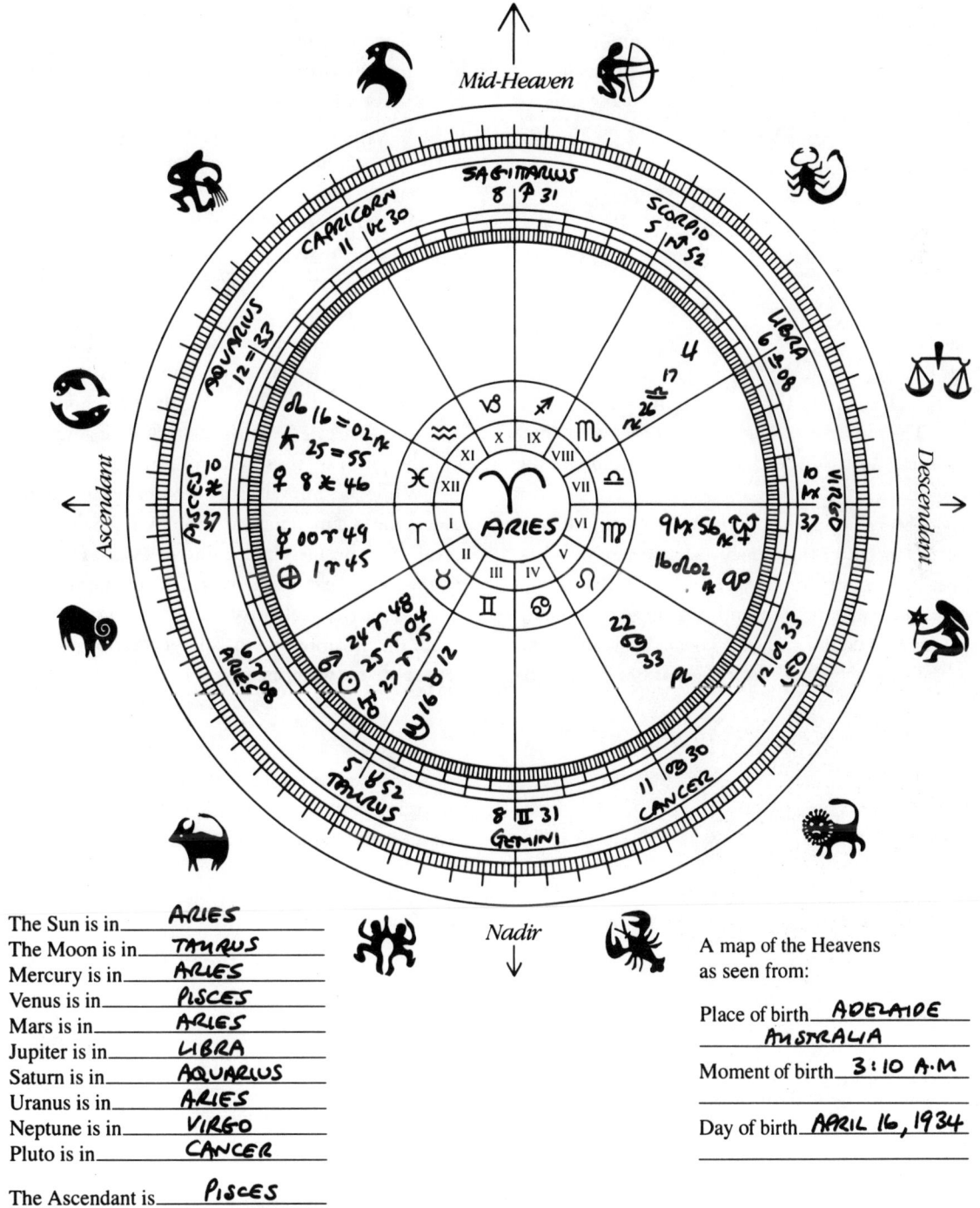

The Sun is in ARIES
The Moon is in TAURUS
Mercury is in ARIES
Venus is in PISCES
Mars is in ARIES
Jupiter is in LIBRA
Saturn is in AQUARIUS
Uranus is in ARIES
Neptune is in VIRGO
Pluto is in CANCER

The Ascendant is PISCES
The Part of Fortune is in ARIES

A map of the Heavens as seen from:

Place of birth ADELAIDE AUSTRALIA

Moment of birth 3:10 A.M

Day of birth APRIL 16, 1934

One characteristic of the philanthropic magicians is their capacity for delegating to and nurturing their "lieutenants." One example proved to be a tremendous success both for Robert and for the lieutenant in question, the brilliant young producer Kevin McCormick, a Leo. I had been doing his horoscope chart for several years when he came to consult me about a difficult decision. He wanted to go out on his own. Was this a good time?

I spent hours going over his chart, looking at the future trends. An astrologer can only give guidance and advice and should try to be supportive of a client's ambitions if possible. But in this instance all the indications showed that Kevin should stay where he was for at least two more years.

Kevin was partially relieved by my suggestion that he stick it out for a few more years, especially when I assured him that by doing so he would have a tremendous success on his hands.

During those two years Kevin took on the personal project he badly wanted to do, under Robert Stigwood's banner. It became one of the biggest film hits of all time when it was released, and the long-playing album broke all records. The movie was *Saturday Night Fever,* starring John Travolta (Aquarius), and the record album was by the Bee Gees.

Robert Stigwood's sun sign is Aries, of course, but his Moon is located in the money-making sign of Taurus, which makes him stubborn but loyal, with an eye to choosing the right type of enthusiastic assistants and associates for his "family." His Ascendant, or rising sign, is Pisces, the filmmaker and storyteller of the Zodiac. A lover of water (like people born under the sign of Pisces), he loves to relax on his yacht and sail around the Caribbean. And, although a bachelor, he entertains lavishly like a true impresario-prince. He has homes in London, Hollywood, New York, and Bermuda, private jets, yachts, limousines, and gourmet meals and champagne for his guests. He spent more than $250,000 on a party to launch *Saturday Night Fever,* held on a vast Paramount soundstage in Hollywood.

Jupiter, the planet of greater good fortune, is located in the eighth house of wealth and income, and his Part of Fortune is in Aries in the first house of personality and self-attitudes. This gives him his innate faith in his own tastes and his intuitive knowledge of what the public wants—and he gives it to them, both in quantity and in quality.

His Venus, the planet of love, is in the twelfth house of solitude and seclusion, and he may have had to sacrifice his personal romantic life in order to get his great rewards in the show business world, like other superstars.

Pluto, the planet associated with big business, is well placed in the area of show business (films, television, stage shows, and resort areas), the fifth house, and this also hints at greater wealth and influence as his ambitions and the goals of those around him expand.

While he himself may not have any performing talents, he is supertalented in knowing what will make a real show business happening or event. He may be the greatest showman in the world at the moment, a generous and magical celebrity whose productions have captured the imagination of all generations—a Sergeant Pepper of show business.

TAURUS
Banker of the Zodiac

SUN IN TAURUS, RULED BY VENUS
April 20–May 21

Gentle, loving, and always happy to lend a helping hand, Taurus is the only sign of the Zodiac that can love any- and everybody, being ruled by the planet of love and beauty, Venus, named for the goddess of love. The creative and sweet traits of this planet lead people born under this sign into positions where they are concerned with the welfare of the mass public, the esprit de corps of the nation (being true patriots), and the loyalty of those who work and play with them.

Always on the lookout for an opportunity to raise the living standards and social environments of their "family," they are attracted to the finer things in life, surrounding themselves with objects of beauty and the tools of the artists, many becoming noted musicians, poets, speakers, and painters as well as great lovers. Others who are blessed with the money-making gifts of the planet (Venus also rules money and luck) have the knack of promoting artists, either as their agents or impresarios or as patrons.

Frustratingly stubborn, especially about their beliefs and emotions, they will not give in once they have stated their position. However, they are the truest and most faithful friends, their loyalty being unquestioning and their devotion to duty almost overwhelming. Almost like the Boy Scouts' motto, which begins "Trusty, loyal and helpful, brotherly, courteous, kind," they are walking examples of the good neighbor, the benevolent dictator, and the gallant crusader.

They are so reliable that they will work well past the time others have left for dinner and their families, not going home until the job is done. They just love to search out information or look for obscure items that someone else needs in the hopes of pleasing them and giving them a token of their love and dedication.

Their effusive devotion is counterbalanced by a cautious and painstaking temperament, which can sometimes cause delays, yet this reliability places them well up on the employable list. That is why one will often meet the cuddly, smiling Taurus bank manager when applying for a loan. Taureans want to help, and may go against their financial instincts in order to see an applicant can get enough cash together to buy a new home, take a vacation, or take the big step of marriage—they are incurable romantics.

It takes a lot to get people born under the sign of Taurus really angry, or even to provoke them into having a friendly argument, but once their wrath is aroused they show great fury and will fight to the bitter end, never conceding or forgetting. When roused, they can also be uncontrollably clumsy.

More long-service awards are probably given to workers born under the sign of Taurus than to those born under any other sign. They stick to their projects, are loyal to the company or organization, and while they are slow in making decisions, their climb up the ladder of success is equally resolute, like the tortoise who reaches the finishing post well before the faster-running hare. They are the trusty workers who eventually become company presidents, bank heads, or shop stewards for having worked in every department in eagerness to learn all the workings of a firm. They can sympathize, and negotiate with every level of employee and management, and they are totally uncorruptible.

They lack the spontaneity of other signs, so their performance, even in risky arenas, appears to be safe, secure, and logical. They make excellent public officials and civil servants, landlords, hotel managers, and stockbrokers. Their only occasional gamble may be in the international currency market; they lose when they try horse or sporting gambles, for they are best at making calculated guesses, their business training giving them excellent hunches and intuition.

They are also drawn to the more creative beauty fields by their ruling planet Venus and have great success working in hairdressing, makeup, cosmetics, jewelry, and fashion. World famous designers, heads of international beauty product companies, as well as models and spokespersons, have strong Taurean influences. The music field, especially singing, is a great outlet, as Venus rules music as well as the throat. Festival managers, promoters, impresarios, and community art committees are full of them, not forgetting the creative, hardworking staff behind the scenes like the wardrobe managers and musical arrangers.

In their personal lives they want security and serenity for every member of their family.

Financial Architects and Comptrollers

TAURUS DECANATE, RULED BY VENUS
April 20–April 30

It is hard to believe, when you look at examples of this Taurus—frequently so delicate, beautiful, and lovable—that underneath they have a brilliant and precise knowledge of how to handle vast amounts of money and how to use it to bring the greatest happiness and joy to the largest number of people possible. Leaders in world trade, they ship their fortunes across continents and oceans and surmount all obstacles by their faith in their luck and ability to make money.

Whether monarchs like Queen Elizabeth II or determined, multifaceted entertainers like Shirley MacLaine, they are doubly blessed by the goddess Venus, ruler of love, luck, beauty, the fine arts, and all the lovely things the world has to offer. And, almost as if they are guilty about receiving so much bounty and good fortune, they are extremely—and insightfully—charitable. Even those with little in their purses will put their energies into earning extra money to help a destitute neighbor or relative, and they are forever scouting opportunities for others to succeed. All they want in return is love and a gesture of respect, and even that is never really demanded. Love is the most important ingredient in this personality; the character attracts warmth and affection and very rarely bitter hate or dissension. The gifts they bestow on newly found friends seem out of proportion to the time they have known each other, but once this Taurus decides to be friends, the bond is as strong as one that has lasted many decades.

In addition to inner beauty, nature also gave them a beautiful countenance—the skin usually being free of blemish, scar, or birthmark, with the texture of a newborn baby's, and big, wide eyes like a gentle, sad maverick in love for the first time, seeking adoration and a hint of approval from a distant lover.

Opponents will misinterpret this gentleness as weakness and their lack of aggressiveness as laziness and lethargy. Yet the same opponents will fall by the wayside long before these Taureans start to tire, well on their way to solid success.

Overly loving and giving, they can coddle and even smother their loved ones. They lack the fire and flare that many relationships need—too much lovey-dovey behavior and not enough passion. But if this romantic temperament is harnessed, it will be hard to find an equal, let alone one so full of subtle and sophisticated techniques.

This Taurus is almost limitless in love and devotion and occasionally can offer love to such an extent that people must refuse them in order to get on with some other activities, especially work and money-making. They like all the fringe benefits of lovemaking—the attention, the music, the candlelight, the flowers, and the little gifts given over the liqueur when dining out—for they are typical lovers of the 1940s Hollywood movie script.

These Taureans would never inflict a deliberate injury—physical or emotional—on a loved one, but their endearing clumsiness occasionally precipitates such injuries.

These are the bedroom lovers, in any case. No open countryside, rooftop, or back of the car for them! Everything must be ready, a picture of love and romance, and overall, their loved ones must look spotless and smell clean. Only then, when all is perfect and the stage set for the big romantic episode to follow, will they charge into the delights that their loved one has to offer, and they wish a similarly discriminating and voluptuous response to their own advances.

RYAN O'NEAL

Like the swashbuckling, devil-may-care rogue, hero, and dandy Barry Lyndon, whom he played in the film of the same name, Ryan lives his life on the edge of a precipice. But there is something very commanding in his adventures, whether on or off the screen; he has a mischievous dignity.

Ryan is a Taurus, born April 20, 1941, at 9:34 P.M., in Los Angeles, with his Mars in Aquarius. It is astrologically appropriate for him to have a fiery, passionate love affair with Farrah Fawcett (Aquarius, born February 2, 1947). Both Taurus and Aquarius prefer freedom, and that is why both of them are quite content to remain unmarried even though they have a son, Redmond. (Farrah's first husband, Lee Majors, was also a Taurus, born April 23, 1940.)

Ryan has Venus, planet of money and good luck, and Jupiter, planet of greater good fortune, in his sign of Taurus, together with Saturn (rewards and work) and Uranus (television—"Peyton Place"). With so much emphasis on money in his horoscope, he has been able to demand, negotiate, and get what he believes his talents are really worth.

QUEEN ELIZABETH II

Reputedly one of the world's richest women, and acclaimed a truly beautiful and majestic queen by all who have seen and spoken to her, Elizabeth II is one of the world's few remaining monarchs. During her Silver Jubilee in 1978, throngs of people lined the streets of London to greet her as she passed by in her golden carriage.

At the time of her birth (April 21, 1926, at 2:40 A.M. in London) the sun had just entered the sign of Taurus and her Moon was in the royal sign of Leo, promising her a dramatic and regal future.

The queen's Venus is located in Pisces, indicating a love of helping the sick, and she is renowned for her support of the sick and handicapped. Pisces, ruled by Neptune, god of the Sea, also dictates attraction to a naval officer, as Prince Philip was, and is also coincidentally, in her house of marriage, auguring well for the match.

The queen's Ascendant, or rising sign, is Capricorn, the sign of great politicians and leaders, and even though her role as queen gives her the titular power to veto or approve new laws or changes within the Houses of Parliament, and personally sign state documents, it is her personal human influence—as ruler, wife, and mother—in all political and social matters in the country and in the far-flung corners of her Commonwealth that has been most resonant.

Taking her role of queen seriously, with Saturn in her chart in the area of religion and foreign affairs, she is head of the Church of England and travels to all parts of the Commonwealth regularly. The Leo influences of her Moon and Neptune give her the grace to see the humorous side of some difficult situations and to enjoy some of the jokes directed at the monarchy with detachment. With such a wit as Prince Philip (a typical fun-loving Gemini, born June 10, 1921) at her right hand, she can keep problems in perspective.

JACK NICHOLSON

Sitting next to Jack at a party in New York in honor of Marisa Berenson, we talked about his Oscar for *One Flew Over the Cuckoo's Nest*. In his acceptance speech he had said that five years previously his agent had "suggested" that he give up acting. But like the stubborn, determined, creative, and persistent Taurus he is, he was soon able to prove him wrong.

He gave me his birthday: April 22, 1937, at 11:20 A.M. in Neptune, New Jersey. His Sun is in Taurus, his Moon in the hardworking sign of Virgo, and his Ascendant is the show business sign, Leo, of course. It didn't surprise me either to find that the planet Neptune was the first planet rising over his Ascendant.

In the tenth house of fame, ambitions, and honors he has Venus in the impulsive sign of Aries and the Sun, Uranus, and Mercury all in Taurus—all industrious, artistic, and dependable. Since winning his second Oscar for *Terms Of Endearment*, he showed that while Taurus the Bull can be bullheaded, his career has certainly been "bullish" and continues to rise in value.

SHIRLEY MACLAINE

Born: April 24, 1934, at 3:57 P.M. in Richmond, Virginia

Few popular entertainers of our time can claim to have made an equal impression in another area of life, but this determined, creative Taurus is almost as well known for her spiritual regeneration and mystical philosophy as she is for her many film roles.

Naturally, this was the side of Shirley I was most interested in when I talked to her at the launching of her autobiography, *Don't Fall off the Mountain* at London's fashionable Crockford Club. I was curious to find out whether she had had any spiritual or psychic reactions to the dramatic and controversial shooting of the exorcism scene in *The Possession of Joel Delaney,* a film she made in 1972.

Director Waris Hussein had confided to me that during the vital scene in which an exorcist performs an actual exorcism ritual, the actor playing the part collapsed, several other actors and crew had unusual and inexplicable metaphysical reactions to the ritual and had to be exorcised themselves. "Even I had to be exorcised," added Waris, "and for the completion of the filming we used a real exorcist, who knew what he was doing."

Shirley was noncommital about her reactions when we spoke, yet I feel that this film and the strange occurrences surrounding it were the turning point of her spiritual awakening, one that later made her such an outspoken supporter of the spiritualist movement in the United States.

The Taurean influence predisposed Shirley to hard work and openness, and these traits were compounded by the industrious sign of Virgo as her Moon and Ascendant. Even as a child she worked hard on her dance routines and acting, a combination of talents that took her into musical comedy.

Perhaps it was her Venus in the sign of Pisces that made her first want to be a dancer, as Pisces rules the feet, yet it was doubtless the Taurean musical-singing influence that made her the great Broadway and Hollywood musical comedy star she was for many years. Destiny took over from inclination in 1954, when she understudied Carol Haney in *Pajama Game* on Broadway. On the fourth night of the show, Haney fractured her ankle, Shirley took over, and the rest is history.

Hollywood producer Hal Wallis saw her and signed her to star in Alfred Hitchcock's "The Trouble with Harry." She soon attracted the attention of major male stars—she was part of Frank Sinatra's Rat Pack, and is sister of Warren Beatty, an Aries. Although in musical comedies such as *Sweet Charity* and *Irma la Douce* she often played sweet, rather pathetic characters, in real life she has always displayed the Taurean impulse toward good citizenship, organization, and charity. A firm political radical, she was the leader of the first American Women's Delegation to China.

In the course of her long career, Shirley has been nominated for an Oscar six times. She lost five times, but after her spiritual regeneration, undaunted, her mystic disciplines combined with Taurean determination and her Mercury in Aries, and she learned to project and visualize what she wanted in life. She made up her mind and "visualized" three important goals: to win an Oscar, to write a bestseller, and to make her nightclub act a hit on Broadway. One after the other her wishes materialized: In 1984 she won the best actress award for *Terms of Endearment;* her book *Out on a Limb* became a bestseller as did its successor, *Dancing in the Light;* and her revue was a smash on Broadway.

Shirley's Part of Fortune is in the fifth house of love and show business together with Saturn, the planet of

hard work and rewards. No one has worked harder on her career, and Shirley is still determined to "keep going until I am 100 . . . and I am going to go on learning." Unlike most Taureans, who dislike change and upsetting the status quo, Shirley feels that her strongest personality trait is "the way she keeps unsettling her life, when most other people are settling down."

She has indeed been the financial architect and comptroller of her own life, ever since she and her brother took off to make it in the difficult world of show business.

Given her own enthusiasm and joy in life, and the help she receives from her "guides on the other side," we can anticipate more exciting adventures, performances, and ideas from this very unique, well-loved, and multi-talented star.

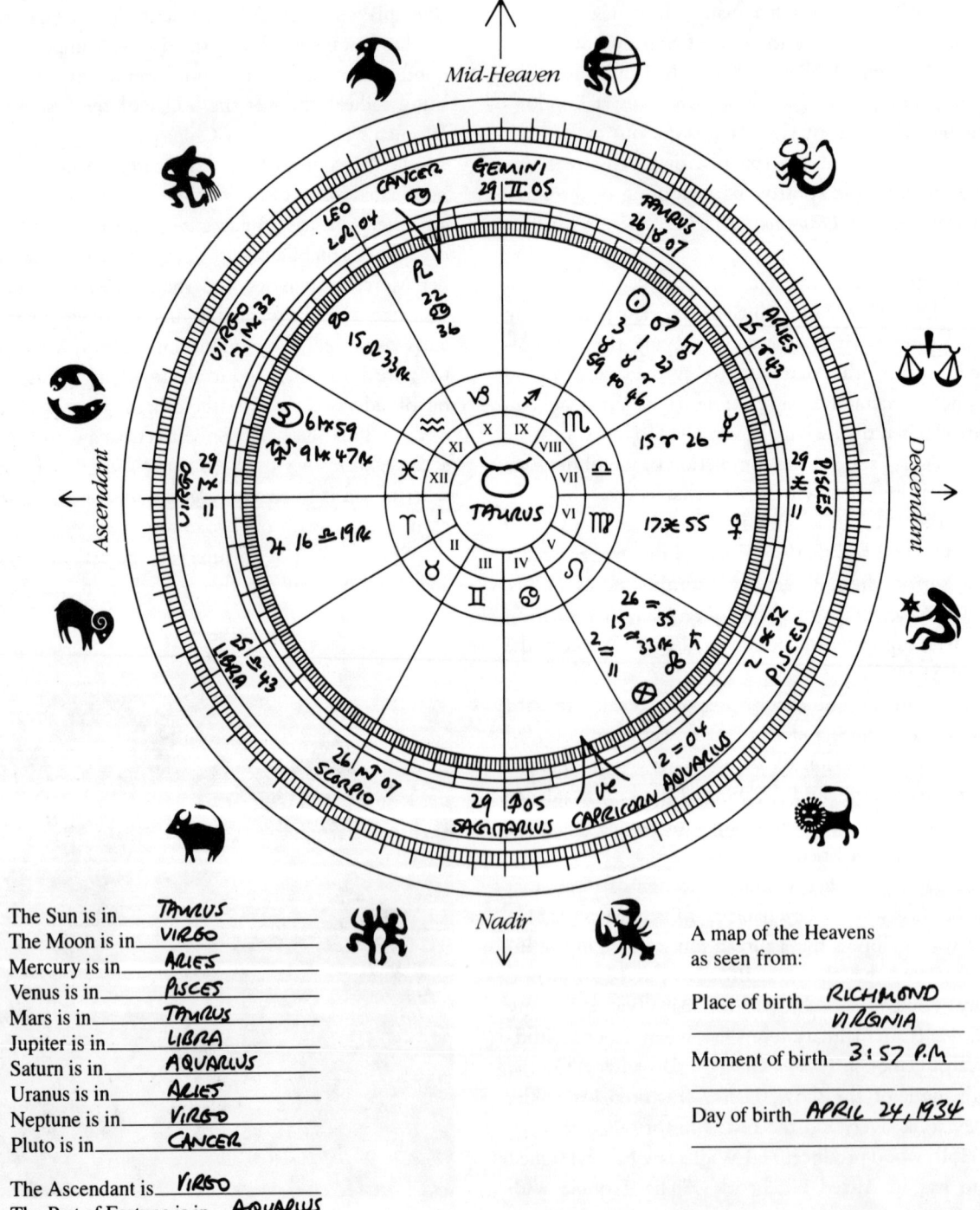

The Sun is in TAURUS
The Moon is in VIRGO
Mercury is in ARIES
Venus is in PISCES
Mars is in TAURUS
Jupiter is in LIBRA
Saturn is in AQUARIUS
Uranus is in ARIES
Neptune is in VIRGO
Pluto is in CANCER

The Ascendant is VIRGO
The Part of Fortune is in AQUARIUS

A map of the Heavens as seen from:

Place of birth RICHMOND VIRGINIA

Moment of birth 3:57 P.M

Day of birth APRIL 24, 1934

Philosophical Street Singers

VIRGO DECANATE, RULED BY MERCURY
May 1–May 10

So methodical and precise in all their business matters, especially in the service of others, it is a wonder that these Taureans find any time at all to make love or play. Even though they have the exuberant love nature of Venus, they combine it with the fickle and changeable traits of the planet Mercury and its Virgo-like love of work.

At their most radiant they combine the two in a creative outlet such as writing lyrics (Mercury) for songs (Venus), or working in an orchestra, writing poetry, or publishing magazines and books. The secretary whose letters and typed copy look like works of art, the chairman of the board whose melodious voice woos all the board members, or the accountant and his spectacular financial reports that look so good it's tempting to read the details are all personalities influenced by this Taurus combination of Venus and Mercury.

Wonderfully diplomatic, they can find the right word to save the day. They invented troubleshooting from the "lip" and can change a few words to give a more winning appeal to any argument. This mercurial ability makes them excellent salesmen, peddlers, beggars, and politicians. They are too honest to want to become con artists, but at times others may feel that is what they are, when they are persuaded to go fishing instead of spending a quiet evening at home or going to a movie. It is this quality, too, that makes them persuasive actors, like Candice Bergen.

They have bright features, and their faces sparkle with personality, curiosity, and the ability to analyze situations with uncanny accuracy. The beauty of Venus keeps them young looking, and Mercury keeps them traveling and learning. They are perennial students, always wanting to learn something more, to make themselves more useful at work and more appealing in the job market, as well as to expand their minds and satisfy their thirst for knowledge.

As children they organized a local band in the back garden and sold tickets to the other children. They were the winners of the poetry-speaking competitions. Their handmade Christmas cards were true works of art that their receivers kept long after the holidays were over. In mathematics they were so advanced that the teachers could not keep up with them. They also had crushes on their teachers and would swoon when they heard their favorite pop singers on the radio during recess.

In love, these Taureans really need an intellect for a marriage partner, someone who will keep up with the current novels and newspaper articles, in fact a "walking reference library" to save economical, time-saving Taureans the chore of having to read everything themselves. It is best if they have the same interests—and they frequently fall in love with people they work with—but if not they will soon learn to have them. These Taureans push their ideas on their loved ones and friends and want them all to enjoy what they consider a perfect way of life. Together they will keep scrapbooks and make special photograph albums so well-itemized and catalogued that they would put the British Museum to shame. They may not want children immediately, even though their lovemaking will be so spontaneous and erratic that there may not be time for the usual birth-control precautions. When blessed by children, they are good parents, giving plenty of love as well as plenty of mental stimulation, which helps their offspring develop quickly, walking sooner than anticipated, reading before they go to school, and growing up to be lovers of books, music, and painting.

PAIGE RENSE

Architectural Digest is one of the most tasteful, chic, and expensively produced magazine in the world today, and editor Paige Rense is the reason for its success.

When I first met Paige in 1974, she immediately asked me to do the horoscope column for the magazine, giving readers the best astrological times for buying, selling, redecorating, or moving, as well as other more personal celestial advice about love and finances. It was an exciting offer, which I naturally accepted.

Just as naturally, I did Paige's chart, and based on her birthday (just before noon on May 4, in Des Moines, Iowa), I realized that it was the great style of her sun sign Taurus combined with her elegant Leo Ascendant that had guided her into the world of show business celebrities and the "who's who" in society to reshape the magazine, raising its circulation by 600,000 readers.

In order to promote *Architectural Digest,* Paige went on television herself as spokeswoman for the commercials. It was a wise choice, for so much of what goes into her magazines *is* herself.

LADY ROTHERMERE

Whether representing Queen Elizabeth at special events in Great Britain; presenting the winner's cup to some sportsperson; entertaining visitors in her Eaton Square home; or helping charities to raise money through street fairs in Berkeley Square; Lady Rothermere always does it with a flourish and a flair that have made her popular with the general public in Britain and also admired and sought after by New York and Beverly Hills society and the press.

Born in Hampstead, London, on May 5, just after noon, Lady Rothermere (Patricia Harmsworth) is a perfect Taurus, artistic and creative (she was once one of J. Arthur Rank's starlets in the movies), capable of making great fortunes through her own talents (her real estate ventures have been incredibly profitable), yet wanting the security of home and family. Pat has four children.

Her Ascendant is Virgo, which attracted her to her husband, newspaper mogul Lord Rothermere (Vere Harmsworth), a Virgo born August 27. Pat's Moon in Aquarius attracts her to helping other people, charitable work, and makes her a popular guest on radio and television interviews.

When she was buying her various homes and properties, I would look at the best possible moment—when the Moon or the planets were in an auspicious location in Pat's horoscope—for choosing and signing the documents. And when it came time for one of her children to marry, I consulted the engaged couple's charts first to make sure that they were compatible and, second, to choose the ideal time for their wedding. For crucial decisions, Pat prefers the planets to lawyers and bank managers.

DONOVAN

Many famous singers are born under the sign of Taurus, but it would be hard to find one who so perfectly fits the description "philosophical street singer." When I first met Donovan in London in the early seventies, the gentleness of his voice and his appearance conveyed this "maverick" feeling.

He was born in Glasgow, Scotland, on May 10, 1946, at 6:15 A.M., a Taurus with his Moon in Virgo and his Ascendant Gemini. His playwright wife, Linda, is a Libra, born October 17.

The combination of Taurus, the singer and musician, and Gemini, the writer and communicator, brought us his great uplifting songs of love, peace, and happiness. He was always a poet, writing rhymes for as long as he could remember. Influenced by Walt Whitman's poems and Chinese poetry, he created his own special brand of poetry and sound and appeared on British television before he even made a record. He arrived on the scene in a sea of flowers, a spokesman for young people who needed a positive direction to follow.

Donovan starts off his record *Cosmic Wheels,* with a reference to the celestial bodies:

> God is playing marbles
> With his planets and his stars
> Creating havoc through my life
> Through his influence on Mars. . . .

CANDICE BERGEN

Born: May 9, 1946, at 9:52 P.M. in Los Angeles, California

If it isn't her incredible beauty or her bright, mercurial intellect that proves overwhelming, it has to be her great sense of humor. In recent years Candice Bergen has proved that she isn't just another pretty face but a talented comedienne (Oscar-nominated for her performance in *Starting Over*) and writer.

Long before she thought about writing her autobiographical book, *Knock on Wood,* I had predicted that Candice would one day write about her childhood and the competitive feelings she had for her nonhuman "older brother," the ventriloquist's dummy Charlie McCarthy, with whom she had to share the love and attention of her father, Edgar Bergen. Her tongue-in-cheek wit and sensitive nostalgia put the book on the best-seller list for weeks.

Candice is not only a brilliant combination of the Venus-Mercury-Taurus influence that presided over her birth—which attracted her to fashion, the arts, and show business—but also has the added talents of her Ascendant Sagittarius, which took her into the world of photojournalism and attracted her to travels in all parts of the world. It seemed fate that she would be asked to play the noted photojournalist Margaret Bourke-White in the 1982 movie *Gandhi.* Candice has frequently accepted movie roles because the locations attracted her and always took along her camera. The Sagittarius influence that gave her her curiosity and love of travel, photography, and film also inspired her interest in anthropology and horses.

Her Moon in Virgo gives her the added talent of the writer and will give her the opportunity to write the script for as well as to star in a major award-winning movie. Candice's Part of Fortune is located in her third house of writing and communication, and there is where her great fortune will come.

The Sun highlights her fifth house of show business and love, but it was ambivalent Saturn, in the seventh house of marriage, that delayed her union with director Louis Malle, a critical but emotionally balancing Scorpio, whom she married in 1980. Saturn tends to delay the area of the chart in which it is located but also brings many lessons and rewards when the goals are accomplished and the restrictions lifted. Now happily married, she has a firm foundation as well as the strong, masculine support she has always needed, allowing her the professional freedom to go after her most desired hopes and wishes.

With Jupiter, the planet of greater good fortune, high in her chart in the tenth house of career and fame, she was destined to have success in anything she wanted to do. Its location in Libra probably took her first into the world of modeling, which she found very boring, for it lacked action and activity. Her Neptune also in Libra, in the ninth house of foreign affairs, makes her a natural diplomat as well as giving her success in filming abroad (Neptune rules moviemaking).

Confident in her own talents and abilities, Candice has taken on such giant assignments as filming an African

expedition for ABC television and becoming photographer for the 1976 Democratic Convention. Her exclusive photo series of President Gerald Ford and his family ran in the *Ladies Home Journal.*

Jupiter well placed in the tenth house, ruling the government, could indicate that Candice will be asked to represent the United States in some official capacity. And there is always the chance she will run for office.

Now that she has nearly everything she desires—love, husband, family, and several careers—she can choose what she wants to do and turn down opportunities that do not fit into her image or life-style. She has come into her own and believes, "It takes a long time to grow up. Longer than they tell you!"

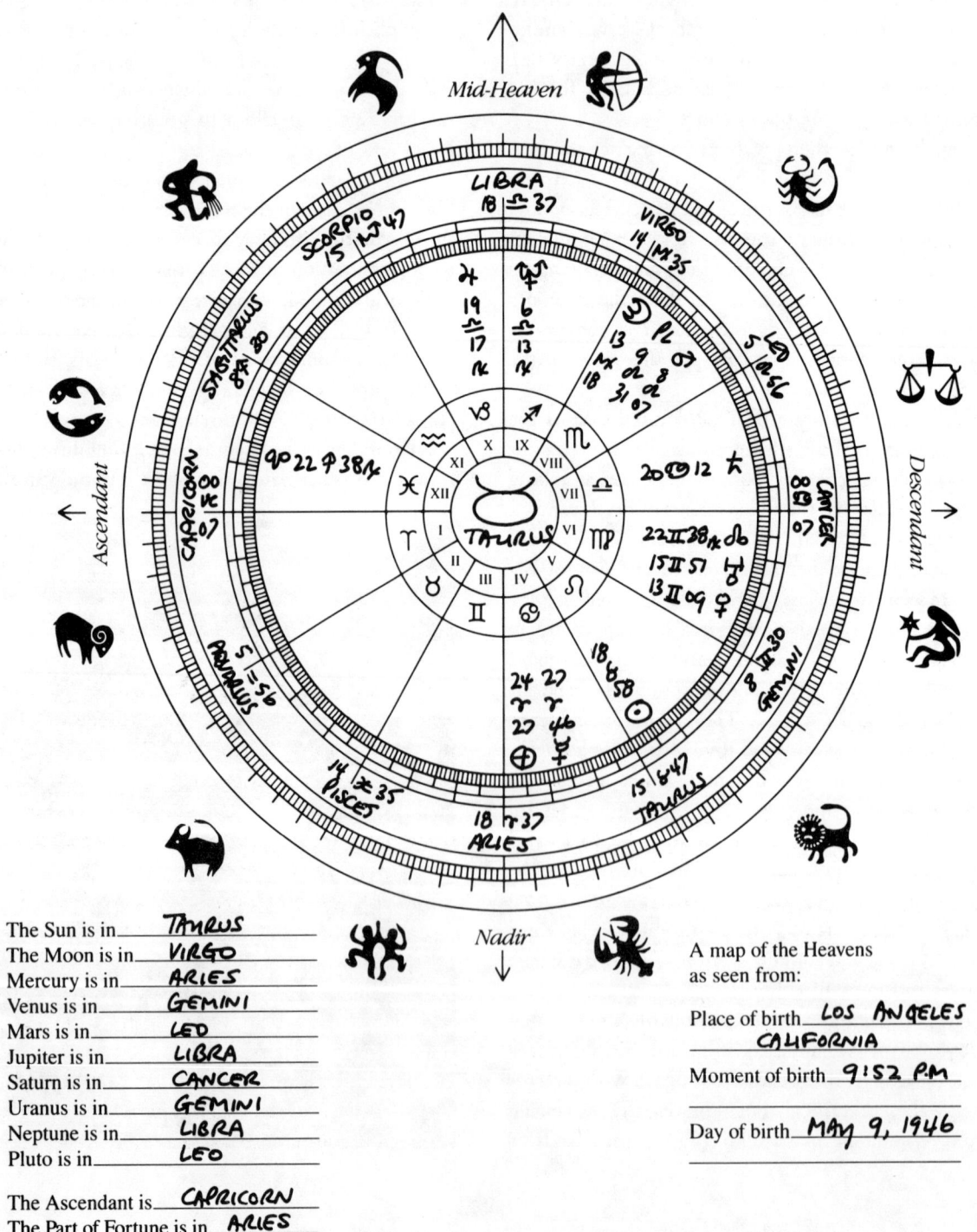

The Sun is in TAURUS
The Moon is in VIRGO
Mercury is in ARIES
Venus is in GEMINI
Mars is in LEO
Jupiter is in LIBRA
Saturn is in CANCER
Uranus is in GEMINI
Neptune is in LIBRA
Pluto is in LEO

The Ascendant is CAPRICORN
The Part of Fortune is in ARIES

A map of the Heavens as seen from:

Place of birth LOS ANGELES CALIFORNIA
Moment of birth 9:52 P.M.
Day of birth MAY 9, 1946

Disco Spinners and Weavers
CAPRICORN DECANATE, RULED BY SATURN
May 11–May 21

These enormously successful and influential Taureans have the luck-and-money influence of Venus—especially, like flamboyant, decorative singer Cher, in connection with fashion, music, and jewelry—and the added Saturnian traits that give them the discipline to persevere long enough to reach a successful climax and financial attainment. They will look at offers and be able to choose the one that will bring the most money in the long run. These aren't the Taureans who must make things happen immediately; they will plot and plan and scheme, and the results, always tasteful, will be fashionable and money-making.

Leaders of style in every way, revolutionaries in the arts, quiet commentators on trends in society, and newsmakers at every turn, these Taureans include the nightclub owner willing to add the latest sensual thrill with lights, lasers, music, and smells; the government leader who supports the arts as a means of attracting publicity and creating extra fundraising outlets in the community; the serious ballad singer; antiwar marchers; as well as conservative socialists, and all have this Saturnian-Venutian outlook on life.

Worldly and successful as these Taureans are, they also have a pull toward nature and solitude. Sometimes, if they could control their vast growing empire from a desert island living off the fruits and fish that nature brings them, they would happily pack their bags immediately or alternatively retreat to a mountain hideaway with a view of panoramic wonder and fresh air that clears the mind to make earthshaking decisions.

It is hard to tell if these Taureans have a sense of humor or not. They tell humorous stories, but in their personal lives it is unwise to tease them or hint at anything with an edge of ridicule. They love detachment as well as attachment, and they need to spend time on their own to think out their moves and seek the answers to life's questions. Excellent teachers, once they have mastered their talents and skills and found the answer to true happiness, they will teach their followers and disciples. As they grow older they want to encourage young people to regard them as big brothers or big sisters—living examples of loving teachers, parents with no children—all who come into contact with them being adopted. And when the time comes and their offspring and foster children are ready to seek their own philosophy of life, they are willing to let them go. This is the spinner-and-weaver side of these go-getters.

When young themselves, these Taureans would make extra money designing and making handicrafts and selling them to neighbors and relatives. They would hand out pamphlets and posters door to door for local politicians. Their musical talents and interests highlighted church fundraising concerts or school proms, and they also decorated the hall to give the right atmosphere to the occasion. They never shirk study, and—though they are inclined toward subjects that interest them or allow them an outlet for their artistic and preaching talents—self-discipline and the encouragement of others are life long.

Generally attracted to the nicer things in life, they can be self-conscious about their status in the community and will want to ensure that their family and friends have the best possible standards of living. They spend well, buying tasteful and expensive gifts, as they need to make a good impression and like to be remembered for their loving and giving natures. This is a serious point for them and must be honored both in the giving and receiving. They have an excellent memory and will notice if a gift has been given away or stored or put in a place of honor.

A working love relationship seems to suit these Taureans best; they love to have a mutual pet project that they and their partners can immerse themselves in and share the adventure together. (Cher, for example, has usually married or been involved with fellow musicians, such as Sonny Bono and Greg Allman.) Otherwise, there can be many lonely days and nights for their loved ones, who will eventually grow to hate the "other" in their Taurus's life, which happens to be their job. These Taureans are susceptible to wining and dining, though routine niceties soon make them restless and bored. Once committed, their love is loyalty and devotion epitomized; in fact they are probably one of the most proficient and attractive lovers in the zodiac. The Saturnian discipline can at times create an atmosphere of puritanism and lack of humor, while underneath the Venus influence brings out the subtle twinkle in the eye that says, "I'm just testing you," and the intense romance that follows is proof of their love. These are the Taureans who, when they become committee chairmen or win an award for public service, want their loved ones beside them to share it, wanting the world to know, "This is the person who helped me get here," and, most important, "This is the person who shares my bed!"

MICHAEL FISH

Michael and I had grown up together, living around the corner from each other in Wood Green, a North London suburb. After many years' separation, during which designer "Mr Fish" had become one of the most famous and fashionable names in London, dressing everyone of note from Lord Snowdon to Mick Jagger, he asked me to do the horoscope chart for the opening of his new shop in Mayfair.

When Muhammad Ali regained his world heavyweight boxing title from George Foreman in October 1974, in Zaire, he was wearing a robe designed by Michael. Into this robe, I had sewn Ali's horoscope chart drawn on a piece of linen, predicting he would win by a knockout. Choosing the exact time for launching Michael's business enterprise was very important, and I took special care to calculate the magic moment. Inspired, I decided to make the chart look very old and mysterious and burned the edges of the parchment with a candle, something I had never done before. With a few artistically placed burn holes and some red candle wax and ribbon, it looked authentic. Little did I realize that I had intuitively picked up from the chart that fifteen months later Michael's shop would be destroyed by smoke and fire.

Michael was born in Clapton, London, on May 11, 1940, at 9:50 P.M., a Taurus with his Moon in the patriotic and home-loving sign Cancer and his Ascendant Sagittarius, the creatively ambitious style maker. With Uranus—the planet that rocketed him to fame at an early age—in the sixth house of clothing next to his Sun in Taurus, the fashion industry was the best outlet for his talents, even though he also revitalized the London disco scene when he reopened the famous Embassy Club.

The Moon in Cancer has made him a successful real estate investor, and he is famous for mixing some of the most interesting talents at his weekly dinner parties. Friends with the older Establishment, he is also an inspiration to new, young artists and designers, adding the particular, charming type of eccentricity so peculiar to Mr Fish to any occasion.

STEVIE WONDER

Stevie Wonder heads a multimillion-dollar empire, and although he has been blind since birth, he is also a man who has been able to do what he loves most and that is to create and perform his own music (and become a superstar and millionaire while doing it).

Born on May 13, 1950, in Saginaw, Michigan, he is a Taurus with his Moon and Venus in Aries. It is the musical talents of Taurus—which also rules the throat and gives Stevie his wonderful melodic voice—and the great determination of Aries to overcome any restrictions in life that made him skilled at the piano, guitar, harmonica, and bongos by the time he was ten. He joined Motown and at the age of twelve recorded his hit, "Fingertips."

Spinning and interweaving the Motown sound with jazz, hard rock, reggae, and other musical influences, he has kept abreast of the times and consistently had one hit after another.

Trying to influence everyone to "love one another," Stevie's Moon in Aries fighter's spirit still comes through his music, as he chastizes the powers that be for ignoring the needs of the minorities, as in "You Haven't Done Nothing." Stevie has the magic to bring young people together and, through his songs, to make a better world.

CHER

Born: May 20, 1946, at 7:31 A.M. in El Centro, California

Cher is a perfect example of a disco spinners and weaver, for not only have her recordings kept every teenager, yuppie and middle-aged American dancing way into the early hours at the local disco, but her outrageous and elaborate fashions have inspired the most daring of designers and trendies alike.

Cher is a Taurus with Cancer Ascendant, which makes her very concerned about having a home base, family, and security. She grew up with her mother, who married eight times in all, after her own father abandoned them when she was only a year old, and she held on to any family, any parental attachment, that she could. She married Salvatore ("Sonny") Bono in 1964, when she was 18, and though the marriage did not endure (but, a true Taurean partnership marriage, it spawned successful music careers for both), she has been involved in marriage and motherhood ever since.

Despite an active career, Cher has taken on the responsibility of bringing up her two children—Chastity Bono, born in 1969, and Elijah Blue Allman, born in 1976. (Her marriage to Gregg Allman lasted eight days, but she stood by him during the next two years while he tried to kick drugs and liquor.) In both romantic and maternal relationships she is a devoted and loyal spirit.

She happily plays mother and housekeeper in an elaborate Egyptian-style setting in Benedict Canyon, another home in Malibu, and yet another in Beverly Hills. In fact, her fascination with Egypt goes back to the early days of Sonny and Cher—their first professional name was Caesar and Cleo—and may also be a reflection of Cher's dark and exotic good looks.

Her Saturn is in Cancer, directly opposing her Moon in the house of marriage. Saturn represents *all* the men in Cher's life and indicates the separation from and loss of the ones that should have meant so much to her. It may have attracted her in later years to men in hopeless situations, in which she could only be a loser.

Realizing that she could no longer rely on her lovers or partners, Cher has taken on her own career and life. Determined to make a success of her acting career, she has wooed a rather skeptical Broadway-Hollywood press into accepting her as a serious actress. Making her mark in New York in the stage production of *Come Back to the 5 & Dime, Jimmy Dean, Jimmy Dean* in 1982 led to her being offered a major role in *Silkwood,* for which she was nominated for an Academy Award as best supporting actress. Since then she has been highly acclaimed for her performance in *Mask*—a film, incidentally, about a courageous and devoted mother.

Her Moon in Capricorn has given her her photogenic qualities and the stamina and guts to work out in order to keep her incredible figure. Because her Moon is located in her seventh house of marriage, Cher needs a husband who can help her take on the responsibilities of her multitalented career. There was much success at first with Sonny Bono, and they were brought back together from 1975 to 1976 to do a new "Sonny and Cher

Show." Even her public affair with record producer David Geffen may have helped develop and encourage her singing career. However, going it alone, she can escape the traumas that go along with most relationships.

Mercury, the planet of communications, is exactly next to her Sun, which enables her to write, speak, sing, and express herself with real candor so that fans and even detractors cannot help but admire her. She may appear flippant and unreliable at times as she has Venus in Gemini (flirtatious tendencies), Uranus in Gemini (unexpected verbal reactions to situations), and the North Node also in Gemini, showing where her lessons must be learned in this life. They are all located in the twelfth house of self-undoing.

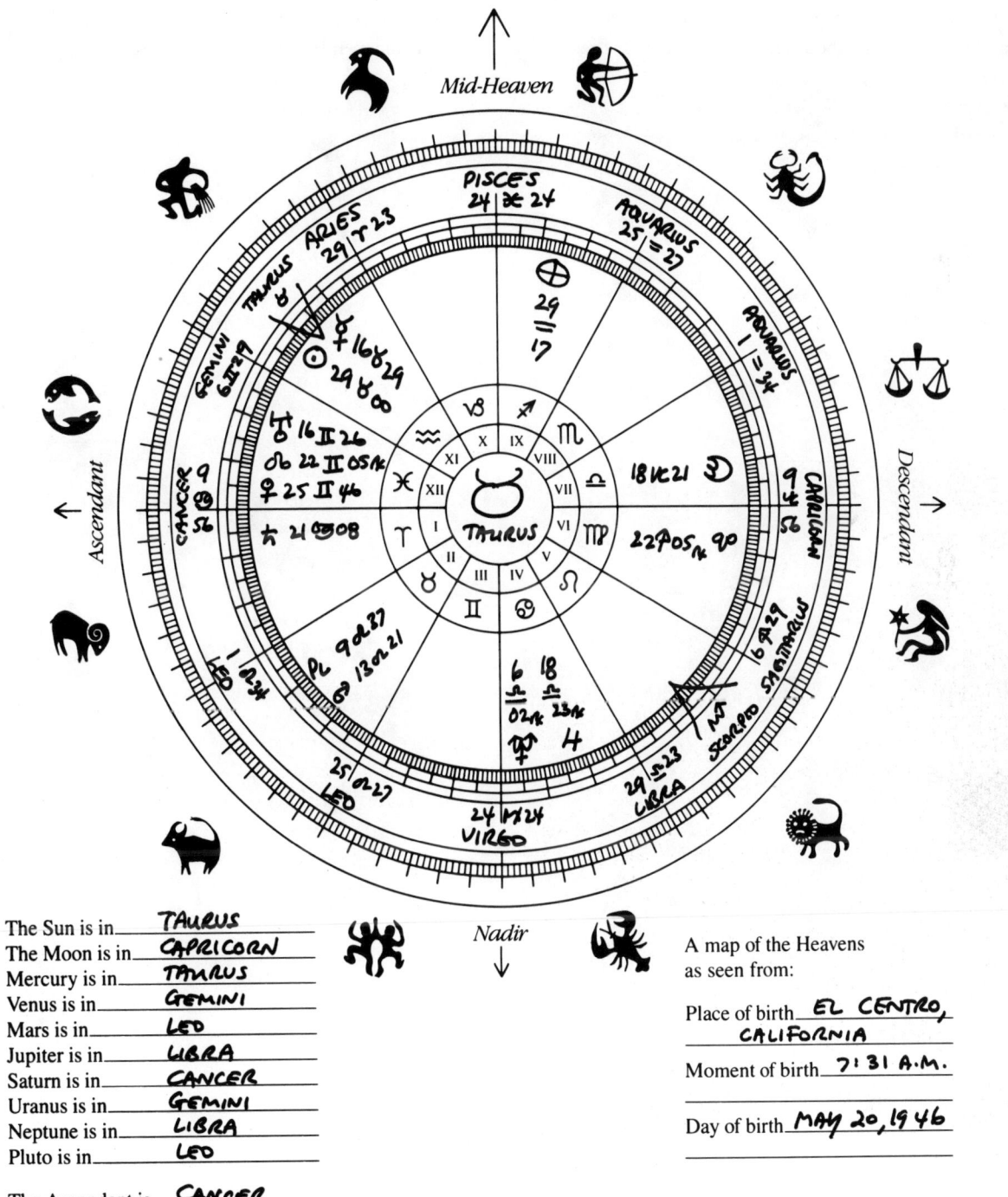

The Sun is in __TAURUS__
The Moon is in __CAPRICORN__
Mercury is in __TAURUS__
Venus is in __GEMINI__
Mars is in __LEO__
Jupiter is in __LIBRA__
Saturn is in __CANCER__
Uranus is in __GEMINI__
Neptune is in __LIBRA__
Pluto is in __LEO__

The Ascendant is __CANCER__
The Part of Fortune is in __AQUARIUS__

A map of the Heavens as seen from:

Place of birth __EL CENTRO, CALIFORNIA__

Moment of birth __7:31 A.M.__

Day of birth __MAY 20, 1946__

So much of the unhappiness we have been witness to in her personal relationships has been self-imposed, yet it may have been that terror of being abandoned, engraved on her memory when she was a baby, that always made her seek a new love while still married to or involved with the main love in her life.

Pluto and Mars are well placed in the sign of Leo, the showman and -woman. This has given her the drive, energy, and aggression to "do her own thing" and to do it so that everyone will remember. Outspoken in political matters and about the concerns of the needy and unfortunate, she can use her charisma to get others to follow her lead.

Still, it is her Jupiter and Neptune in the fourth house of home that give her the greatest security—even though at times it is a fantasy one (Neptune)—knowing that however the professional winds blow, she will always have a roof over her own head and those of her children. She will make a fortune in real estate.

As a charismatic singer, actress, and celebrity, and as a passionate and devoted mother, she has always been more independent than she realizes.

GEMINI
Orator of the Zodiac

SUN IN GEMINI, RULED BY MERCURY
May 22–June 21

Chatter, chatter, chatter. It is easy to recognize a Gemini anywhere in the world, whether on a crowded bus talking to strangers and giving them directions; keeping guests enthralled at a cocktail party with witty anecdotes and humorous stories; painstakingly editing the third revised news item for the late edition of the best-selling city newspaper; or speaking out either on a street corner, a pulpit, or a platform about some public cause or concern to which they have the answer. These are the Mercury-ruled people and, like the "messenger of the gods," they are reliable and anxious to do their duty, even though it may involve lots of extra travel, late hours, and headaches. The anxiety that gives them all that nervous energy also gives them an enormous lust for life and a desire to be helpful to others and to be wanted in return. Very much like the Red Cross, at every accident crisis or sickbed the sparkling, bubbly, and reassuring Gemini will be found.

Their enthusiasm for life and their curiosity can exhaust others, who will become nervous with the reports of all the activities that Gemini is involved in, and as deadlines and events turn up in their lives, this fun can turn into hysterics and panic if they do not work out a practical schedule. But somehow or other they *can* cope and appear pretty happy most of the time, their charm being the ability to escape from life's real problems by letting their imaginations and creative abilities take over.

Geminis just love to talk; they will easily take over the whole conversation, and they are so charming and persuasive they can sell others on something they either don't want or can't afford. Their wide, innocent eyes, with a slightly mischievous twinkle, can trap the most stubborn person in romance and business. Geminis are never boring, as they have so many interests and are always looking for new and exciting projects or books.

Reading is almost an obsession for them. They just cannot go past a bookshop and would rather spend their last money on a book or magazine and have to walk home than feel that they have missed the latest publication. Their shelves are already filled with thousands of extra books bought on a whim to be read later, and friends—knowing their weakness—are always donating their collections to Geminis. Unlike some signs, they hang on to the printed word as if it were gold. It almost seems as if they will throw away their furniture and give away their clothes and jewelry but take their books and papers with them to the grave if necessary. But, knowing their generous and neighborly attitudes, they are actually more likely to give them to the local library, school, or orphanage at the last moment, so that others can share the adventure of the printed word and the ideas that jump off the pages that made their lives so full and adventurous.

Gemini is the third sign of the zodiac, the house that rules communications of all kinds—speaking, writing, theater, radio, television, the telephone, and recordings—and also studies, usually short educational courses, particularly crash courses in languages and job improvement. Mercurial both mentally and physically, it is the sign that rules short trips and travels and means of travel such as cars, bicycles, and local transportation. And it is the house of brethren, neighbors, teachers, or students—people whose interests and ideas one is forced by choice or chance to share, people with whom to discuss and communicate problems, and people to think of when making important decisions.

It is funny to think of Gemini as being the sign of communications, for those born under it are notoriously late for appointments, not deliberately or by accident but because their minds have been captured by the sight of some exciting new concept that momentarily takes them off course, or a conversation with someone with a problem keeps them on the telephone long after they should have left for an appointment. They are not punctual but strangely reliable. They will get the medicine and go out of their way to do it—disregarding their own needs on occasion—but deliver it late and so create a worry that might have been avoided. They will bring packages and messages themselves rather than trust other means of communication, like the post office and like the Saint Bernard dog in the Alps, will come to the rescue of anyone at any time no matter what the obstacles.

One problem is their apparent superficiality, but if

their witty, bubbly, and brilliant minds at times give the impression of no real substance, they are among the very sincerest, emotional, and alert people to have around. On the other hand, this lightness also helps lift all involved onto a much more realistic and philosophical plain, especially in times of loss and sickness.

In their eagerness to make friends and show genuine interest in others' points of view or vocations, they can be overly energetic and enthusiastic, causing many relationships to be short lived through sheer exhaustion of the other person involved.

They just love to be a part of all that is going on—this multiplicity of character is a reflection of the twins who are the Gemini symbol—but at the same time to be free and independent of responsibility, loving change and diversity. They have the best type of sense of humor, they are clever with their wittiness, and their laughter is contagious.

Geminis just love to travel, and any work that involves movement and adventure is good for them. Because they excel in the communicative arts they are excellent salesmen and -women, knowing just the right phraseology to turn a difficult customer into a happy and friendly one. Most will not, however, cheat others deliberately, even though there have been some very clever and brilliant confidence tricksters born under this sign. Fun-loving people will find them at the local resort area, on the cruise ship, or at the travel agency enjoying planning others' travels equally well as planning their own. Since they hate to work on their own, as they enjoy conversation and company, jobs involving the public are much better and more fun for them. Clearly, they make good entertainers.

Their excellent reasoning powers and investigative minds attract them to the newspaper business as journalists and editors, and to radio and television either on or behind the screen. Having great dexterity, they can often work in two jobs at one time, doing an excellent job in each case and enjoying every minute of it. Lots of astrologers are Gemini, as they are attracted to the services offered by the psychic arts and sciences—first aid of a different kind. More modest and introverted Geminis might own a bookshop, run a messenger or limousine service (there's that winged Mercury again!), or become librarians or museum curators.

As many will write their own books, or get into publishing (of poetry and music also), they naturally get themselves into the public eye. Their great skill with words and communicating their ideas will be of assistance to others as well as to their ambitions, and public relations and publicity are other ideal outlets for their energy.

The main thing to remember with Gemini is that they are, or can be, two distinctly different personalities in one body. One minute doing and saying one thing, and the next doing and saying something else.

Champagne Conversationalists

GEMINI DECANATE, RULED BY MERCURY
May 22–May 30

This is the purest, most mercurial Gemini, with twice as much ability to communicate with other people and to pass on the gods' words of wisdom either through research and clarity of expression or jumping on the bandwagon to spread the gospel—even guiding others in what stepping-stones to take in life's journey. Mercury, the messenger of the gods, works night and day for these Geminis, who include radiant Joan Collins, entertainment ambassador par excellence Bob Hope, and "bubbly" Beverly Sills.

Curiosity and analysis go hand in hand with all their ventures. They will not enter into new projects without first exploring the future possibilities and what the end results could be. Spiritually as well as mentally, these Geminis will set up research committees and delve into the realms of the supernatural as well as the area of science. They will speak out boldly about their findings, often against public opinion, and keep to their beliefs however much they may be in the minority. Communication between human beings is sacred to them, and they will not allow any personal biases to influence their report or add a single inflection that might alter its meaning.

Refiners of their language—whether it be English, Spanish, French, Swahili, or any other from any remote part of the world—they have a knack of coining a phrase to fit the exact moment or feeling. They are the world's translators, the people who pass on the beauty of the language from one generation to another, the people who, with a wave of their hand, capture the imaginations and ears of the masses. Many have talents in speaking, writing, acting, and singing. Others are drawn to helping the United Nations or to international business as translators or couriers. Some travel around the world as explorers, teachers, missionaries, and tour guides. But all have this amazing ability to relate verbally to others, and once they decide to put their thoughts on paper, they may have a best-seller on their hands.

Worrying about other people, however, takes them away from their normal course of action. They are forever the rescuers, and whether it is a cat that is trapped in a neighbor's cellar or the child who is lost and cannot remember its name or a sick relative who needs round-the-clock care—all and each get the attention and help of these Geminis. They are true crusaders.

To balance these wonderful qualities, one has to put up with their patter and continual need for sound, either music or speech, as this gives them more thoughts and ideas. They love to be topical, their conversations are the best at cocktail parties, and their facts—though often embroidered by their creative imaginations—are the latest from the *Times*. As teachers they encourage debate and the exchange of ideas, even though they can at times leave their students more confused than when they began with the bombardment of information they generously pass on.

It is the chairperson of the board giving a summation of the meeting, as well as the drunk on the corner keeping passers-by entertained with his words of wisdom; the actor who becomes a cultural emissary, as well as the evangelist shouting his own philosophy from the back of an open truck who epitomize this energetic and communicative Gemini.

These flirtatious Geminis need a very mental love relationship, with sharing of ideas and long periods of conversation. They love to delve into their loved ones' minds, and sometimes to challenge them, and with the double Mercury influence of this decanate twin sign, it is often a case of "two-upmanship." They want to know the history of their partner's family, the idiosyncrasies of each brother and sister, and what they think about each other. Their fascination for detail is what makes them such good narrators of incidents and such good storytellers. Love and love of words go together for them.

BARBARA PARKINS

At the table in my house in Chelsea, I was faced with several important questions and decisions that had to be made by Barbara Parkins. A television starlet, Barbara had been rocketed to fame in 1964 as Betty Anderson/Harrington/Cord/Harrington on "Peyton Place," having married twice on the series like a good Gemini. She had done many movies in Hollywood, including *Valley of the Dolls*. Now, in 1972, she had to decide between the many offers of movies in England and Europe or going back to Hollywood. It helped her to know that astrologically London was the best place for her to be in this upcoming period of her life. Since making her base in the United Kingdom, she has worked solidly in many British movies and on television.

Born in Vancouver, Canada, on May 22, 1942, Barbara has the Gemini trait of being a wonderful conversationalist. Sitting next to Art Buchwald, Peter Ustinov, and many others celebrating the Fourth of July at a buffet at the popular-chic White Elephant club in Mayfair, she kept everyone enthralled with her charm, wit, and ability to make lighthearted comments that made everyone feel she had known them for years. Seeing me returning from the dessert table, from which I had taken samples of every cake, pie, Jell-O, fruit, and English trifle, she remarked that my plate looked as if I were at a children's party. A wonderful observation I cherish to this day, as I go on "sampling," a habit rooted in my childhood.

Knowing the right location to live in is as important as choosing a career or spouse and Barbara had discovered that London, a Gemini city, was very compatible and lucky for her.

BRUCE WEITZ

I was directing and emceeing a gala benefit, "A Knight of Stars and Stripes," at the Kennedy Center in Washington, D.C., promoting bulletproof vests for the police. It was Bruce Weitz, one of the stars of "Hill Street Blues" (on which he plays the ferocious but compassionate Mick Belker), who most immediately responded to the producer and fundraiser Tammy Kennedy Wolfe's invitation to participate. "A cause to help the police," he said. "I'll come immediately." How popular he was when visiting various parts of the city to meet with his fans or to aid antidrug programs, with which he is involved, and to do his famous "dogbreath growl" to the delight of adults and children alike. At the gala he helped introduce many of the important celebrities, and Marion Barry, the mayor of Washington, declared a Bruce Weitz day, on which he was given the keys to the city and a personal visit to the White House to speak to President Reagan.

As he and "Hill Street Blues" co-star Michael Warren read the names of the police officers killed in the line of duty, two singers, male and female, dressed as police officers, sang "What I Did for Love," accompanied by the Kennedy Center Orchestra, while the honor guard presented their colors. There wasn't a dry eye in the audience, which included Presidential Press Secretary James Brady, Senator Edward Kennedy, Chief of Police Maurice Turner, and many other leading political dignitaries. President Reagan sent a specially filmed message to start the evening, which he finished by saying, "In the words of Sergeant Esterhaus, 'Hill Street's' tough duty sergeant in the early season, 'Let's be careful out there.' "

Bruce was born in Norwalk, Connecticut, on May 22, 1943, at 3:17 A.M., and has four planets in the sign of Gemini, giving him the wonderful ability to teach, entertain, and win a place in everyone's heart. His Ascendant is in the 8:37 degrees of Aries, the sign ruled by the planet Mars, god of war, thus his affinity to the police and uniforms. Although Bruce had had great success in films, television, and on Broadway, it was the television series, "Hill Street Blues," that made him and his character a household word.

Like many others who have had great success in the United States, he has his Venus near that special degree of the birthday of the United States of America, in Cancer.

BEVERLY SILLS

By the time she was seven years old she already knew and could sing twenty-three arias. When she took over as director of the New York City Opera—situated on the plaza at Lincoln Center in the New York State Theater—in 1979, she had been the company's leading coloratura for twenty-five years and was determined to make it a still greater success. Her mercurial Gemini instincts came to the fore: "I think with a little bit of luck I can make this *the* place. I have a feeling," she told the *Washington Post's* music critic.

Born in Brooklyn, New York, on May 25, 1929, she has only the Sun in Gemini. Her other planets are spread widely around the zodiac, giving her the appearance of being all things to all men (and women) and capable of doing everything from administration to performing.

It was her Mercury in Taurus, the sign that rules the throat and singing in particular, that gave her that incredible instrument—her beautiful voice—and her charming way of wooing audiences. Nevertheless, it must have taken many conversations over many glasses of champagne for Beverly to keep the New York City Opera going, winning the enormous financial support necessary for such an endeavor.

In any event, her feelings proved to be correct. She did make the New York City Opera *the* place.

ALLAN CARR

I couldn't write about champagne conversationalists without a brief mention of the amazing genius of show business producer Allan Carr, who has done much to rejuvenate the traditional Broadway musical by bringing us *La Cage aux Folles,* among numerous other production credits.

Born in Highland Park, Illinois, on May 27, 1941, Allan has five planets in the sign of Gemini including the Moon, making him a dazzling communicator. He was born on a New Moon and was drawn at a young age toward show business.

He never allowed his weight problem, which he has finally overcome, to stand in his way. In fact, the battle he had with it from his youth may have made him more determined to be a success.

One hit after another has been directly or indirectly influenced by the now-almost-legendary Allan Carr. As manager of such stars as Ann-Margret, Marlo Thomas, Marvin Hamlisch, Melina Mercouri, and Peter Sellers as well as in other capacities, Mr. Carr has played a vital role in the entertainment world.

It must have been his mercurial attraction to Broadway that gave him the ability to talk both the young and the mature into trusting his knowledge and success. After all, by the age of twenty, he had become a name to be reckoned with. With *Grease,* starring John Travolta (Aquarius), Allan had produced the highest-earning movie musical in history. And it is reported that Allan collects over $100,000 a week from *La Cage aux Folles.*

Never give up, whatever the obstacles. Keep an eye on childhood dreams, and there is no reason whatsoever for not reaching at least some of them, perhaps all. Allan Carr did; so can anyone.

BOB HOPE

I can't think of anyone in the world with sharper wit, more delightful repartee or wicked humor, and truer patriotism than Bob Hope. He is a perfect example of the champagne conversationalist, though he is as at home with a USO mug of coffee in his hand as with a glass of champagne at the White House.

When I talked to him at the Westbury Music Fair, where he was on the same bill with Debbie Reynolds, he showed a sensitive vulnerability that made him nervously aware if any of his guests showed signs of timidity or of being ill at ease. It's interesting to watch him in action, and one can see why he has had such an influence on the troops all over the world, often entertaining in battle zones, impervious to warnings of danger by his friends and family.

Born in London, England, on May 29, 1903, at 3:36 P.M. Bob has the Sun, Mercury, and Pluto in the sign of Gemini. His personality (Sun), his witty jokes and introductions (Mercury), and his attraction to big business and the armed conflicts where he has brought so much comfort (Pluto), have combined to make him one of the most formidable yet affectionate entertainers in the business.

"Big business" is really an understatement—he is worth approximately $250 million. Those Gemini planets are located in his eighth house of income and wealth, yet his Ascendant Libra makes him a born diplomat, often representing the United States at special political and charitable events. Success is indicated in his horoscope, as his Moon is in 14:33 degrees of Cancer. His Moon coincides with the birthday of the United States, July 4, 1776.

He is the recipient of more than a thousand awards and citations for humanitarian and professional efforts, including the Kennedy Center Honors for Lifetime Achievement in the Arts and the President's Medal of Freedom, his most cherished award.

With all the natural advantages in his chart, Hope, like many other stars, still wound up changing his name. Born Leslie Townes Hope, as a child he was called "Les," a name that quickly modulated into the not-very-stellar "Hopeless." And so Bob Hope was launched, a name admirably suited to a man who has given hope to so many soldiers on the front lines and who inspires other eighty-year-olds with the knowledge that life doesn't have to be over when you grow old. There are still wonderful adventures, romances, and happiness ahead, as long as you start by making others happy first.

JOAN COLLINS

Born: May 23, 1933, at 3:00 A.M. in London, England

Sitting with Joan, very pregnant with Katyana Kennedy Kass in 1972, we talked of metaphysics, her career, her loves, and her new baby. Joan, already one of the biggest box office successes of the British screen, was looking ahead.

"You won't fulfill your great potential until you move to Hollywood," I explained to her. "Los Angeles is a Virgo city (foundation of the Spanish settlement September 4, 1781), and your Jupiter is in Virgo in the exact degree that the Sun is in Los Angeles' horoscope. It will be fantastic for you and make all your dreams and ambitions come true."

Hollywood was not new to Joan; she had made *Land of the Pharaohs* in 1955, but the time was not right for the superstardom in her horoscope. She had to wait until she portrayed Alexis Carrington Colby on television's "Dynasty" twenty-six years later to become Number One on American television.

Joan is an amazing combination of her sun sign Gemini, her Moon sign Taurus, and her Ascendant sign Aries. There is no doubt she is a champagne conversationalist. She looks perfect talking to friends and business associates over a glass of champagne.

The witty, fascinating chatter of the Gemini, plus the wealth sign Taurus, made her the ideal choice for the ambitious, greedy, and bitchy Alexis, so unlike the private Joan Collins. She has devoted her private life to her daughter Katyana, who was in a car accident when she was eight and whose doctors predicted, after her eight-day coma had ended, that she would suffer from brain damage.

Joan, who has Mars-ruled Aries as her Ascendant, refused to accept this and miraculously nursed Katyana back to health. A fighter, too, Joan is also sensitive, caring, and helpful to those around her and has had many ups and down in her life, proving herself a winner over and over again.

During the last days of her pregnancy with Katyana, Joan was concerned about her own happiness and compatibility with her new baby. We had looked at the various planetary aspects around the expected time of arrival. It was a choice between Cancer and Gemini. As the last days of Gemini arrived, Joan made an important decision. The child must be a Gemini, and on June 20, 1972, the final day before the Sun would move into Cancer, Joan had Katyana induced.

This decision also played a vital role in her next choice of sweetheart, Peter Holm, who became her husband for a short time in 1986. A fellow Gemini, born on June 16, 1947, Holm was the husband Joan was looking for—a husband who would be compatible not only with her but also with her daughter. Joan's Venus, planet of love, is in Gemini, and she felt that finally the two most important loves in her life were Geminis.

Luckily, Pluto, the planet of big business, is located in the fifth house of show business in Joan's chart. Not only is she an actress but also a very successful businesswoman. Her own company produced the 1985 miniseries "Sins," in which she starred for television; and she has also starred in film versions of the novels *The Stud* and *The Bitch,* written by her sister, best-selling novelist Jackie Collins.

Geminilike, Joan is ever hungry for new projects and injects new life and panache into every character she

GEMINI

plays, leaping with the inborn dexterity of the twin sign from scoundrel (suitably, the name of her perfume) to heroine.

Joan's much-publicized nude photographs in *Playboy*, taken when she was fifty, gave all maturing women a boost. The careers, romances, and personal sexual pride of millions have all been helped by Joan's successful life, giving everyone a new sense of ambition and dreams. Instead of planning to retire from life, people are now just starting to live it after fifty.

In 1958, when Joan was making her name in Hollywood, she said, "England is a marvelous place for someone who likes gracious living, but for someone young and ambitious, give me America." There's no question about it—ageless, buoyant Joan was talking about herself.

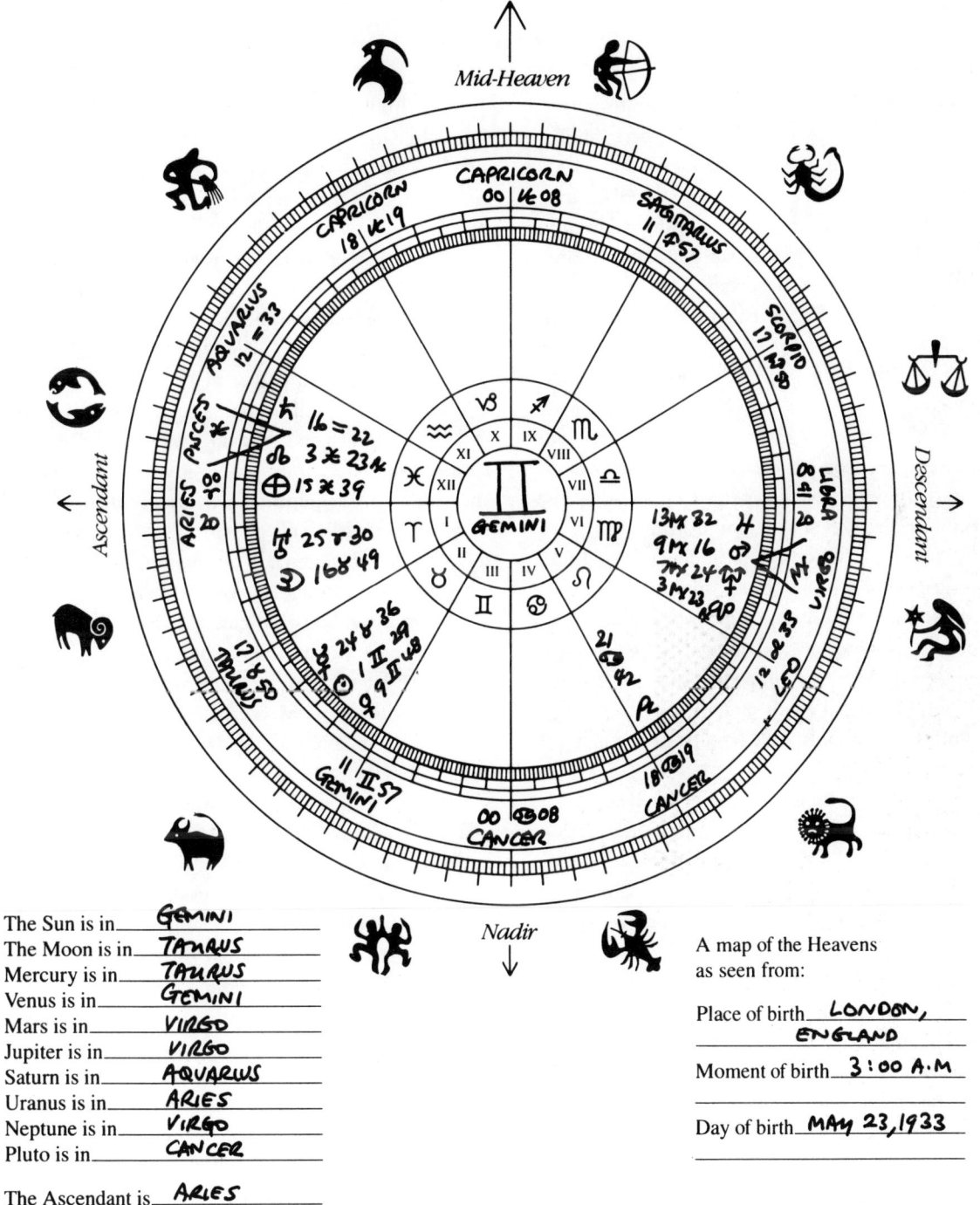

The Sun is in __GEMINI__
The Moon is in __TAURUS__
Mercury is in __TAURUS__
Venus is in __GEMINI__
Mars is in __VIRGO__
Jupiter is in __VIRGO__
Saturn is in __AQUARIUS__
Uranus is in __ARIES__
Neptune is in __VIRGO__
Pluto is in __CANCER__

The Ascendant is __ARIES__
The Part of Fortune is in __PISCES__

A map of the Heavens as seen from:

Place of birth __LONDON, ENGLAND__

Moment of birth __3:00 A.M__

Day of birth __MAY 23, 1933__

Beautiful Nightingales
LIBRA DECANATE, RULED BY VENUS
May 31–June 10

These Geminis make the most exquisite music, either literally, by their singing or performing, or symbolically in their beautiful thoughts and ideas. They have the combination of the lively and distinct variations of Mercury plus the love, warmth, and beauty of Venus and all the gifts of music, painting, dancing, and the other fine arts that this planet brings. They want to be loved for what they do. They need an audience that will cry for them when life treats them badly, a fan club that sends flowers and cards when they are ill, and a public that will forgive them when their emotional life affects their performance. They want to go out into the darkness and know that there are people there to hug and understand them. Beauty combined with a childlike hopefulness is characteristic of Brooke Shields, for instance.

Nightclub singers who have retired and come back again and again; poets—even of sentimental verses for greeting cards; hit songwriters, whose words and music express our every emotion and give us goose bumps when we listen to them; and all people in the world of entertainment connected with singers and musicians have this mixture of Venus and Mercury somewhere in their horoscope.

They are always willing to entertain at parties or to volunteer their time to fix the disco music for the weekend party or the sound system at the local fundraising concert. Their sincere need to be an accepted member of the community makes them offer to take on more chores and committee work than others do. They enjoy seeing other people in love, so they will organize an engagement party or plan a blind date for two of their dearest single friends, and they will play a very active and dominant part in the actual marriage ceremony. They know just the right way to present things—not only tasteful but highly original and imaginative.

As children they would write beautiful verses and sing while they played with their toys. They would win verse-speaking competitions and the more agile and theatrically inclined would go regularly for tap- and ballet-dancing classes. Others would edit the school magazine, as well as have a paper delivery route. And as they grew older their communication skills would become more sophisticated, and they would be hired by the local newspaper as editors and at the local radio and television stations to gather news.

Their charm and excitement over ideas and events make their speech and writing lively and full of imagination. Like all Geminis, these love to talk and gossip and leave you delightfully exhausted when they come to the end of their talk or narration. With so much to tell, they try to cram all the material into one story. They find it easier to edit others than themselves.

Love is the best medicine for these Geminis. They need not only romantic love but to have a loving entourage of friends and associates around them. They are in love with love. Mercurial as they are, they need balanced, supportive partners—whatever their signs—to counteract restlessness or melancholy.

These are the loving Geminis, and they must feel that everyone loves them at all times. They cannot cope in a loveless world, and they want to spread the "love conquers all" message. You need never worry about knowing if these Geminis love you or not . . . they will tell you over and over again, writing romantic notes, playing love songs, and announcing to all that they are in love. Remember, they will want to escape from you like the "air." But just try to escape from them and they will be on your tracks, and envelop you in words and ideas that will seem impossible to contradict. After all, if someone loves you, what defenses do you have?!

TOM JONES

Here is a perfect example of a "beautiful nightingale"—just ask any one of his fans, especially women, for Tom has one of the most melodious voices in show business. Tom's physical gyrations on stage, which would put Elvis to shame, only add to his sexy image.

A Gemini, born June 7, 1940, at 1:00 A.M. in Pontypridd, Wales, he has his Sun and Moon in the sign of Gemini (the great communicator), and his Ascendant is Aquarius (the ruler of television shows and recordings). Born during the New Moon, Tom was destined to start a new life, and escaped from the family tradition of working in the coal mines.

As Gemini rules the hands, it is no surprise to learn his interests include boxing.

His Mercury, Mars, and Venus are in the sign of Cancer (the homelover), and one of his first big hits was "The Green, Green Grass of Home." And as the United States is a Cancer country (July 4th is its "birthday"), it is the place he chooses to woo, whether on tour, appearing in Las Vegas, or living in his Bel Air mansion. He lives with his wife—his childhood sweetheart Linda—and his son, Mark.

Aquarian's love masses of people, and his ascendant helps him turn on his fans, many of whom throw their hotel keys to him during his performance.

JOAN RIVERS

When you go to a party or gathering and a group of people are being entertained by a nonstop raconteur of the most outrageous, shocking, and funny stories, you can be sure it is a Gemini, especially one of "the beautiful nightingales."

Though I am sure Joan would never claim to be such an exotic bird, her chirpings and New York–accented oneliners have the same kind of hypnotic magic over the viewers or listeners. There is no way to stop her once the motor is turned on.

It is no wonder. Joan is a triple Gemini, and she has her Sun, Mercury, and Venus in that quixotic, curious, and investigative sign. It gives her the brilliant, comic mind, the memory that is necessary to recall, remember, and deliver her monologues, and the love and compassion that enable her to reach the audience on a sympathetic, yet vulnerable, level.

Born in Brooklyn, New York, on June 8, 1933, and during the Full Moon in Sagittarius, she is likely to say and do things (sometimes on purpose) that shock the listener; she can easily put her foot in her mouth, and people love it when she does. After twenty years appearing on the "Tonight Show" and doing one week a month as host for Johnny Carson since 1983, Joan was finally offered the "Late Show" on Fox television.

But like all "nightingales," Joan comes out at night to lift the spirits, to bring a little joy to the lives of her devoted followers. She makes them laugh.

MICHAEL J. FOX

Watching him closely during the shooting of his new movie, *The Secret of My Success,* I was aware of the perfect timing and professional discipline that he gave every retake, adapting quite quickly, though thoughtfully and seriously, to new actions from the director.

Being a Gemini, Michael is able to think twice as quickly as most people, always one step ahead of other actors and actresses and capable of handling other people's temperaments and emotions.

He was born in Edmonton, Alberta, in Canada, on June 9, 1961, and with his Mercury in Cancer, the family sign, it is only natural for him to hang on to his role in the hit television series "Family Ties," for which he receives more than 500 fan letters a week. His 1985 movie *Back to the Future* rocketed him into a career as a movie actor.

Michael's Jupiter in Aquarius, which rules the media, will always bring him good luck with television, no matter how successful he is with his films.

With the quick-witted timing of Gemini, he will always be popular, entertaining, and perceptive. Should he finally play James Cagney (Cancer, born July 17, 1899) in his life story, perhaps he will be a "beautiful nightingale," another "Yankee doodle dandy."

BROOKE SHIELDS

Born: May 31, 1965, at 1:45 P.M. in New York City

When I was asked to do Brooke's horoscope chart, she was only twelve years old, and I was astounded at the incredible grouping of planets at the time of her birth.

At the time I wrote (*The Brooke Book,* Wallaby Pocket Books, 1978):

> Success at a young age and international fame are the two outstanding factors in Brooke Shields' birth chart. At the time of her birth, Jupiter, the planet of Greater Good Fortune, and the Sun were in exactly the same position in the sign of Gemini. A few degrees away was the planet of luck, beauty, love and money—Venus—close to the Moon's position, also in Gemini. Being born on the New Moon, while having the additional luck and support of these other planets of fortune, whatever Brooke was to do would zoom her into the limelight.

This powerful grouping of planets at the top of her chart emphasized, first, a major career success when the planet Jupiter returned to its original position (it takes twelve years to do so) and triggered off the luck, as well as the benefits of the rest of the planets, one by one. The aspects from the other planets to this celestial conjunction look like spotlights keeping her in the public eye and supporting her talents both with luck and ease, and also with diligence and hard work.

Brooke is now entering her big career period despite the great success already achieved. She is destined to be one of the great stars of the world, and while she may bear the burden of hard work and fame at an early age, she will develop the wisdom and philosophy that will enable her to handle all obstacles and enjoy the rewarding personal life and stardom that she is destined to have bestowed upon her.

There is no denying the accuracy of the planetary prognostications and, by following her life and career, it is obvious that Brooke is also seeking success and personal fulfillment in the academic world. All those planets in the ninth house of higher education gave her the mind and intellect to go to Princeton University. It was just as important for her to achieve her goals in education as it was in show business.

Like Marilyn Monroe, whose birthday was the day after Brooke's, June 1, Brooke has always been determined to prove herself as an intellectual as well as a sex symbol. They both shared the ability to turn on photogenically as soon as the camera started clicking.

Brooke's Ascendant is Virgo, the sign of hard work and service to others. She is always there to help fellow actors and actresses promote their careers, or to raise money for charities.

Legend has it that while wheeling Brooke as a child down Fifty-second Street in New York, her mother Teri met Greta Garbo, a Virgo born September 18. She stopped to pat and admire the child. Perhaps Greta added that touch of Virgo magic and awe that made her one of the greatest beauties of the screen.

GEMINI

Her Part of Fortune, which indicates what will bring the greatest success, wealth, and fortune to an individual, is well placed in Libra in the first house of her chart. Her fortune will come from herself, her public image, disposition, personality, and appearance.

In *The Brooke Book* she very astutely said, "Sometimes I feel like a million bucks because I look like a million bucks."

Like all "beautiful nightingales," she thinks of success for herself, thinks of beauty, wealth, and love, and somehow her thoughts make her the international star she dreams of being.

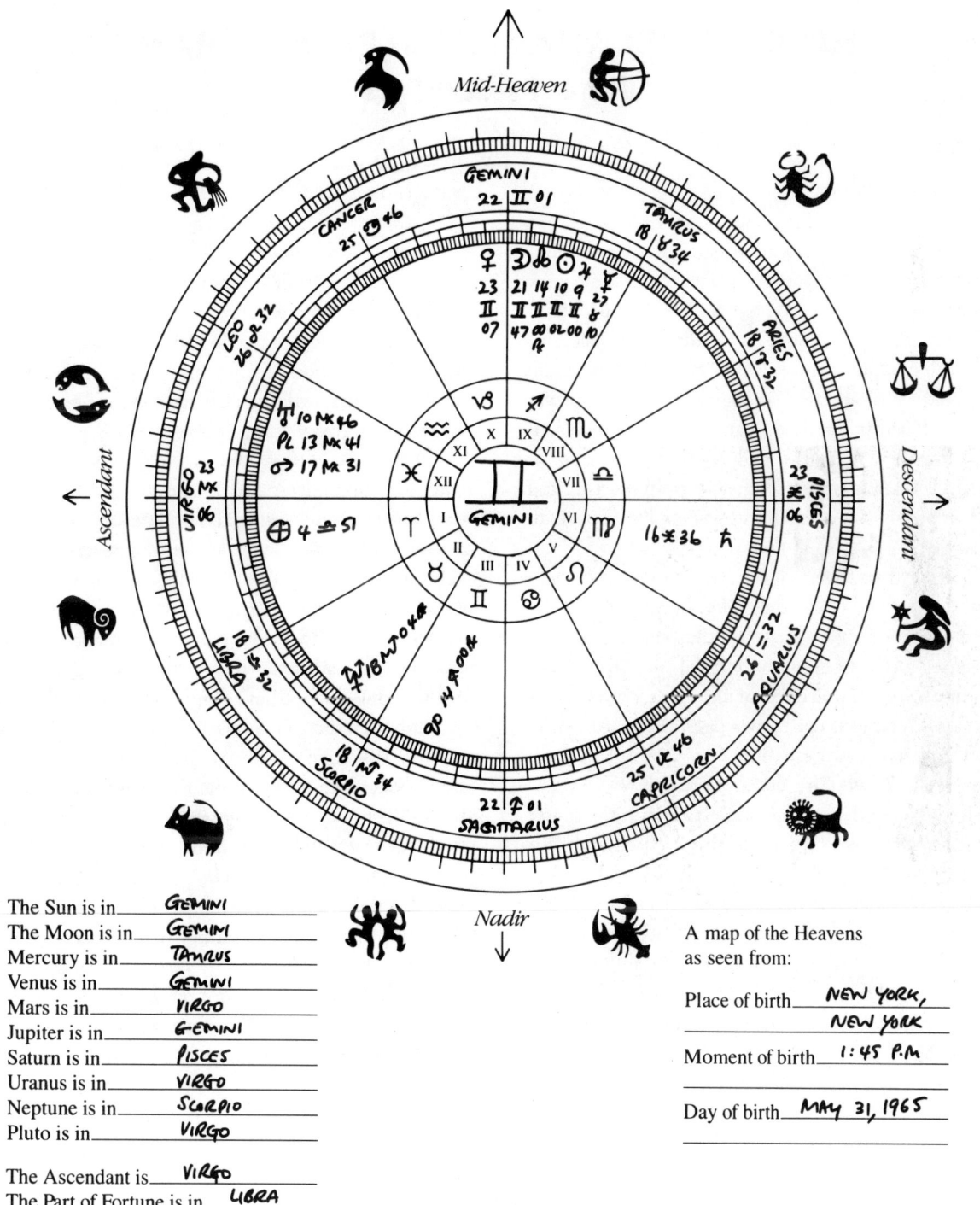

The Sun is in GEMINI
The Moon is in GEMINI
Mercury is in TAURUS
Venus is in GEMINI
Mars is in VIRGO
Jupiter is in GEMINI
Saturn is in PISCES
Uranus is in VIRGO
Neptune is in SCORPIO
Pluto is in VIRGO

The Ascendant is VIRGO
The Part of Fortune is in LIBRA

A map of the Heavens as seen from:

Place of birth NEW YORK, NEW YORK

Moment of birth 1:45 P.M

Day of birth MAY 31, 1965

Scientific Heralds

AQUARIUS DECANATE, RULED BY URANUS
June 11–June 21

These Geminis—born with a mixture of Mercury and Uranus, the planet of exciting new changes—are the most inventive and unique people in the zodiac. They can zoom in on ideas with the efficiency of a computer and solve problems with brilliant new creative thoughts and through systems never dreamed of before. And as Uranus rules the world of electronics, these Geminis will control the realm of modern sound systems, becoming recording artists and jet-set travelers like legendary groundbreaker Paul McCartney.

Strange, unexpected happenings occur for them over and over again, and they take the punches of life in their stride. They evaluate all the obstacles as new experiences and lessons to be learned and store them away in their computerlike brains. Readers of great depth and retainers of knowledge, they are encyclopedias of information, which they can organize and explain to those who are not so alert and retentive.

They change their minds and go off into the sunset at the drop of a hat. They hate to be bored and will refuse routine jobs and commitments in favor of careers that offer excitement, adventure, new investigations and discoveries, and flying. Uranus is the planet of modern-day travel, the superjet Concorde, the intergalactic space probe, and mental travel through the wonders of television and radio, via satellites and computerized photographs.

There is an element of another world about these Geminis. At a party it is impossible to tell whether they are mischievous pixies, crazy inventors high on life, or serious yet eccentric futurologists making scientific predictions for the guests. They bring gadgets and pocket-size devices that thrill the viewers, and they love to share the latest discovery with everyone.

In the past, they would have enjoyed playing with radio kits and electrical inventions. In the modern world, they would have walkie-talkie sets to communicate with friends on the next street and never be without their tape recorder, either recording or playing cassettes of their favorite rock group. They are the reporters for the school newspaper who gather information by interviewing with tape and who do the news summary before spinning a few discs of the Top Ten for the week.

Although these Geminis are more talkers than readers, they still love to snuggle up on the couch with a good book, more likely nonfiction than fiction, for they are absorbers of knowledge and are insatiable in their search for new and ambitious discoveries. The information they get they pass on by writing or being interviewed; music, composing both the words and lyrics; television, through playwriting, documentary production, or research; and generally through public speaking to large audiences or over a beer at the local pub.

Means of travel is important, and many will learn to fly a small plane in order to have more independence and freedom of movement. They love to fly and whether in a Piper Cub or a jumbo jet, they spend more hours per year in the air than do most other signs. Some will find jobs as traffic directors and wardens handing out traffic violations all over the city. Others will drive trucks, buses, trains, and taxis, hating to be boxed up in an office or factory.

While they do not as a group go in for sports, there are many talented stars of local football teams whose techniques help to win weekend games and whose strategies others recognize and respect. Likewise, while they love to create music for the general public, singing or playing in a band, they tend to be wallflowers (male and female) at the dances. However, once encouraged, some of them become the champions of ballroom dancing competitions, for they study and learn at an amazing rate.

These Geminis are in love with humanity; they really have no need for marriage as they are in love with the world, and the world is in love with them. Yet, somehow, they do not cope so well without the support of a loved one, someone to share the interest, work, excitement, and satisfaction. Daring in love and curious about what makes other people tick, they could gear their thoughts into doing research in the area of love—comparing, testing, investigating, and enjoying new sexual conquests—making them appear very flirtatious and fickle. If not careful, they could meet someone who is the opposite in love—possessive and jealous, and unwilling to be another sample for the laboratory shelf—and though strong love could grow into passion, these Geminis may not be able to stand being cooped up. Much suffering and hurt could come from what should have been a harmless little flirtation. They must remember that when they open up a long-locked heart even for a minute, they cannot just leave it hanging there or put it back. Curiosity killed the cat, and these Geminis must keep in mind that they do tend to venture into very dangerous territory and so must arm themselves with wit, understanding of the emotional needs of others, and superintuition to tell them when to say no.

GRACE JONES

Sensational singing star and futuristic beauty Grace Jones brought us amazing visual as well as aural experiences in her slightly S & M stage act and shocked us with her villainy in the 1985 James Bond movie, *A View to a Kill,* in which she played May Day.

Born on June 12, 1954, in Jamaica, British West Indies, Grace is a Gemini with her Moon and Saturn in the sign of Scorpio. Saturn is the disciplinarian, which may explain her use of whips and other paraphernalia in her show. Translating feelings into a performance is not easy: Grace's Gemini traits give her her communication talents. (She speaks several languages.)

With her Mercury, planet of speech; Venus, planet of music and love; Jupiter, planet of greater Good Fortune; and Uranus, the media planet; all in Cancer, it was destiny that Grace would become a big media star in the United States. (She had to leave the United States and work in France and West Germany to develop her reputation, but her photographs soon covered the pages of *Vogue, Elle,* and *Stern.*)

A very sensitive, moody, intense, and unique individual, she rebelled against her home environment (her father was a clergyman and her granduncle a bishop) and created her own form of stage ritual and passion. Using her sexy image to get her message across the screen, she starred opposite Arnold Schwarzenegger (Leo, born July 30, 1947) in *Conan: The Destroyer*. Grace is a "scientific herald" of what is yet to come.

DONALD TRUMP

To me it was a symbolic move, not necessarily astrological, for Donald Trump to play his "trump card" and become a partner in Harrah's at Trump Plaza in Atlantic City and then play his second "trump card" by opening another casino hotel, Trump Castle.

Because Gemini rules the hands, the sign also influences playing cards, and whether shuffling real estate contracts or encouraging others to gamble, Donald is certainly a magician.

He was born in Jamaica Estates, New York, on June 14, 1946, during the Full Moon in Sagittarius, which probably accounts for his daring speculative moves. As a Gemini he is able to talk to people, to convince them or sell them on an idea, and to present and resolve ideas and schedules that seem to conflict.

Mercury, which rules the way we think, and Venus, the creative and artistic planet, are located in the same sign as his planet of work and rewards, Saturn—all in Cancer.

As Cancer is the home builder, the hotel and restaurant owner, the contractor and constructor, he can use his natural Gemini gift of talk to persuade others that his real estate ideas are profitable and exciting.

As a "scientific herald" he has shocked the sleeping realtors of New York, and is reshaping the Manhattan skyline.

PAUL McCARTNEY

Born: June 18, 1942, at 2:30 A.M. in Liverpool, England

One of the richest men in the world, Paul is also one of the most prolific and busiest. Just one important factor of his incredible career—that he has sold over 60 million gold singles, apart from millions of record albums, and that he holds rights to some of the greatest musical properties of the pop world—would be enough for one man to achieve in a lifetime.

But Paul McCartney is not just another man, he is a brilliant creative artist with four important astrological positions in Gemini, the sign of the writer, the communicator, and the great "scientific herald" of this period.

Born during World War II, he may have had a genetic as well as an astrological predisposition to music, as his father played the piano and the trumpet. The history of the Beatles, the group that evolved in his home city of Liverpool, is, of course, legend—the group shot to international fame during the sixties and revolutionized not only pop and classical music but the philosophy of the world.

In true Gemini fashion, Paul wrote and composed as well as performed (he was the group's bass guitar player) some of the most outstanding ballads and melodies, all of which are now standards in record libraries around the world. With John Lennon, he wrote most of the group's songs.

Since the breakup of the Beatles, he has remained as prolific as before, recording major hits with Stevie Wonder, Michael Jackson, and others, as well as starting his own group, Wings.

A charmer, with great wit and his own particular brand of humor, he can see the light side of every difficult situation and happily entertains his audiences and his house guests with his outgoing personality.

Married to Linda Eastman, he has two homes, which fits the Gemini character well. One is a London town house and the other, a large, sprawling farm in Scotland, where they live with their four children.

On the day he was born the Sun was in Gemini, and so were Mercury, the planet of communications; Saturn, the planet of work and rewards; and Uranus, the planet of recording, video, electronics, and new inventions. His Ascendant was Aries, showing that he excels and is a pioneer in the world of words, music, and communication, heralding the future for us.

The Moon in Leo, together with Mars and Pluto, attracted him to show business and gave him the business instincts and radical qualities necessary for his special star to shine.

His Part of Fortune is in exactly the same position as his Venus, the planet of music and singing—the first planet rising in the first house, well placed in Taurus, the sign of the singer. Venus is the goddess of love, and the beauty of his words and music have tugged the heartstrings of his many thousands of fans. In the sixties, girls would scream his name, their eyes overflowing with tears, each time he sang his melodies and songs.

Mercury, the communicator, in Gemini makes his

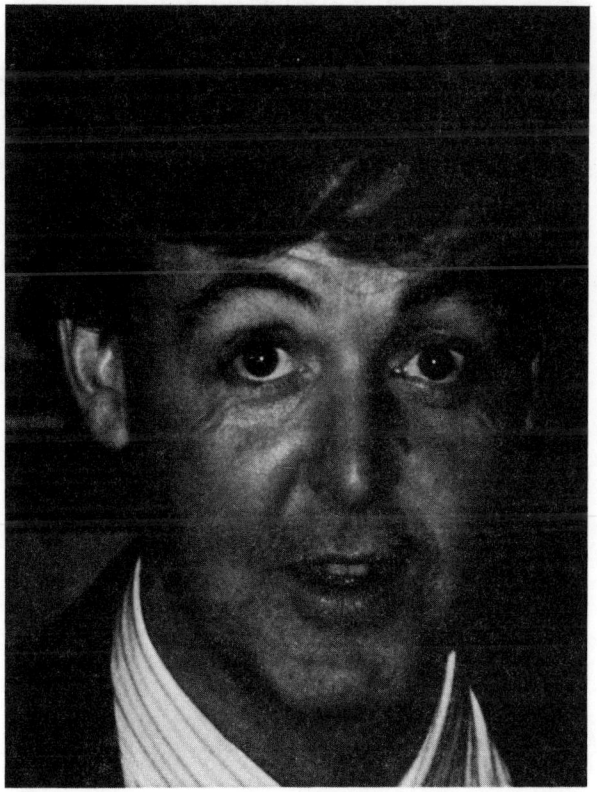

everyday conversation just as musical, lyrical, entertaining, and compassionate as when he is on stage, and it gives him the unique style to capture moods by his choice of words and awareness of nuance.

The messages of this "scientific herald" have been spread throughout the world by the Uranian electronic influence on radio, television, and recordings. Not a day, perhaps not even a minute, goes by without his music being played in some corner of the world.

A true herald of the troubles of his generation, the joys of love and companionship, and promises of happiness and peace of mind to come, Paul lifts his listeners out of their environment, their sadness, sorrows, and loneliness onto a higher and more spiritual plane where they can understand the reality of life and laugh at it, argue back at it, and see it for what it really is.

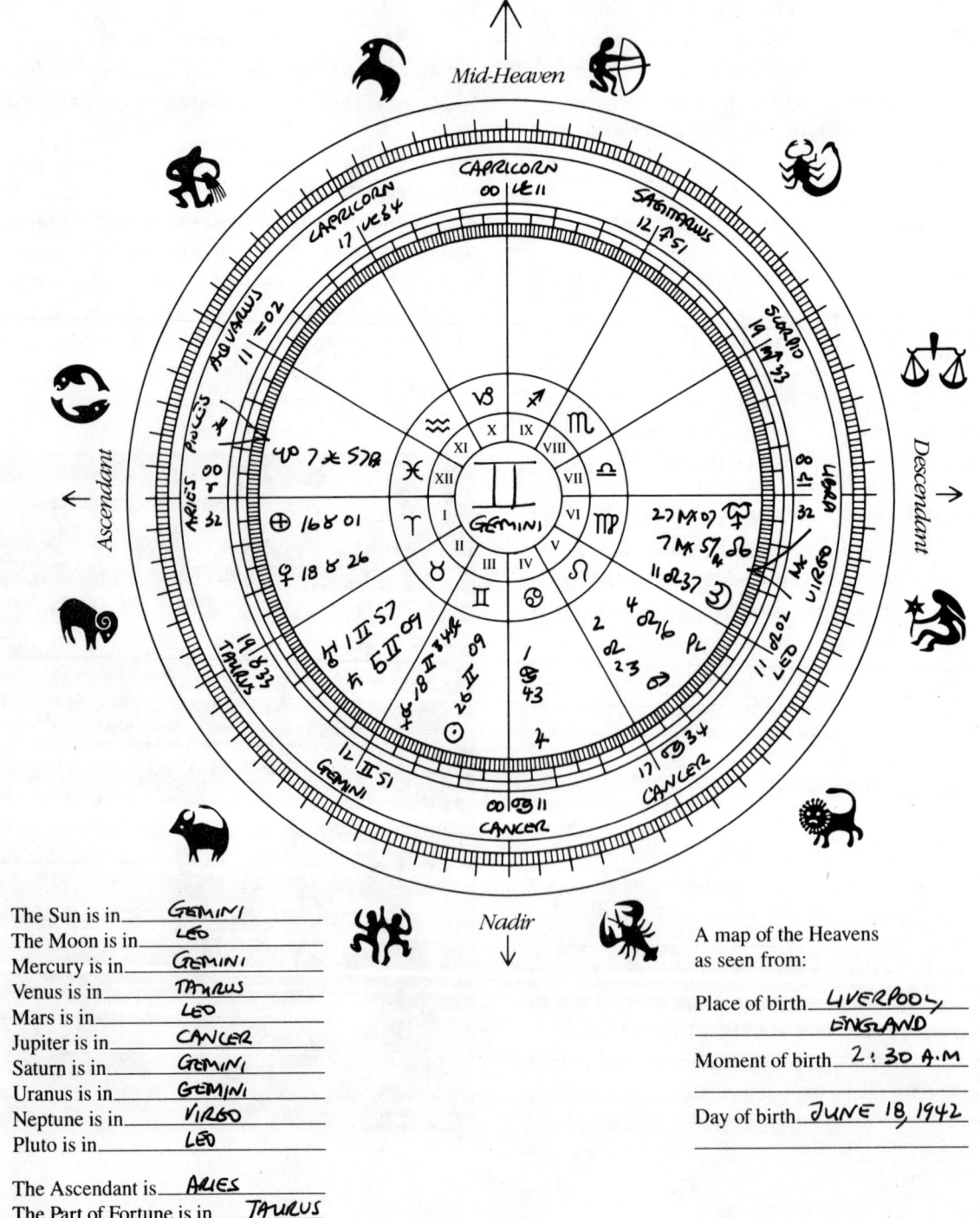

The Sun is in _GEMINI_
The Moon is in _LEO_
Mercury is in _GEMINI_
Venus is in _TAURUS_
Mars is in _LEO_
Jupiter is in _CANCER_
Saturn is in _GEMINI_
Uranus is in _GEMINI_
Neptune is in _VIRGO_
Pluto is in _LEO_

The Ascendant is _ARIES_
The Part of Fortune is in _TAURUS_

A map of the Heavens as seen from:

Place of birth _LIVERPOOL, ENGLAND_

Moment of birth _2:30 A.M_

Day of birth _JUNE 18, 1942_

CANCER
Mother of the Zodiac

SUN IN CANCER, RULED BY THE MOON
June 22–July 22

As the Moon rules the night and opens our hearts to the romance of life and to the mysteries thereof, so people born under the sign of Cancer are the protectors of the rest of creation. They are natural parents, the earth mothers and earth fathers, protecting their young. Like the Moon, they are a beckoning light in the growth of every individual, affecting the emotions and the development of every soul and spirit as the Moon pulls the tides.

It is no good trying to escape the protectiveness and tenacity of this overly emotional sign. They care as much for strangers and their needs as they do for those close to them. They hate to see anyone hungry or wearing threadbare clothing, and they will overfeed people as a symbol of protection and security.

If teased, even lovingly, they will retire into their shells like the crab that is their symbol. Being overly sensitive toward other people's opinions and feelings about them, the Cancer's greatest fear is ridicule. Any hint of a joke at his expense will change a happy-go-lucky individual into a tearful, retiring bowl of jelly who seems likely to escape into a monastery or, more likely, into a bottle of whiskey.

Home is part of the Cancer's vocation. Cancers are great home lovers and worship the family, and their houses or apartments are shrines to their friends and relatives alike. They will always want to improve their surroundings, and everything centers around this base of operations. Loving businesses associated with the buying and selling of homes, many go into real estate; others make money from their residences, either by renting rooms or restoring and improving them and then selling for a profit. Of course, they would really like to hang on to all the places they have lived in, and it takes great effort and decision making to get them out once they have established roots anywhere. Lots of decorators have some of their planets in Cancer. Another outlet is the restaurant and fast-food business, where they can feed others and care for them indirectly. Thus, combining all their natural instincts, hotels and motels give them an ever-growing family, many of whom return year after year to spend their vacations with their newly adopted "mother" or "father" figure.

It is interesting to note that the official birthdate of the United States of America—July 4, 1776—makes it a Cancer country, and on the Statue of Liberty is written, "Give me your tired, your poor, your huddled masses yearning to breathe free. . . ." America has become the mother and protector of the world, even in places where this maternal influence is unwanted. Like all Cancerians, it wants to feed everyone, sending vast amounts of food supplies to needy areas. And (like all mothers) thinking it knows what is best for its new children, it forces its opinion and ideals on them, which they often rebel against. Although the United States is concerned about feeding its own poor and giving them shelter, many live on welfare, handed out by their "mother," the government. The United States probably has more restaurants, snack bars, hotdog and hamburger stands, supermarkets and grocery stores per capita than anywhere in the whole world.

Cancer is the fourth house of the zodiac, and it rules home, property, parents, and family. It is where our roots are embodied, where we go for solace and comfort, and where we can feel secure and know that no harm will come to us.

Cancer is very influenced by the Moon, and produces changing moods in those born under this sign. Once Cancers can accept this tendency as a normal rhythmic pattern, neither thinking they are to blame nor trying to change it, they will be well on the way to accepting these variations in personality, which—like the ever-waxing and -waning moon—can shift from moment to moment. Cancerians cannot be made completely happy all the time—they just cannot cope with it. All their lives they have been used to fitting in with their regular emotional ups and downs and are only truly content when they have a balance of optimism and pessimism—they are trained to handle it. Yet, they can comfort and nurse others, for they want them to be healthy, happy, and secure.

While we may often want to escape from the overprotection of this mothering sign, we must also realize that much of our personalities and attitudes to life have been guided by this influence. In times of trouble we will always seek out and pour out our souls to them. They know our intimate secrets, and by sharing them will not only lift the burden off our shoulders but place our dreams and goals up there among the stars.

Lamplighters of Darkness

CANCER DECANATE, RULED BY THE MOON
June 22–July 1

These are very special Cancers, with a double helping of Moon influence in their personalities. These are pioneers in the spiritual and religious corners of the soul. They can illuminate the most sensitive parts of our personalities, can carry our thoughts across oceans and continents to communicate with loved ones, and can break down the most stubborn barriers and hardest hearts in their own gentle yet firm way. The Princess of Wales, who has won the hearts of the world, is an ideal representative of this lunar aspect.

Willing to sell all their belongings to help raise money for a special operation for their child, friend, or neighbor, their time on earth is spent more in giving than in receiving. Their happiness is that of the giver, both a gracious need and a fulfilling gesture. These Cancers will smother the objects of their affections with love and gifts, often substantial and practical.

Devotion is their strong trait. With very little training or experience, they are able to take under their wing both young and old and lead them into a better way of life. They can heal the sick and give joy to the poor. Their presence is welcomed and very rarely rejected.

At another person's home they quickly fit in and help where they can, occasionally going overboard with their gifts of things for the home. They will help with the meals, allow the hostess to entertain her guests while they do the clearing up or the dishes, at the end of the evening offering lifts home to those without transportation. They are the protectors of others during the hours of darkness and partners, aides, and helpers to others during the day.

Exceptionally intuitive or psychic, they follow their hunches and put into action preventive measures to deal with what they foresee or feel. With close loved ones they can sense danger and other problems over long distances. They will call to warn them of their feelings, and the recipient will confirm the cause of their concern. Others will sense great joy and happiness and will know well in advance the imminent announcement of a marriage, birth, or other happy family event.

Once they have done their duties, they love to retire into their shells and relax, building up their energies for the next occasion. Their energy levels may regularly be very dependent on the phases of the Moon, and once they have worked out the ups and downs, the periods of activity and the times of necessary rest, their work is most efficient, and they will rely on their body clocks to initiate any move, not try to do things at the wrong time.

These Cancers are among the best prospects for love and marriage. They marry young and quickly have families, for they want to enjoy every minute of parenthood and can't wait to have grandchildren and, if the gods allow, great-grandchildren. Pregnancy is usually a joy, and both Cancerian mothers and fathers will follow the developments of the growth of the embryo with scientific and spiritual awareness, and will obey all the doctor's instructions in order to have a healthy and strong baby. These mothers will readily change their eating, smoking, and drinking habits.

They are gentle in lovemaking and require lots of soft light, gentle music (especially love ballads), and, most important, a good meal, whether at home or at a good local restaurant. When the stage is set and the atmosphere conducive, these Cancers will spend more time with loving than with any other emotional or creative outlet.

MERYL STREEP

From the time Meryl Streep was born, the stars, the celestial ones, have guided and directed her, every step of the way. Despite her feelings about her looks as a child ("I was ugly"), Meryl is now one of Hollywood's leading dramatic actresses, having won two Oscars (plus nominations for another three), a television Emmy, and a Tony nomination.

Born in Summit, New Jersey, on June 22, 1949, she was named Mary Louise but chose to use her mother's nickname, Meryl. The Sun was in Cancer, and the planet of talent and television, Uranus, was in exactly the same degree, giving her a radiant personality and star quality that began to show in her late teens and certainly emerged once she started performing.

Her Moon is in Taurus, the sign of the singer, and at first she thought she would become an operatic soprano. But the sensitivity of acting appealed more to her emotional Cancerian personality traits. After finishing her dramatic studies she took New York by storm. She was nominated for a Tony for her role in the Broadway production of Tennessee Williams's *27 Wagons Full of Cotton*. She used her trained singing voice at the Martin Beck Theater in the Brecht-Weill musical *Happy End*.

Her hard work won her an Oscar nomination for her supporting role in *The Deer Hunter*. She was nominated as best Actress for her work in *The French Lieutenant's Woman* and *Silkwood*. She won the best actress Academy Award for *Sophie's Choice* and best supporting actress for *Kramer vs. Kramer*.

Jupiter, the planet of greater good fortune, in Aquarius, the sign of television, may have helped her win the role in the TV miniseries *Holocaust*, for which she was awarded an Emmy.

It is very important for Cancers to have a home and family, and Meryl lives with her husband, sculptor Donald Gummer, and their son and two daughters in Litchfield County, Connecticut.

Her Mars and Mercury—the planets of energy and action and of speaking, writing, and communication, respectively—in the sign of Gemini gave her the strength and intellectual determination to graduate from Vassar College and from the Yale School of Drama. Her mind and body work nonstop, and she is capable of doing two things at once—to relax, she may read one script while shooting another.

To achieve so much in so few years, Meryl has had to keep working on her craft, whether rehearsing, rewriting her scripts with her directors, or taking classes. Ready when opportunities turn up, Meryl is always well prepared to do any part offered to her.

To the next generation of serious dramatic actresses and actors, Meryl is a "lamplighter," showing them the way to get out of their "darkness" into the limelight.

DIANA, PRINCESS OF WALES

Born: July 1, 1961, at 7:45 P.M. in Parkhurst, Sandringham, England

No event could have been more exciting, uplifting, and inspiring than the royal wedding of Prince Charles and "Lady Di," as the whole world by then fondly called her, in 1981. The future Queen Consort of England, Diana Spencer, certainly became a "lamplighter of darkness" as she restored the romantic aura of the royal family.

Everyone loves a wedding, but the whole world loves that fairy-tale romance, a Royal Wedding. It is estimated that over 600 million people worldwide watched the wedding on television. It was just as nerve-racking for the British public as it must have been for the royal family to follow the romantic escapades and courtships of Charles, Prince of Wales and heir to the British throne. Over the twelve years prior to his wedding, hardly a month had gone by in which a journalist, astrologer, or "friend of the family" hadn't announced that Charles was about to get engaged to this or that debutante or foreign princess.

During most of those years, Diana was not even a teenager. Born on the royal estate of Sandringham, her closest friends during her childhood days were Charles's younger brothers, Prince Andrew and Prince Edward, who would come over to her neighboring home to swim in her family's heated pool.

It wasn't until she was in her mid-teens that she officially met Charles, when he was guest of honor at a dinner at her home. Charles was dating Diana's elder sister Sarah at the time, and their own romance didn't start until 1980.

Since Diana was born under the sign of nurturing Cancer, it is not too surprising that her first jobs included being a part-time cook, a nanny, a governess to an American family, and a kindergarten teacher. Her natural love of children made her a perfect choice for the future queen of England, as the continuation of the royal line by having children was an important factor in the final selection by Prince Charles and his advisers. Not that this wasn't a love match. Prince Charles, a Scorpio, an excellent lover for a Cancer, was born November 14, 1948, at 9:14 P.M. in London, and he has the royal sign of Leo as his Ascendant. Diana's Part of Fortune is in exactly the same location, making this a very strong romantic bond. Her fortune was with the "royals."

It is her Ascendant Sagittarius that endears the Princess of Wales to the public, for it gives her that honest, frank, and open spirit that often gets her into trouble with other, more conventional members of the royal family.

Saturn, the planet that represents the husband (and the father) in her first house, being her rising planet made her more mature in her outlook on life and attracted her to an older lover (Charles is thirteen years her senior). Her Saturn is in Capricorn, the zodiac sign of the United Kingdom (the official birthday of the United Kingdom is January 1, 1801, when Great Britain—England, Scotland, and Wales—became the

55

SIGNS OF THE STARS

United Kingdom of Great Britain and Northern Ireland), so Diana's place in the future of the United Kingdom was written in the stars, as well as in her lineage. The Spencer family goes back to the early sixteenth century and her father is the eighth Earl.

Both the Moon and the planet Venus have played great parts in romance through the ages, and Prince Charles's Moon and Diana's Venus are both in Taurus. This made for another bond of love, so important for both of them. Charles's mother, Queen Elizabeth II, is a Taurus (born April 21), and so the two important women in his life both have this Taurus influence. This determined quality may also account for the acknowledged tension between the two women, who have been known to lock horns occasionally.

Having her Venus in the fifth house of children, in

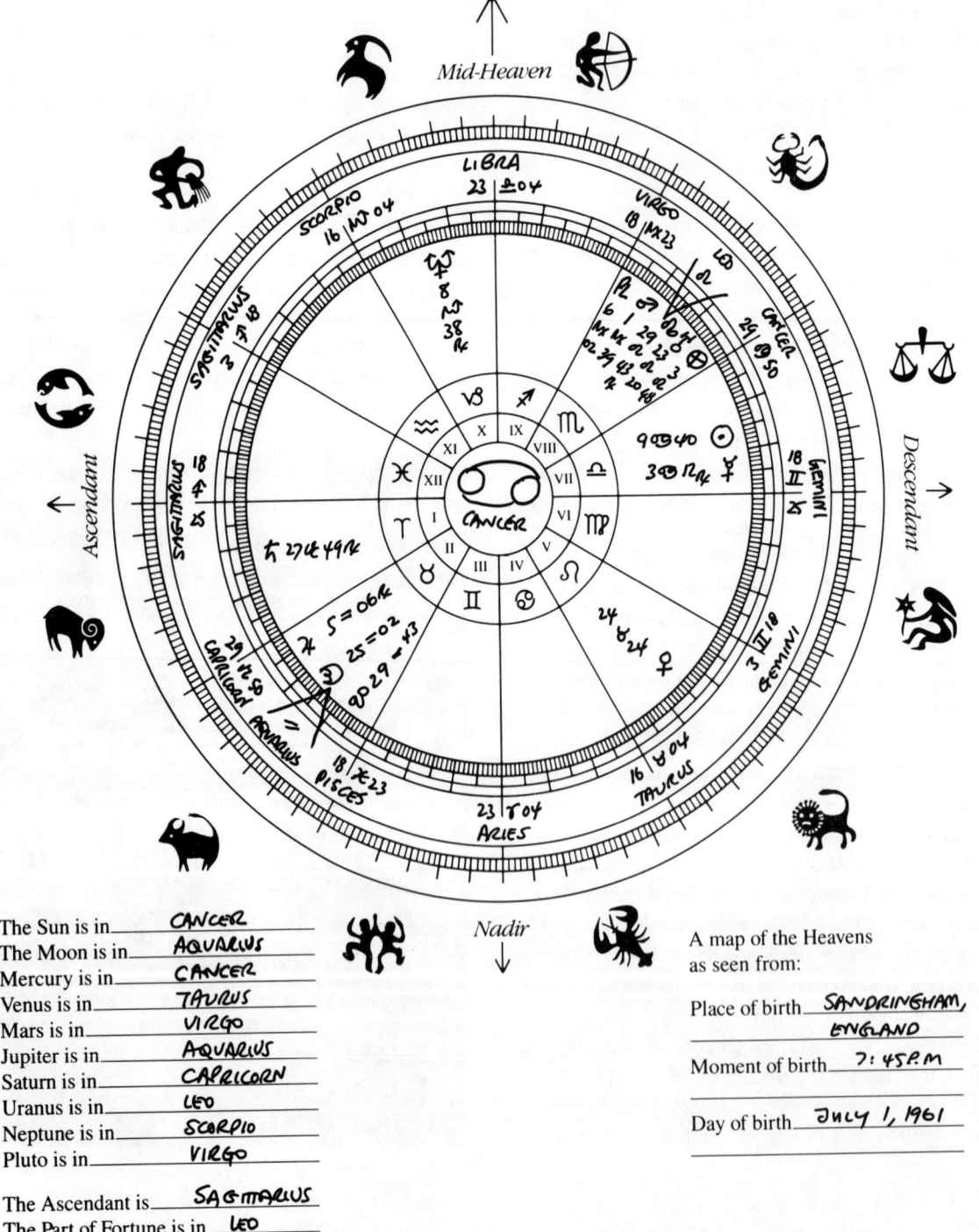

The Sun is in _CANCER_
The Moon is in _AQUARIUS_
Mercury is in _CANCER_
Venus is in _TAURUS_
Mars is in _VIRGO_
Jupiter is in _AQUARIUS_
Saturn is in _CAPRICORN_
Uranus is in _LEO_
Neptune is in _SCORPIO_
Pluto is in _VIRGO_

The Ascendant is _SAGITTARIUS_
The Part of Fortune is in _LEO_

A map of the Heavens as seen from:

Place of birth _SANDRINGHAM, ENGLAND_

Moment of birth _7:45 P.M._

Day of birth _JULY 1, 1961_

the earthy sign of Taurus, made Diana very fruitful. Her first child, Prince William, was born June 21, 1982, at 9:03 P.M. in London, a Cancer like his mother, and with his Jupiter, the planet of greater good fortune, in the same degree of Taurus as Charles's Moon and the queen's Sun—the natural inheritance of a future king.

Diana's second son, Prince Henry (known as "Harry"), was born September 15, 1984, at 4:20 P.M. in London. He is a Virgo with Capricorn rising, and his Moon is also in Taurus.

The strong Taurean influence in the royal family dates back to the first Act of Union between England and Scotland on May 1, 1707, which formed the political unit of Great Britain.

In the tradition of the royal family, Diana plans to have many more children. However, I believe that when Prince William inherits the throne, his brother, Prince Harry, will become prime minister, a political situation not previously allowed by British law.

Diana's role is that of the Cancerian earth mother, for she has to bring up her children in such a way that she sets a good example to all the other mothers of her generation, still maintaining that special mystique in order to remain slightly distant from her worshipful and admiring fans.

Diana still has the beautiful, happy-go-lucky, carefree quality that she had in her not-so-public days—when, as she later confided to dancer Mikhail Baryshnikov, she stood with other teenage girls outside the Royal Opera House in Covent Garden to get his autograph.

It was out of this same wonderful spirit that she responded to the press questions about what she thought when she met Prince Charles the first time. She immediately replied, with stardust in her eyes, "I thought he was pretty amazing!" And so it all must have seemed to her when she walked down the aisle in St. Paul's Cathedral to say "I will" to her prince.

Prophets of the Times
SCORPIO DECANATE, RULED BY PLUTO
July 2–July 11

The combination of the Moon and the planet Pluto in this Cancer frequently makes them the most influential people in the community. Pluto—the modern planet of big business, radical thoughts and action, gangs, groups, trade unions, and political parties—gives them the ability to think big and on a scale that would frighten others. Leona Helmsley's confident management of a vast real estate empire and Sylvester Stallone's rampant, monumental film career show them to be exemplars of their sign. The Moon collaborates here to help humanity, to further the causes of the downtrodden, to solve great problems in health and government, and to throw these Cancerians into the public eye to be worshipped, respected, and followed. Their great perception makes them "prophets of the times."

They are sure to be found somewhere influencing every election, organizing programs for television (Cancer loves to bring entertainment into the home), raising funds for needy third-world countries, speaking at strike rallies, and always writing their memoirs or plans for the future of mankind.

Reliable when there is a crisis, they will get their workmates or business partners to help finance big-budget projects that will remain monuments to them. Like the Pied Piper, they can call on the people to follow them. Their strength lies not only in their ability to put up cash when needed but also to follow through with devotion and sincerity. Honest to a fault, they will not play secret games and be deceitful; they know they have to live with themselves and their families afterwards.

As young adults their energies are likely to be geared toward local improvements in the arts, in commerce, and in the community as a whole. They want to be proud of the place they live in and would be willing to give their free time and spare cash to build a monument, clean up historic landmarks, and plant trees, shrubs, and flowers in the parks.

Their skills in cooking and entertaining give them the impetus to organize large outdoor picnics and concerts, moonlit dances, street theater, and public competitions. And in most affairs they take an active part as well, willingly donning an outfit to liven up the occasion, hilariously entering competitions or races that they can only just handle, and standing for hours cooking over an open fire when necessary. They win the hearts of all who meet them.

They can, however, be very secretive, and underneath is a growing desire for power in the world, knowing that their philosophy and wealth (of ideas if not money) call pull people out of their depressing environments and help them to live happier lives. They are not content with little changes even for themselves; they want big, radical, almost rebellious changes and are willing to go out on a limb to accomplish their noble ends. To themselves they are true, yet others may see them as scheming and dangerous opponents or bedfellows.

When they can make room for romance, these Cancers are big-timers in that area too. They are usually up to date with all the latest gadgets and toys, and they have fun with their partners as they are not inhibited and shy in the bedroom. They are not concerned with age, either; they can happily fall in love with someone very much younger or very much their senior, for they have

CANCER

a way of seeing each romantic encounter as something special, even bizarre. These Cancers want successful and visible marriages and will want someone who is on a par with them financially or who has the mind to keep up with the duties and work load they will have to share. They see family dynastically, as an empire to build as well as shelter in a domestic environment.

These are most powerful people, and those who fall in love with them immediately put their own lives in danger, not necessarily from violent outside sources but from the emotional and sheer physical exhaustion that a relationship with this type of Cancer can produce. But for mutual satisfaction, both mentally and physically, they are among the best.

MERV GRIFFIN

Merv is one of the big profit makers of our times. His production company, which produces some of television's most popular game shows, is worth millions.

Not just a pretty-faced, blue-eyed television host, Merv Griffin is the brains behind most of his empire.

He was born on July 6, 1925, in San Mateo, California, at 4:45 A.M. and is a Cancer with his Moon in the business sign, Capricorn, and his Ascendant also Cancer.

Cancers like to keep people together, especially at home eating or watching television, and Merv has devised family-type shows that play in the early evenings, bringing his special type of entertainment into the homes of his audiences, which are in the millions. His own syndicated talk show was beamed to over 100 stations nationwide before he retired from it.

His Jupiter sits in exactly the same degree as his Moon in Capricorn, which gave him his uncanny negotiating abilities and the imagination to achieve so much. Next to these is his Part of Fortune, also in Capricorn.

The Sun in Cancer is exactly conjunct with his Ascendant and Pluto (the planet of big business) and all are within two degrees of each other, making Merv's appearance, personality, and disposition factors in his success.

Though he has Mercury, Venus, Mars, and Neptune all in Leo, he doesn't claim to be an actor, although he was once a singer—an Irish tenor on a San Francisco radio station, a band singer with Freddie Martin's orchestra, and a performer in many nightclubs.

He raises quarter horses, flies a plane, and plays tennis in his spare time, when he isn't at business meetings or involved in production negotiations.

Born on a Full Moon in Capricorn, Merv is very independent and self-sufficient; he likes to handle his life, emotions, and his business himself. That way, should anything go wrong, he has nobody else to blame.

With Uranus, the planet of television, sitting at the top of his chart in the tenth house of career, his destiny was television. And we await with excitement and anticipation what his fertile imagination will bring us next, as he takes us into the twenty-first century, a prophet and creator of the media.

ARTHUR ASHE

I was asked to do Arthur's horoscope chart when he was in London playing at Wimbledon in 1974, and I predicted that he would be the Men's Singles winner. He was.

Arthur Ashe, Jr., was born in Richmond, Virginia, on July 10, 1943, at 1:55 P.M. and with such a magical chart it was no wonder that he had such a major influence on tennis, opening up one of the most restricted sports in the United States to blacks. He is a Cancer with his Moon and Ascendant in Libra, the sign of the diplomat, the ambassador, and of justice.

The Sun and Mercury in Cancer in the ninth house of long distance indicated his success abroad and also at college. Arthur attended UCLA on a tennis scholarship. In the tenth house of ambitions and fame he has Jupiter and Pluto, the planets of good luck and big business.

Mercury, the long-distance communicator, explains his success with his syndicated columns and his frequent television appearances to analyze tennis matches.

He married photographer Jeanne Moutoussamy, also a Cancer (born July 9). Arthur shares his birthday with Virginia Wade (born July 10, 1945). The English tennis player won the U.S. Women's Singles tennis championship in 1968, the same year that Arthur won the U.S. Men's Singles. He was the first black to win a major tennis championship in the United States.

SYLVESTER STALLONE

Born: July 6, 1946, at 7:20 P.M. in New York City

The highest-paid actor in Hollywood in 1985, Sylvester Stallone can thank his lucky stars (the celestial ones) that his mother was an astrologer.

"Hang in there," she told her restless son. "You're gonna make it in seven years, and as a writer, not only an actor."

Seven years later when *Rocky* hit the screen, he could look back on her words and be grateful that he hadn't accepted the tempting $300,000 he was offered for the script, but for a name actor to play Rocky. He was the writer *and* the star of this sensational underdog that won the 1976 Oscar for best picture.

It's no wonder that Sylvester is a patriotic and heroic role model, since he shares America's sun sign (Cancer—July 4, 1776). Before she became an astrologer, his talented and beautiful mother was a Billy Rose chorus girl; his father had a chain of beauty salons.

I was not surprised to discover that his Ascendant was Sagittarius, the sign of the archer, aiming the quivering arrow with the taut bow at the enemy, prey, or target ahead. His talent with bows and arrows, hunting knives, machine guns, and rockets almost surpass his skill as an actor. Sagittarius is the sign of the moviemaker, and what movies he makes!

Astrologically, the Ascendant shows the areas in which he should excel, and he was able to put all his many talents into filmmaking, as well as the suspense-making techniques he had learned over his many years in show business. He had worked long and hard on his career, made his off-Broadway debut in a nudie drama called *Score,* written (unpublished) novels, and gained attention for his role in *The Lords of Flatbush.*

It is also very symbolic that his nickname, the "Italian Stallion," should so perfectly reflect the Sagittarian horseman of his Ascendant as well as the enormous sex appeal of this powerful man.

Having seen every one of his movies at least three times I was impressed by the Cancerian determination and stick-to-itiveness that his characters all possess. Like the sign's symbol, the crab, they hang onto their objectives, are protective of those under their wings, and can disappear into the natural surroundings and camouflage. Remember Rambo under all that oozing mud, just like the Long Island crabs basking in the sun.

His Moon and Jupiter are both at the top of his chart in the sign of Libra. The Moon is in his tenth house, making him a household word, and granting him honors and great success, especially in connection with governmental matters and affairs. And Jupiter is in the ninth house, bringing him great fortune in connection with foreign affairs. True to this Cancer's tendencies, even his films, like *Rocky* and *Paradise Alley,* have been about the downtrodden, unions, and the poor. The *Rambo* films, on the other hand, reflect the governmental and foreign-affairs aspects of the sign.

Having Taurus in the fifth house of children, Sylvester consulted astrological charts to make sure that the time of conception would bring him a Taurus child. His son Sage Moonblood was born a Taurus in 1976. He has one other son, Sergio.

Divorcing his wife Sasha in 1985, he married fellow Cancerian Brigitte Nielsen the same year.

With Mars, the god of war; Venus, the goddess of love; Pluto, god of the underworld; and Mercury, the messenger of the gods, all in his eighth house of money, his financial success is no surprise, and neither are the crusading, violence, and motion predominant in his work.

As his mother said, he would also make it as a

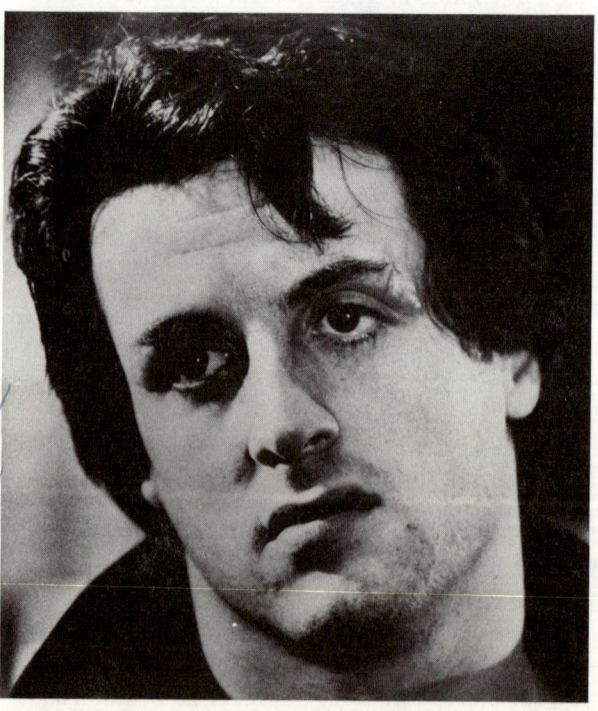

writer. His Part of Fortune is in the third house of writing and communication, giving additional luck to his planet Mercury (the writer) and Pluto (big business) in his house of money.

Paradise Alley, his autobiography, was a best-seller, and we can look forward to many more action-packed books and movies from his fertile and creative mind. With Libra in his mid-heaven he is an artist; he has made violence and terror visions of great beauty and he personally supervised the remaking of John Travolta's already beautiful body for *Saturday Night Fever.*

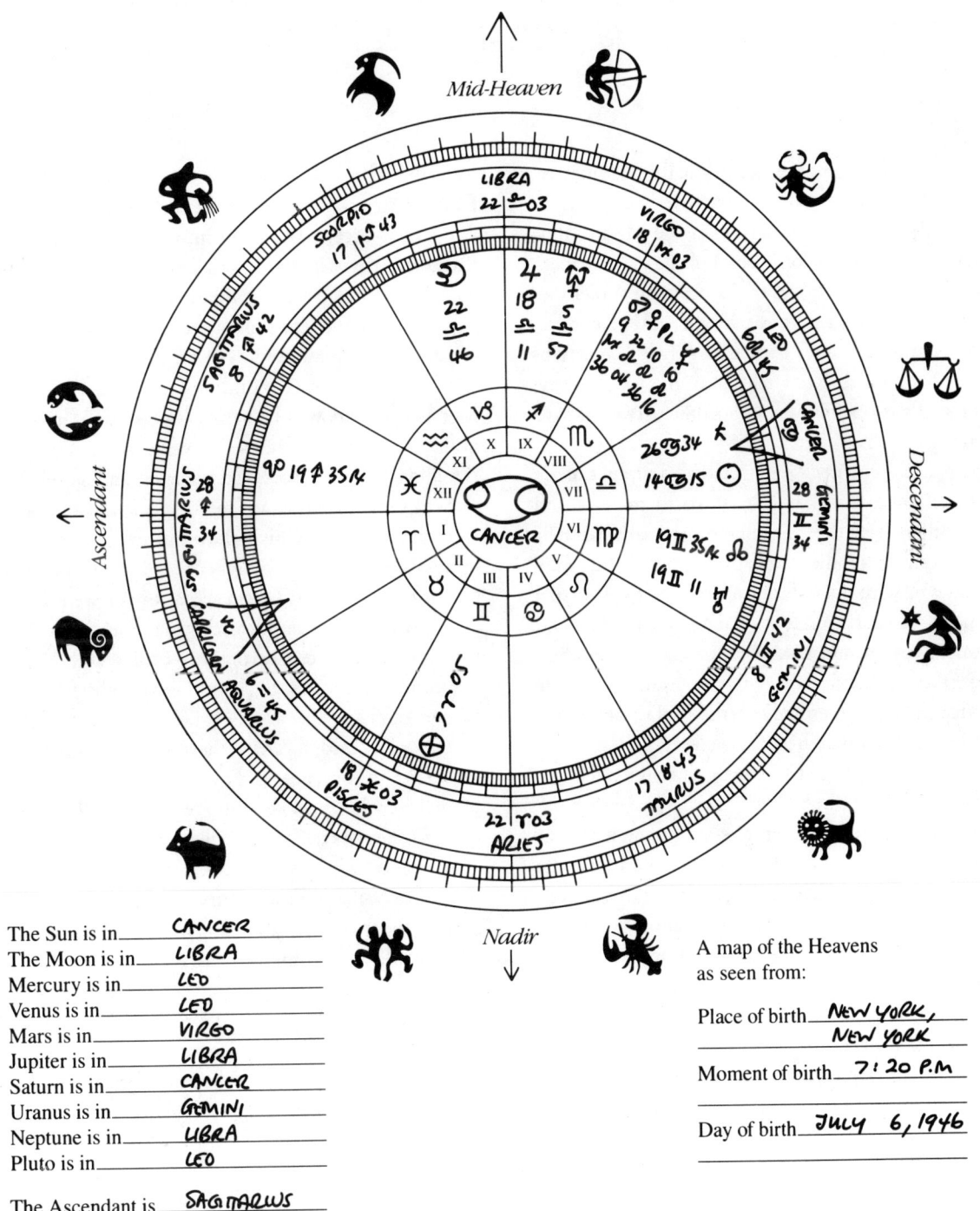

The Sun is in __CANCER__
The Moon is in __LIBRA__
Mercury is in __LEO__
Venus is in __LEO__
Mars is in __VIRGO__
Jupiter is in __LIBRA__
Saturn is in __CANCER__
Uranus is in __GEMINI__
Neptune is in __LIBRA__
Pluto is in __LEO__

The Ascendant is __SAGITTARIUS__
The Part of Fortune is in __ARIES__

A map of the Heavens as seen from:

Place of birth __NEW YORK, NEW YORK__

Moment of birth __7:20 P.M__

Day of birth __JULY 6, 1946__

Inspirational Faith Healers

PISCES DECANATE, RULED BY NEPTUNE
July 12–July 22

These Cancerians are exceptionally imaginative, both in their worldly activities and in their spiritual development. Not only does the Moon influence their moods and personalities, but the equally mysterious planet Neptune plays tricks on them sometimes and at others gives them great insight into the well-being of the people under their care. These Cancerians would die for a cause. They may even die for someone else's cause, if they believe enough in the person or love them enough.

These noble-spirited and spiritual people can be found in all religious groups, faithful to the end and inspiring others with their genuine charity toward their fellow creatures. Commentators on life's tragedies, they will want to be with the suffering after an earthquake or a battle and to see for themselves what terrible tortures and pain human beings and nature inflict on one another. They are the journalists who will not glamorize or lie about what they have seen and felt, the civil rights leaders who are willing to march for what they believe in.

In youth, they would be likely to center their activities around the church. They would be among the first to offer their time and services to anyone who was ill in the parish. At public events they would help the Red Cross or other auxiliary workers, willingly running messages and doing the most menial of chores, for their thoughts are not on what they do but what they are helping to accomplish by doing it.

Very creative, too, their talents, including woodwork, sewing, knitting, painting, and performance will be very salable. They would make most of their Christmas and birthday presents for family and friends, and the love that they put into each item would make a gift from them not only beautiful but priceless.

Their careers take them into rather exotic areas for Cancers. They will get into the arts, like vital and intelligent Diana Rigg, and religious professions, which in turn get them into the public eye, especially in their own communities. Some will even set up retreats or holiday centers where whole families can come and worship together. Others will be nature lovers and help organize nudist camps where the body and spirits can roam free. Running seaside resorts, restaurants, and hotels where they can feel the fresh air and taste the salt on their lips is another area in which they can excel. Cruise ships, houseboats, and simple rowboats can all be moneymakers for these Cancers. Operating a convalescent home on a lake would offer an ideal combination of the Moon's love of nursing and caring for others and Neptune's emotions, dependent on water surroundings such as a lake, a river, or the sea.

Though faith healers, these Cancerians may have little faith in romance, as they tend to be very suspicious of anyone who shows any interest in love. They are not sure if others like them for themselves or if wooers are after something—money, shelter, attention, or their bodies. In both males and females born in this Cancerian period, there are many unhappy, suspicious, and defensive people. They must open themselves up to life's romantic adventures; there are very few dishonest lovers in the world, so they must be less critical of people they meet. Their humanitarianism can also sometimes take the form of martyrdom, so they may prefer to suffer for a cause rather than abandon themselves to affection.

BILL COSBY

An inspiration to everyone young or old, "The Cosby Show" is the number one prime-time show on television. It is the Cancer influence that made Bill want to do a family-type show, entertain children on television, and earn a Ph.D. in education from the University of Massachusetts.

Born in Philadelphia on July 12, 1937, he was attracted to study and to helping others. A Cancer with his Moon in the sign of the schoolteacher, Virgo.

His planet Mercury, the communicator, in Cancer probably got him the television commercials for Del Monte and Jell-O, as Cancers like food, cooking, and eating!

Venus, the planet of good looks, luck, and money, in Gemini, the sign of the writer, speaker, and actor, also gave him his brilliant sense of humor. He has won eight Grammys for his comedy and children's records, and six Emmys for his "I Spy," "The New Fat Albert Show," and "The Cosby Show."

Many Cancers are always willing to lend a hand, and in addition to education, Bill is devoted to uplifting others and social work.

Loving his home in Amherst, Massachusetts, his wife Camille, and his five children, all with first names beginning with the letter *E*—daughters Erika, Erinn, Ensa Camille, and Evin and son Ennis—Bill needs his family environment to balance his hectic work and lecture schedule. He is an inspiration to all.

PHYLLIS DILLER

If Phyllis had been male, one could have called her a knight in shining armor, for she has never hesitated to help anyone who has gone to her for assistance. She is another star who responded immediately to my invitation to appear in *A Knight of Stars and Stripes*.

Arriving at the theater for rehearsal, she immediately confided, "I'm Cancer with Gemini rising. What's happening to my love life?" A great astrology buff for many years, she is very knowledgeable about the science and extremely intuitive and sensitive to other people.

Born on July 17, 1917, at 1:00 A.M. in Lima, Ohio, the mercurial qualities of Gemini give her the great sense of humor and timing that makes her one-liners so hilarious as she fires them at rapid speed one after another.

"How would you like me to introduce you?" I inquired. She slipped me a small piece of paper. When the time came for her to appear in the blackout I announced, "And now ladies and gentlemen, the sex symbol of the geriatric set, Phyllis Diller."

Always willing to poke fun at herself, she is very sensitive to how people treat her. Beneath that outrageous facade, she fears being ridiculed by others and prefers to get one step ahead of them by doing it herself, though she is no longer the "fright" that made her famous. She used to claim that Earl Scheib Auto Paint Shops did her makeup, and that she created her hairstyle by rolling her hair in sticks of dynamite and lighting them. Now, thanks to the cosmetic skills of the plastic surgeon, she has become one of the beautiful ladies of show business over the age of—fifty?

Having the planet Mars, which rules her appearance and public image, in her first house, she was destined to have plastic surgery on her face, as the first house is also ruled by Aries.

Her Moon in Cancer, as well as the Sun, Pluto, and Mercury, gave her the inspiration to base her humor on being the typical wife and mother (she has five children and didn't start her career until she was thirty-eight), and she even created the fictitious "Fang" as her husband so that other wives would identify and sympathize with her.

That her Ascendant is Gemini says a lot for her choice of dress. For her stage comedy routines she appears dressed in something that is a cross between a butterfly and a clown's costume. Both butterflies and clowns come under the sign of Gemini.

Like other Geminis, Phyllis is determined to remain a child forever, overcoming her Cancer sun sign's influence, which made her devote the first half of her life to her husband and children. Now, having divorced twice and looking better than ever, she wrote the best seller *The Joys of Aging and How to Avoid Them*.

DIAHANN CARROLL

Television was always waiting for Diahann Carroll. She had always had success in her career, whether doing her nightclub act, appearing on Broadway in the musical *House of Flowers* and later Richard Rodgers's *No Strings,* which he wrote for her and for which she won a Tony, or appearing in the Hollywood movies *Carmen Jones, Porgy and Bess,* and many others.

Diahann was born in New York City, on July 17, 1935, at 9:35 P.M. She is a Cancer with Aquarius as her Ascendant and also her Moon sign. With this powerful combination, she was destined for great success in the media, as Aquarius is the sign for television and all things electronic, including recordings.

Pluto, the planet of big business, is exactly conjunct with Diahann's Sun, in the sixth house of work, health, and service to others. This combination rocketed her to superstardom when she joined the cast of "Dynasty," even though she had had her own television series before ("Julia," in 1968). Playing Dominique opposite John Forsythe (Aquarius, born January 29, 1918), Linda Evans (Scorpio, born November 18, 1943), and Joan Collins (Gemini, born May 23, 1933), she is in her element.

Though her eye was on show business, Diahann studied sociology while at New York University, and she recently played the psychiatrist in *Agnes of God* on Broadway. She has always been an "inspirational faith healer."

DIANA RIGG

Born: July 20, 1938, at 4:00 A.M. in Doncaster, Yorkshire, England

I was always a great fan of television's Emma Peel, the martial-arts-fighting, seductive, and tongue-in-cheek witty heroine of *The Avengers*. She was a guest on my "Star Power Show" when she was in New York appearing at the St. James Theater in *The Misanthrope*.

She was born with both her Sun and her Ascendant in Cancer and her Moon in the fighting sign of Aries.

Though the skills of karate-chopping and fighting off villains she displayed as Mrs. Peel came through the Aries influence of the Moon (Aries is ruled by the planet Mars, god of war) and brought her to a greater audience through television, her more sensitive Cancer traits have been responsible for her other critically acclaimed performances in such classics as *King Lear* and *Pygmalion*, as well as challenging newer plays like *Abelard and Heloise*.

Saturn, the planet of work, and her Moon are both in Aries in her eleventh house of personal hopes and wishes, giving her great ambition and the desire to attain her goals.

In the tenth house of fame and career, Diana has her Part of Fortune also in the sign of Aries, giving her the energy and enthusiasm for that physically exhausting action in her movies and television series.

Her Sun and Mars are next to each other in Cancer in the first house of personality, which may explain the rather self-protective manner in which she converses. Diana says that she is just "frank," but the overly sensitive Cancers try to hide their vulnerable natures and therefore develop compensating habits and techniques. Cancers hate to be teased or ridiculed and Diana is no exception.

Mercury in Leo in the third house of communications directed her toward the theater. After working in repertory companies in England, she joined the Royal Shakespeare Company at Stratford-upon-Avon and later the National Theatre in London.

Jupiter, the planet of greater good fortune, in her ninth house of foreign affairs and travel gave her the international success and stardom, especially with *The Avengers,* and her love affair with Israeli artist Manachem Gueffen, who became her first husband.

And while most of her stage work has been done in England, she has had great success on Broadway. America is lucky for Diana because her Ascendant is 14:17 degrees of Cancer, which translated into the monthly calendar is July 4, and the Ascendant indicated where she would most excel.

It is easy to see how that powerful combination of Sun and Mars and the Aries Moon took Diana into roles that were anything but domestic—James Bond's *On Her Majesty's Secret Service, Theatre of Blood, The Assassination Bureau,* and *Evil Under the Sun*.

Her more lighthearted movie performances include roles in *The Great Muppet Caper,* and *A Little Night Music*.

SIGNS OF THE STARS

Her spiritual interests and openness to the world's religions and philosophies may have been partly influenced by her guru planet, Jupiter, in the ninth house of metaphysics and the higher mind, but they were probably effected by her father, who was a British government official posted to India, where she grew up until she returned to England to study acting.

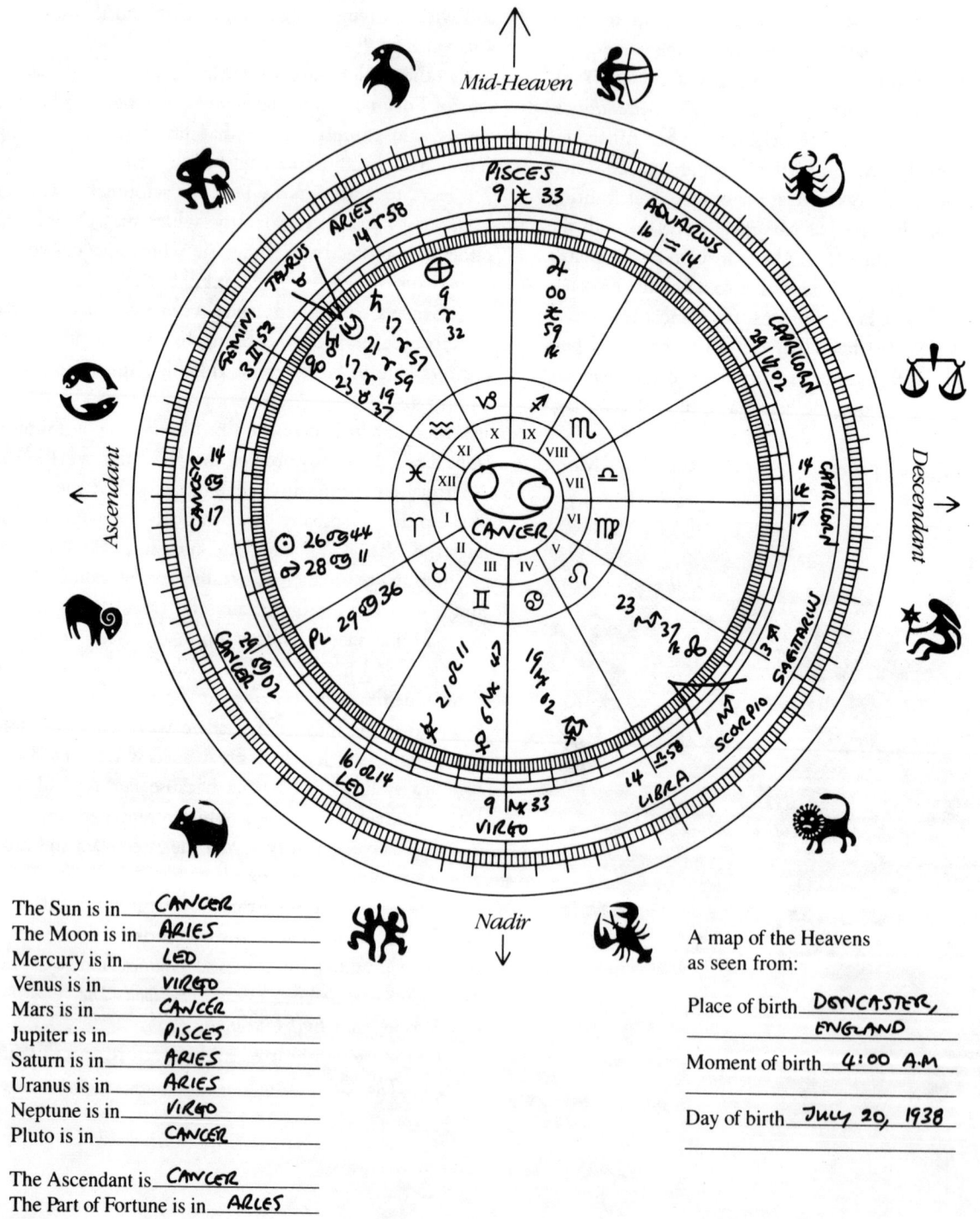

The Sun is in _CANCER_
The Moon is in _ARIES_
Mercury is in _LEO_
Venus is in _VIRGO_
Mars is in _CANCER_
Jupiter is in _PISCES_
Saturn is in _ARIES_
Uranus is in _ARIES_
Neptune is in _VIRGO_
Pluto is in _CANCER_

The Ascendant is _CANCER_
The Part of Fortune is in _ARIES_

A map of the Heavens as seen from:

Place of birth _DONCASTER, ENGLAND_

Moment of birth _4:00 A.M_

Day of birth _JULY 20, 1938_

LEO
Royal Sign of the Zodiac

SUN IN LEO, RULED BY THE SUN
July 23–August 22

Like the blazing Sun that rules them, Leos exude a radiant, glowing, overpowering, blinding, and enveloping disposition, and like the energy and heat given off from this heavenly body, Leos can either help others grow and bloom with their philanthropic and generous guidance or dry them up, exhausting less overpowering signs with their excess of showmanship, vitality, pomp, and pride.

They are always onstage, whether asking questions at the local community meeting, courting their loved ones, or even being at home alone. Everything they do must have drama, and such flamboyancy that their deeds (both kind and cruel) will be recalled by all members of their "audience" for the rest of their lives.

Leos always seem to be happy, even though they may be acting and covering up their hurt pride, their crushed ego, and their jilted affections. Whatever the crisis, they smile, shine, show off, make a gracious gesture, and sail into their next adventure, having written the recent drama in their already full autobiography. Energetic and egocentric, they start to write this early in life, just in case they are too busy by the time they are famous—and the public clamors for more knowledge of what makes Mr. or Ms. Leo tick, and for all the juicy details of the love affairs and broken hearts left in their wake.

We should not judge stellar Leos by their gold-plated Rolls-Royces or ninety-nine-carat diamonds. These are the right accessories for these true kings and queens of the zodiac, who are above mere earthly people.

Leos' constant sunny attitude toward all of life's troubles and their cheerfulness while working at some of life's chores is a total bewilderment to the less happy and more timid signs of the zodiac. They are likely to raise the level of life in Harlem, or to present entertainment in the park in some deprived area of East London.

Astrologically, Leo is the fifth house of the zodiac, the area that rules all the wonderful and happy elements of life—love affairs, sexual pleasure, theaters, places of amusement, gambling casinos, resorts, and beaches as well as all the beautiful-people places. It is the sign of jet-setters, each competing with the other for more radiance and attention. The public is often infatuated by their blinding exteriors, though some less than admirable traits may be disguised by all that Gucci, Chanel, or Bill Blass.

Love is a great satisfaction to Leos, both because they adore making other people happy and because being loved satisfies their egos. These actors and actresses of the zodiac also enjoy the performance aspects of courtship and romance.

Many people consider Leo the royal beast of the jungle, the gracious regal creature ruling a wild, unsophisticated environment with laziness and unconcern; others, on the contrary, call them alley cats, always on the prowl, always in hot pursuit of the local feline Persian, flirting with the ginger tom from the next street, or parading the garden wall followed by at least three recent offspring.

Pleasure is the main drive for them, and whatever gives them pleasure is what they will try to be the best in—the winner, the gold medalist, or the chairman of the board.

Everything from their stationery to their hair must have flamboyance and flourish. They are big show-offs, naturally, but who can help but love them? Likewise, they have such great feelings for their fellow humans that they will go to great extremes to help them directly or indirectly with charitable and philanthropic works. It helps if the edifice, hospital, memorial, or scholarship has their name attached to it, for they like their names to be remembered, but should this be inappropriate or tasteless they will magnanimously wave their hands and let it be known that they don't really mind and, with a royal gesture, pull the unveiling cord to display the cornerstone or launch a ship.

Non-Leos might conclude that pride is the Leo's biggest weakness. Leos, on the other hand, will acclaim that pride is their greatest personality trait. However, this overbearing characteristic causes many a downfall, not only in their business and careers but also in their personal lives. A hint of boredom, a glimmer of interest in someone else, lack of response to their amorous behavior, disapproval of some grandiose financial gift to the arts, or ridicule of their choice of color for their car, hair, or new suit—any and all will crush their seemingly strong, metallic exteriors, pop their big yellow balloons, and send them off damning the recent past and everyone in it. Even their temper tantrums are performances, with everyone around them as featured players.

While they lose their tempers easily, upsetting their dignified aura and toppling (temporarily) from their pedestals, they forgive quickly and easily but hate to be forgiven. They may appear to be rather bullying or pushy at times, but it is their way of royally getting their own way, and what is good for the king should be good enough for everyone else.

It is little wonder that more Leos enter the theatrical profession than any other sign. It is natural for them, and in most cases they do not even have to enter or join—they are from birth part of that group of life's actors that create their dramas on the world's stage, either in entertainment or in the flourishes of battle.

Sun Kings and Queens
LEO DECANATE, RULED BY THE SUN
July 23–August 1

These are the true Leos, for they are doubly influenced by the Sun. It throws both men and women born during this period into the limelight and gives them the glory and the position in life that they seek. They are life's royalty—it was as much because of Jacqueline Kennedy (Onassis) as John that the Kennedy era was America's Camelot—yet these power-happy Leos can discard a crown as easily as they accept one. If you want an actor who will love a live audience whether he is onstage, behind a bar, on the football field, or in a department store, this is the one—always onstage and yet happy only if the masses are entertained or helped or uplifted, for this is not a selfish Leo. King or Queen of all who come in contact with them, they will do all they can to help as long as they feel they are treated with the respect and honor they deserve.

They have but one weapon to fight life's indifference, and that is to dramatize and to publicize every situation and event that may fail because of lack of interest. Their drama will involve everyone, even to the point of war.

The moment these Leos enter the scene, they are the dominant characters, well rehearsed, lines memorized, looking immaculate, and with a retinue of lords and ladies who will happily do Leo's bidding and make sure that Leo is happy all the time.

Deeply concerned over their achievement potential and their ambitions, they will concentrate on getting what they want, even to the point of appearing ruthless and using force if necessary to get exactly what they feel is rightly theirs. This hard streak is covered by an eager vitality, sunny, healthful looks, and a spirit of adventure, yet underneath this Leo's pride is doubly in need of satisfaction, on the sports field, at the conference table, or in a duel.

Unlike Leos born later in the sign, once these Leos' pride is hurt, it takes a long time to heal. Their homes and private lives are of none or of little importance. And they want to succeed in the outside world, be internationally acclaimed and loved, sought after or feared. While they need the support of others, the loyalty to those close to them will often be in question; they have a great detachment that does not allow personalities and emotions to stand in the way of communicating.

Yet their tremendous willpower is the envy of all, and thus they become heroes or heroines, their deeds occasionally splashed across the pages of the local newspaper.

Romantically there is no better lover than this passionate and uninhibited Leo as long as they can be the king or queen of the relationship. They need to be served and flattered, and they will reward their loved ones generously.

While Leos will try to make each and every relationship work for them as part of their basic need to make everyone happy, they soon give up if their efforts are not appreciated. It is impossible for these Leos to have a "bad" relationship with any sign; however, some will prove more difficult than others, with some obstacles that even the most generous and understanding Leos will not want to submit to or bulldoze their way through.

I have always been strongly attracted to the Sun Kings and Queens, probably because my own ascendant in my horoscope chart is 8 degrees of Leo.

MICK JAGGER

The Rolling Stones captured the imagination and spirit of a whole new generation, and sexy, feral Mick Jagger had a lot to do with it.

It is not surprising when you see his performances—he is dramatic, entertaining, wild and ranting, a renegade, and a rebellious bad boy—that Mick has five planetary positions in Leo and his Ascendant is also in Leo. He is a natural show-off, and he also has a frantic sense of humor.

Mick was born in Dartford, England, on July 26, 1943, at 6:30 A.M. His Part of Fortune is at the top of his chart in Taurus, the sign of the singer and musician, and combined with the showmanship of Leo, this gives him the devil-may-care charisma (whether you have *sympathy* or not) to pull off outrageous stunts like wearing a dress by Carnaby Street designer Michael Fish in order to recite a poem written for a special occasion.

Described as "the rhythm-and-blues Nureyev" in his early career, Mick's athletic, creative abilities dominated his hysterical, panic-causing, suggestive, and explosive singing.

Coming from an ordinary middle-class family, he soon developed in his childhood a great love of music and, adding Leo's starlike qualities to his talents, he rocked to stardom.

While he spends much time on tour, loving a Leo environment because of his Ascendant, he has been restoring the eighteenth-century La Fourchette Château in the Loire Valley in France, quite suitable accommodations for a "Sun king."

Fellow Rolling Stone Ron Wood, also a Sun king, was born August 1, 1948. I was delighted when asked to do the horoscope for his new baby Jesse James Wood, which showed "paternal" Saturn in Leo.

SUSAN GEORGE

It was when I was starring in the BBC-TV "Star Signs" in 1979 that I first met Susan George, whom I had always loved and admired from afar. As well as being one of the most popular and talented actresses in England, she had taken on a certain amount of genuine Sun-queen tendencies by being one of Prince Charles's favorite dates, and for a long time they were an item in all the gossip columns.

"Star Signs" was a weekly show on prime-time television, and part of it was an astrological guessing game. I was given the birth data July 26, 1950, at 2:00 A.M. in Surbiton, Surrey, and told only that it was the chart of a female.

When it came time for me to describe the chart, I spoke in glowing terms about the past and future of the individual born at that time and place. When the host of the show asked me to guess who it was, I said, "I predict I will have lunch with this young lady next week. . . . I think it is Susan George." Of course, I was right, and we became instant friends. In all the times I have seen her since, I have always been aware of her positive, optimistic, and enthusiastic disposition.

When Susan arrived in New York in 1984 to publicize her new movie *The Jigsaw Man,* I visited her at her suite at the Mayfair Hotel. We pored over her chart and discussed the important question of marriage. For years I had been telling her that the time wasn't right, but now, she was thrilled to hear, the chart showed that October 4–6, 1984, was the ideal time for her to wed longtime sweetheart Simon MacCorkindale (a star of "Falcon Crest"), an Aquarius. They married in Fiji the first week of October. Simon's Ascendant is 2:15 degrees of Leo, exactly on Susan's Sun, making him a magnanimous king and a fitting consort to a Sun queen.

GEOFFREY HOLDER

When I met Geoffrey he was working on the black Broadway musical *Timbuktu,* adapted from *Kismet,* shifting the setting from Baghdad to Timbuktu in Africa. It starred the legendary Eartha Kitt, an Aquarian, a natural creative partner for Geoffrey's Leo Sun.

As the choreographer and costume designer of the

show, he was a shot in the arm to a rather dull Broadway season, with all the flamboyancy of a Leo Sun king. He was already riding high on the success of *The Wiz,* for which he won two Tony Awards as choreographer and costume designer.

Geoffrey was born in Port of Spain, Trinidad, on August 1, 1930, between 9:00 and 9:30 A.M. His Sun in 8 degrees of Leo and Moon in the sexy sign of Scorpio give him a talent to bring sensuality to his performances, whether as an actor, dancer, or choreographer. This was vividly depicted in his bizarre role in the James Bond movie *Live and Let Die.*

With his Sun high in his chart in Leo, and with Jupiter, the planet of good luck, in Cancer, he was destined to be a success in the United States, a Cancer country. His own dance company made their first appearance in the United States in 1953, and he made his Broadway debut in 1954 in the musical *House of Flowers.*

TOM WILSON

I was already a big Ziggy aficionado, sending greeting cards and gifts bearing Ziggy's words of wisdom, uplifting and inspiring, to my friends and clients when they needed that extra-special boost. So I was not a stranger to his creator, Tom Wilson.

Tom was born August 1, 1931, in Grant Town, West Virginia, with his Sun in 8:37 degrees of that magical sign of the Leo Sun king. He was born at 3:00 P.M. with the witty, philosophical, and visually creative sign of Sagittarius rising over the horizon.

His chart augured the upcoming expansion of the Ziggy empire into many American homes. Uranus in his fifth house of show business indicated an opportunity to do a television special at the end of the year. This gave millions of viewers great happiness and good entertainment when Wilson's show was aired during the holiday season. "Ziggy" had become rich and famous.

Tom has made Ziggy autobiographical, turning the artistic, creative, and lovable little prince into a benevolent Sun king.

GIANCARLO GIANNINI

I opened the door of my New York apartment, and there, radiating from an incredibly friendly and Leo-like countenance, were those incredible eyes that have dominated the screen for many years. Already a fan of his since seeing *Love and Anarchy,* I had just seen his *Seven Beauties,* and he was in town promoting the movie and making plans to expand his career.

"Your chart shows that you could be a great director as well as a star," I told him, and I was very supportive when he indicated that his own thoughts were going in that direction.

Born in La Spezia, Italy, on August 1, 1942, between 4:00 and 5:00 P.M., Giancarlo has four planetary positions in Leo, and his Part of Fortune is in exactly the same place as his Sun, in 8 degrees of Leo. His fortune comes from being himself and pushing his good looks. His film career was launched by Lina Wertmuller (Leo, born in Rome, August 14, 1928).

JACQUELINE KENNEDY ONASSIS

Born: July 28, 1929, at 2:30 P.M. in Southampton, New York

Jackie is a typical Sun queen Leo, a true flamboyant, dramatic, and regal queen of the zodiac. Everything she does has a touch of drama about it, and the public is fascinated by her every action, whether shopping, horseback riding in Central Park, or attending the ballet in her latest fashions. She is always dignified, loyal, magnanimous, and cheerful.

The American public thought of her and her handsome husband, President John F. Kennedy (Gemini, born May 29), as their "royal family," and their ideals for the United States were the ideals of Camelot.

I first did Jackie's horoscope for British *Vogue* magazine in 1971, three years after her marriage to Aristotle Onassis (Capricorn, born January 15). Her Ascendant Scorpio makes her both ambitious and temperamental, and she has the pridefulness of all first-degree Leos. It adds an air of mystery to her personality. She is capable of attaining any goal she sets out to reach, especially with Mars, the coruling planet of Scorpio, at the top of her chart on the midheaven, in the tenth house of government, ambitions, and foreign affairs.

Gemini in the seventh house of marriage made Kennedy the perfect partner. Venus, the planet of love, is in Gemini, attracting her to a Gemini husband. As most Gemini influences represent a double effect, she was destined for more than one marriage. Jupiter is also in that sector of her chart; this planet is symbolized by an older, wiser, benevolent god who symbolically would represent the older Aristotle Onassis (Capricorn).

Her Moon in Aries in the fifth house of love and romance, sports, resorts, places of amusement, theaters, and all the good things of life has thrown Jackie into the spotlight—few international superstars have captured the imagination of the press and the public as has Jackie over the years. She is a symbol of love or romance on a high level and of a glamorous jet-setter flying from one resort to another. Yet this Moon also makes her a compassionate champion of needy children, the handicapped, endangered species, and the arts.

The planet Jupiter (good fortune) and Venus (good luck and love) in the seventh house of marriage made her successful in winning two wealthy and generous men, but as a Leo queen she would love to have a title, and this may still be in the stars.

Pluto, the planet of the underworld and mystery, is in the eighth house of death, legacies, inheritances, big business, and income, reflecting the assassination of President Kennedy and the mystery and violence surrounding it as well as the vast wealth, much of it passed on to Jackie, of Aristotle Onassis.

Her love of horses is a result of the Sagittarian influence in the first house of the zodiac, the area that represents environment, personality, and disposition. Her Ascendant Scorpio and the influence of Saturn give her a slightly secretive and serious personality—very few people have heard Jackie speak publicly. Yet as Saturn rules Capricorn, the sign of government, she has probably had a great influence on the government both as first lady and as a crusader.

Uranus, the planet of sudden changes and happen-

ings, affects home and property in her chart, explaining her many homes and sudden moves. The Sun, representing herself, and Mercury, the planet of communications (traveling and writing), are both in the area of money income, too. This means that Jackie has the ability to make a fortune for herself. Now that she is an editor in publishing (with Doubleday in New York) she is indeed earning her own money through the communications field.

Jackie's Part of Fortune is in the ninth house of long distance, foreign affairs, and international business, and it is located with the planet Neptune, which rules shipping (her great fortune is partly from Onassis's shipping empire). It also rules oil, liquids, and

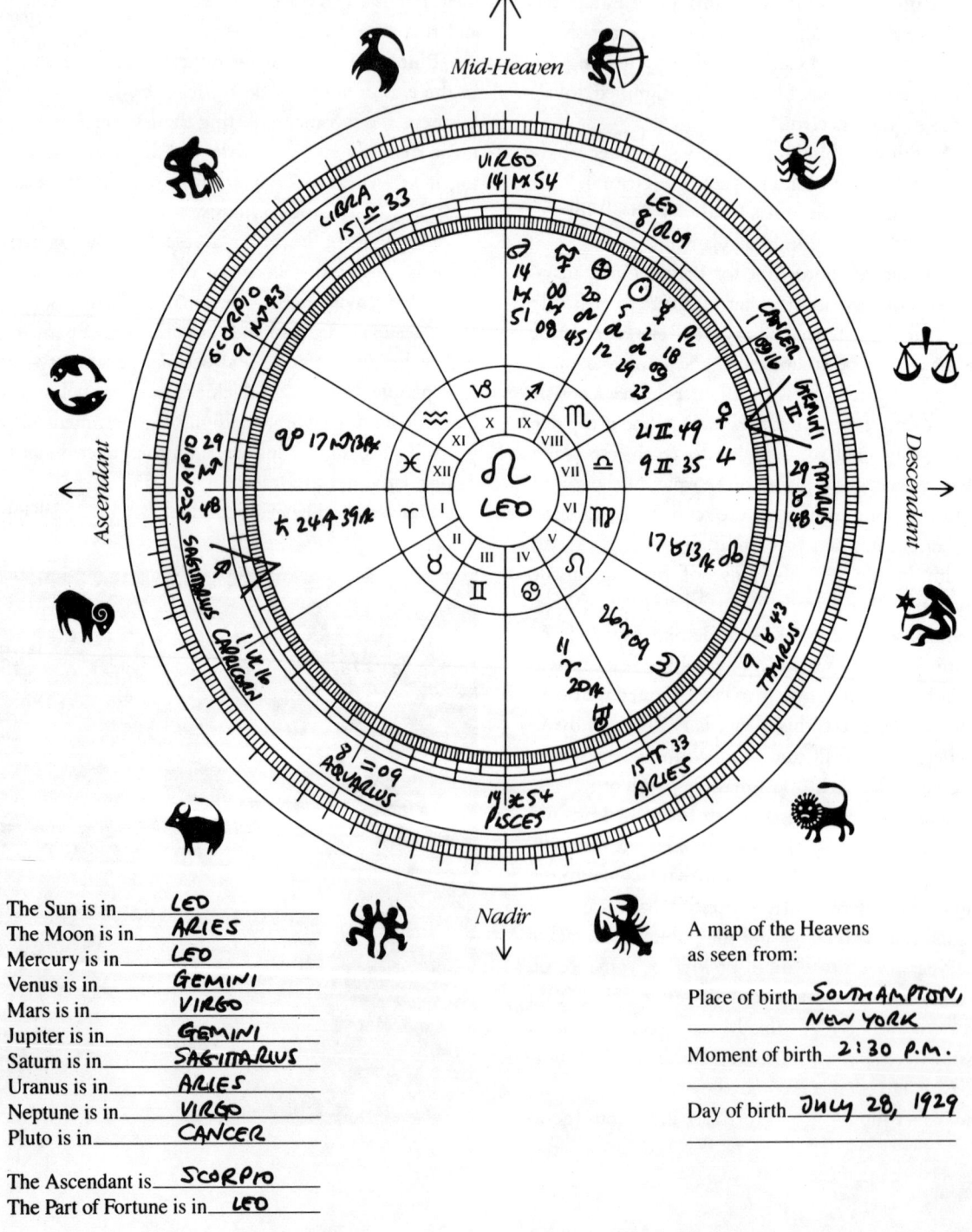

The Sun is in _LEO_
The Moon is in _ARIES_
Mercury is in _LEO_
Venus is in _GEMINI_
Mars is in _VIRGO_
Jupiter is in _GEMINI_
Saturn is in _SAGITTARIUS_
Uranus is in _ARIES_
Neptune is in _VIRGO_
Pluto is in _CANCER_

The Ascendant is _SCORPIO_
The Part of Fortune is in _LEO_

A map of the Heavens as seen from:

Place of birth _SOUTHAMPTON, NEW YORK_

Moment of birth _2:30 P.M._

Day of birth _July 28, 1929_

movies (Kennedy's fortune came from whiskey and the film industry). As Neptune is in Virgo it is not surprising that Boston, Kennedy's hometown, and Greece, both traditionally considered ruled by the sign of Virgo, had an important influence on her life. (Cities and countries, like people, have characteristics and traits associated with the zodiac signs.) Mars, the planet of energy, action, and enthusiasm, is on the top of her chart, giving her that tremendous success, yet she is still a Sun Queen, for these ambitions and achievements all help to shine more light and publicity on her. Perhaps it was the warlike planet Mars that triggered the assassin's bullet that killed her husband on November 22, 1963. Yet the Double Grand Trine (when three planets within approximately 120 degrees of each other form an isosceles triangle—Jackie has two) in her chart protects her, despite all the tragedy in her life, and has enabled her to keep a regal Leo composure despite emotional torment. It is interesting to note that the degree of the zodiac represented by November 22 is 29 degrees of Scorpio, the exact degree of Jackie's Ascendant. As described by "Charubel" in his book *The Degrees of the Zodiac Symbolized,* first published in 1898, November 21 (28 degrees of Scorpio) is "A tiger crouching ready to spring on its prey. A revengeful, treacherous, and cruel person. This degree is an evil mixture of Saturn and Mars." November 22 (29 degrees of Scorpio) is "A man with a bow and arrow in the act of taking aim at some object in the distance. A good marksman; very expert; fond of chase."

Regardless of how the pendulum will continue to swing for her from tragedy to great achievement and happiness, Jackie will always appear to be the epitome of the true Leo, and she will be treated as the Sun queen she really wants to be.

Glorious Travelers and Philosophers
SAGITTARIUS DECANATE, RULED BY JUPITER
August 2–August 11

These Leos are misleading, for their need to dash off to foreign countries (or, as in the case of pioneer astronaut Neil Armstrong, other planets), hunt in jungles, join missionary settlements, enter the religious service can be misinterpreted as being very un-Leo-like. But while the Sagittarian influence accounts for the spiritual, religious, and philosophical inclinations, the Leo drive is still underneath and will produce the radical bishop, the charismatic guru, or the renegade nun who leaves the convent for Hollywood, as well as deterministic political thinkers. These Leos will use all of life's illusions, adventures, and physical activities to get noticed.

Thanks to Jupiter's benevolence and witty disposition, many will try to influence the population with a satirical comedy act or social commentary, poking fun at the politicians and political reformers of the day. They will take themselves and their ideals seriously, and they will not allow themselves to yield to any others. Dustin Hoffman's sardonic intensity and his roles in such movies as *The Graduate, Midnight Cowboy,* and *Tootsie* are characteristic of these Leos.

Like all other Leos, they will be generous to a fault and yet unlike the others, they will not claim the pomp and glory and jewels and decorations. These Leos believe in a more spartan regime, a pure world, and would be as happy with a hill as a kingdom, with a simple altar as a cathedral.

Despite their love of philosophy, these Leos will love to join the team after the football match and drink with them, explaining how they handled a bunch of rowdy spectators while they were getting their third down. Or the female Leo will welcome her boyfriend by demonstrating a newly learned karate chop or kung fu kick. Witty and with a wealth of stories and anecdotes (all about themselves), they are great performers and will be prepared to do their own stunts in life—horseback riding, leaping tall fences with a single bound, boxing, wrestling, hanging from the twenty-eighth-floor window ledge for realism, and doing a somersault in a Piper Cub. These are real, up-front people. In fact, their honesty, which they always kick themselves for afterward, is usually their weakness. They will be frank and tell others straight out that they hate that new sweater, that hair color, or that new book. And others cannot help but love them because they are genuine and real and love getting lots of attention by being rather outrageous. They accumulate their knowledge by being life students, and they are always rushing off to buy the latest nonfiction, attend lectures at colleges and local adult education centers, and take courses in various mystical arts and sciences.

Their strength, their audacity, and their showmanship as well as their ideals for bettering mankind (and themselves) attract all whom come in contact with them.

The Leo independence and cheerfulness are reflected in their love lives, as are the impulse toward spontaneous behavior and witty speeches. They can charm and bewilder, offering their breathless lovers voyages, travels, expansion in the philosophic and religious senses, karmic lessons and peace of mind, whether they are balancing precariously on a mountain slope in Switzerland or attending the annual convention of a subcommittee of the United Nations working to aid deprived children in Africa.

NEIL ARMSTRONG

There is no better example of "the glorious traveler and philosopher" in modern times than this Sagittarius-influenced Leo, the astronaut, Neil Armstrong, the first man to set foot on the Moon. Not only was he born in the decanate ruled by Sagittarius, but the Moon, which rules his emotions and ideals, was also in the sign of Sagittarius, rule of long-distance travel.

Neil was born on August 5, 1930, at 12:31 A.M. in Wapakoneta, Ohio. His sun sign is Leo, which is well complemented by his Ascendant, Gemini, which foreshadowed the environment in which he would most excel—he served as command pilot of the Gemini 8 space mission in 1966.

Uranus—the planet of space, electronics, computers, and travel—is in Aries, the sign of the pioneer, the leader, and crusader. And Mars, the god of war, is in Gemini in his first house, drawing him toward the military and flying. Neptune, the god of the sea, is in Virgo, the sign of the detailed analyst and teacher, next to Mercury, the planet of travel and communications, also in Virgo. He flew many combat missions from 1949 to 1952 and in 1955, he became a civilian research pilot for the National Advisory Committee for Aeronautics (NACA), and the National Aeronautics and Space Administration (NASA). His many incredible achievements and daring feats at NASA, led to his appointment as an astronaut with the Gemini flight missions, which included the first successful docking in space by two vehicles and later, the historic Moon flight, during which he set foot on the Moon on July 20, 1969.

His planet Jupiter, which brings him the great fortune in his life, is in Cancer, and Pluto, the planet of big business, is also located in Cancer. Many modern-day astrologers call Cancer Moon Child instead. Clearly, Neil is a Moon Child who could not escape this great moment that destiny bestowed upon him.

A world hero, he has been honored and decorated by seventeen countries and holds numerous awards. Neil Armstrong has added a new philosophy to life with his immortal words, "One small step for man, one giant leap for mankind," heralding the new-age philosophy of travel, exploration, life, and spiritual awareness in the universe.

LUCILLE BALL

Lucille Ball took her brand of humor and philosophy to seventy-seven foreign countries, and she didn't even have to leave Hollywood to do it. Her legendary show "I Love Lucy" was broadcast around the world and is still being rerun today.

Lucy was born on August 6, 1911, at 4:00 A.M. in Jamestown, New Jersey, a flamboyant Leo with the home-loving sensitive sign of Cancer as her Ascendant and her Moon in Capricorn, making her a practical businesswoman. She became president of Desilu productions when she bought out ex-husband Desi Arnaz's share of the company for $3 million; three years later she sold her share to Gulf+Western for $17 million.

Her Part of Fortune is in Sagittarius, in her fifth house of show business and speculation, and she was always one step ahead of others in negotiation, despite her scatterbrained public image.

The Cancer Ascendant gave her the right personality for having a family, and her children Desi Arnaz, Jr. (Capricorn, January 19, born 1953), and Lucie Arnaz (Cancer, born July 17, 1951) both appeared in "I Love Lucy." Lucy was able to run her home, bring up her children, and still manage her television empire.

Asked by the press to express her feelings about the death of her father in 1986, Lucie Arnaz said, "Desi was the 'I' in 'I Love Lucy.'"

We all love Lucy.

DUSTIN HOFFMAN

Born: August 8, 1937, at 5:57 P.M. in Los Angeles, California

Dustin Hoffman shows the maverick traits of this Leo—he has always been an antistar, enjoying a private social life yet willing to chat with and tease his fans when eating in a Greenwich Village restaurant.

Dustin is a Leo with Aquarius ascending, and his Moon is in the hard-working sign of Virgo, which probably explains his perfectionist approach to acting.

His Part of Fortune is in Pisces in his first house, giving him the looks, attitude, disposition, and personality to attract the right sort of success. The dynamic intensity he projects has played a large part in his fame and success. Venus, the planet that rules music, drama, and the fine arts, is in his fifth house of show business and this at first influenced him to become a concert pianist. Later he realized he wanted to be an actor. Whether Venus gave him this good luck or whether his Aquarian intuition led him to this decision, it was obviously the most important revelation in his life.

The fifth house also represents children, and as well as being fulfilled in his acting career, Dustin has two children by his first wife, dancer and actress Ann Byrne, and three by his second wife, lawyer Lisa Gottsegen. With the Sun in his seventh house of partnerships, marriage is very important to him.

The Moon, representing the public, and Neptune, representing the film star, are right next to each other in the sign of Virgo (the worker) in Dustin's chart, which accounts for his status as one of our most successful and popular stars. He has been nominated for an almost unprecedented number of Oscars—for his roles in *The Graduate, Midnight Cowboy, Lenny, Little Big Man, Papillon, Marathon Man,* and *Tootsie,* as well as for his winning performance in *Kramer vs. Kramer.* These planets intensify Dustin's workaholic tendencies, and Mars, in his tenth house of career, gives him the energy and drive he needs to succeed.

With his Sun in Leo in the seventh house of partners, it was a natural choice for Dustin to team up with fellow Leo Robert Redford in *All the President's Men.*

Another vital career link was to Jon Voight, with whom Hoffman first worked on an off-Broadway revival of Arthur Miller's *A View From the Bridge.* Soon friends, the two went on to do *Midnight Cowboy.*

The Dustin Hoffman we see is the artist obsessed by his work, demanding and craving perfection for his audiences as well as for his own realization of artistic excellence.

About Willy Loman, the character Dustin played in Arthur Miller's *Death of a Salesman,* Miller wrote, "Willy was a salesman.... He's a man way out there in the blue, riding on a smile and a shoeshine. And when they start not smiling back—that's an earthquake. ... A salesman has got to dream, boys. It comes with the territory."

Dustin is not going to wait for others to direct and control his life. He is determined that whether he is tragic or comic, his audiences will keep smiling. A Leo wants nothing more than to please others, to entertain, and to be loved. It comes with the territory!

LEO

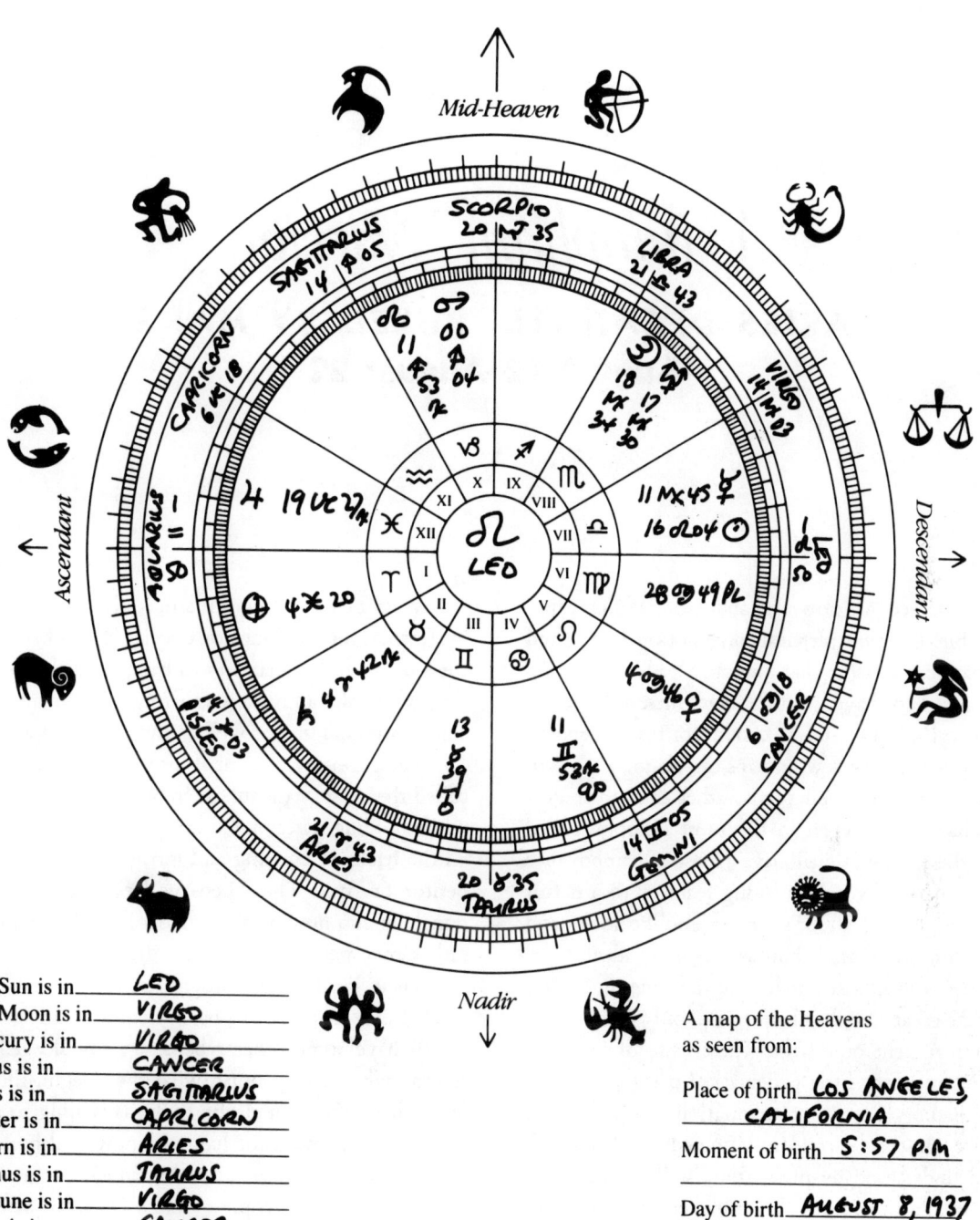

The Sun is in _LEO_
The Moon is in _VIRGO_
Mercury is in _VIRGO_
Venus is in _CANCER_
Mars is in _SAGITTARIUS_
Jupiter is in _CAPRICORN_
Saturn is in _ARIES_
Uranus is in _TAURUS_
Neptune is in _VIRGO_
Pluto is in _CANCER_

The Ascendant is _AQUARIUS_
The Part of Fortune is in _PISCES_

A map of the Heavens as seen from:

Place of birth _LOS ANGELES, CALIFORNIA_

Moment of birth _5:57 P.M_

Day of birth _AUGUST 8, 1937_

Triumphant Warriors

ARIES DECANATE, RULED BY MARS
August 12–August 22

These Leos are powerful and strong leaders capable of intense physical and emotional drive and such dynamic leadership that it usually leads to heroism. Where most Leos have great courage, these will go far above the call of duty and be known for feats of endurance and strength that few humans can claim. They will win a following for their deeds rather than their dramatic behavior, yet even in the most unsophisticated situation these Leos will still have a sense of flamboyance and give panache even to a losing team or to a defeat in battle. Robert Redford's almost godlike looks and vigorous film roles mark him as this Leo's ideal.

These Leos can hate and love at the same time; their passions are great, and they believe that only good comes from an argument or a fight. Their sense of justice is instant, having very little patience for petty discussion, long-winded arguments, or negotiation. Their decision or verdict must be carried out immediately. Though wise and understood by many, they will attract many enemies in life because of this impatient attitude. Devoted and loyal to those they work or fight for, these Leos appear very serious, stern, and businesslike yet are compassionate, sympathetic, and helpful to causes and to the downtrodden. They make great leaders or partners either in business or romance.

Subtly domineering, these Leos use tactical stratagems to impose their wills, and agreeing with their plans will bring a whole new energy and vitality to any relationship.

With a childlike enthusiasm for life, these Leos cope by fussing. Simple kings or queens, they like to go out for a picnic rather than have a banquet at the castle, and they will take musicians, boating equipment, friends, and relatives along, as well as the best food and wines.

These Leos are combat prone; they can truly be called the beast of the jungle in business and in love and, while holding a very regal bearing or position, will use all the tricks of cunning and intrigue to outwit a competitor or rival. These Leos will probably resort to a punch in the nose as a method of resolving problems rather than gentle and "royal" discussion.

Their business philosophy is, "Do it now. Next week I may not want to be in charge of this company. I will have some other scheme up my sleeve." Great starters who hate to finish what they begin, they must leave that to some underling who is willing to execute their plans in return for having a powerful boss who is a hero to all. It is this excitement, adventure, and enthusiasm that attracts people to these Leos, for with them there will never be a dull moment, only one moment of glory and victory after another.

In love these Leos are ardent and chivalrous as well as prone to jealousy. Variable as Leos are, they might do well with a fellow adventurer, a politician, or someone who shares their great love of books. Inclined to quick fights, they are exhausted by emotional scenes. Like the third-decanate Sagittarians, they are fighters and lovers.

PRINCESS ANNE

Regality is in the blood—as well as the temperament—of this "triumphant warrior," always sitting on her favorite horse, hunting or competing in international jumping events, and always valiant in handling the press.

Born in London, on August 15, 1950, at 11:50 A.M. Princess Anne is a Leo with her Moon in the critical but methodical sign of Virgo, and her ascendant is Libra, the sign of peace and tranquility.

Perhaps this Libra influence made her choose horses rather than people, so she could escape from the duties of the royal family—all the pomp and ceremony that Leos usually love yet against which her Virgo instincts may rebel. (Virgo is the sign of the worker or the servant.)

Her riding skills have been helped by the positioning of Mercury (riding and communication), Saturn (discipline), and the Moon (public), all together in Virgo and with the unaffected style these Leos are known for, she enjoys grooming her horses herself.

Not known for Libran tact and diplomacy, she may have learned to roar like a lion in order to protect her peace of mind.

MADONNA AND SEAN PENN

A woman of great character and talent, Madonna has been able to keep ahead of the press that assails her for being so sexual. She is a "material girl" who has been triumphant in overcoming all the traumas and crises in her life. Her mother died when she was only six, and she grew up with a very strict stepmother.

Born in Bay City, Michigan, on August 16, 1958, she is a Leo with her Moon and her Mars (emotions and energy) in the sign of Gemini, and her performances reveal the spirit of another misunderstood star, Gemini Marilyn Monroe (June 1). The routines in Madonna's videos recall Marilyn.

Emotionally, too, Mars has attracted her to a rather combative husband, Sean Penn, born the day after her two years later, August 17, 1960, in Santa Monica, California.

They both attract the same type of controversy and intensity, and both have the same exciting appeal of the oldtime stars, whether or not one approves of their behavior. Their performances are what makes them stars, and Sean, like Madonna, has given excitement and entertainment to his fans and audiences on Broadway and in the movies (*Racing with the Moon, The Falcon and the Snowman, Taps,* and *Bad Boys*).

Obviously warriors when it comes to their private lives, they are triumphant professionally.

ROBERT DE NIRO

An actor who creates a totally different character and personality for each of his roles, often gaining or losing weight or learning new skills, Robert De Niro is one of America's greatest stars, yet very little is known about his private life.

It was his Sun in Leo that finally brought him into the world of show business. Born at 3:00 A.M. on August 17, 1943, in New York, he has Pluto, the planet of big business, and Jupiter, planet of good luck, both in Leo, and his moody, intense, slightly withdrawn personality is due to his ascending sign Cancer. He likes to curl up in his shell, his home.

His Moon in Pisces took his creative talents into the movies, and being located in the ninth house of foreign affairs, he is internationally famous.

As a "warrior," Robert's characters in his movies ranged from *Raging Bull,* for which he won the best actor Academy Award in 1981, to the lonely, obsessed Vietnam veteran in *Taxi Driver,* not to mention his roles in *The Deer Hunter, The Godfather Part II,* and the more recent *The Mission.*

Uranus and Saturn, the talent and work planets, in Gemini highlight his subtle sense of humor, and his lighter, yet still intense, roles include *New York, New York* and *King of Comedy.*

Whatever part he plays, he is "triumphant."

ROBERT REDFORD

Born: August 18, 1937, at 8:00 A.M. in Santa Monica, California

When I met Robert he was filming the last scenes of *The Great Gatsby* at Pinewood Studios in England. According to director Jack Clayton (Pisces), though it was near the end of shooting, he was still as enthusiastic as on the first day. He was still working hard on the character of Gatsby. Between scenes he would go over his lines, work on subtle details of character, and analyze the previous scene. At the end of the day it would be rare for him to socialize, for he was eager to retire and study for the next day.

"I was born in Santa Monica, California," he told me as he grabbed a quick lunch at about 8 o'clock in the morning. "That's probably why I like to start work early!"

Robert is a fascinating mixture of his Sun sign Leo, and his hard-working Ascendant Virgo, plus the effect of his Moon in Capricorn, which gives him those wonderful photogenic lines and a grim determination to stick things out.

While many of his obvious traits seem very Virgoan, for he has Neptune, the filmmaking planet, and Mercury, the communicator, also in Virgo, the Leo Sun sign still forces itself to the surface, making him popular with friends and coworkers and happy and content most of the time.

Since his Sun sign, which represents the person he is deep down inside, is Leo, he has a tremendous determination to be the "king" of his profession. Yet he also has the weakness of pride, which in his case means that he can be easily hurt, both professionally and in his personal life, but he will keep it to himself. The martial side of this Leo personality was demonstrated even in his first film, *War Hunt,* and since then he has played a wide range of men of action—athletes, cowboys, outlaws, and politicians.

He is basically very honest and frank and often outspoken when it comes to causes he believes in. Though he is forceful and can lose his temper, he is easily appeased, and very forgiving. He rarely holds a grudge.

He is happiest when making others happy—as actor, director, husband, or friend.

His work load is certainly helped by his Virgo Ascendant. It makes him a perfectionist in everything he does and gives him an innate sense of what is right for every occasion, as does the good taste bestowed by the Leo-Virgo combination. Fortunately, he has the wealth necessary to satisfy his desires.

A lover and defender of the beauties of nature, he is happiest when relaxing in his hilltop retreat in the Rocky Mountains of Utah, which he named Sundance, after his character in *Butch Cassidy and the Sundance Kid.* Capricorn, his Moon sign, rules mountaintops, and attracts him to the spectacular natural mountains and views. His cabin, which he built himself, blends into the landscape. In his very Virgo way he describes it as being "uncluttered and harmonious with the mountain." But like all Virgos, he needs a telephone and working area right at hand. And the teacherlike qualities of Virgo encourage him to allow the mountaintop retreat to be used for film study and workshop groups.

The Capricorn Moon also drives him to cultivate the land, to grow vegetables and plants, and to protect the trees. This is a place where Robert's Leo Sun can dance free, away from the public and the pressure of being a superstar.

His Part of Fortune in Aquarius is located in the fifth house of show business, film, and television. Venus, the planet of good luck and love, is located with Pluto, the planet of big business, in his tenth house of career and fame.

Leo is ruled by the Sun, and Robert is an outspoken advocate of solar power and environmental issues.

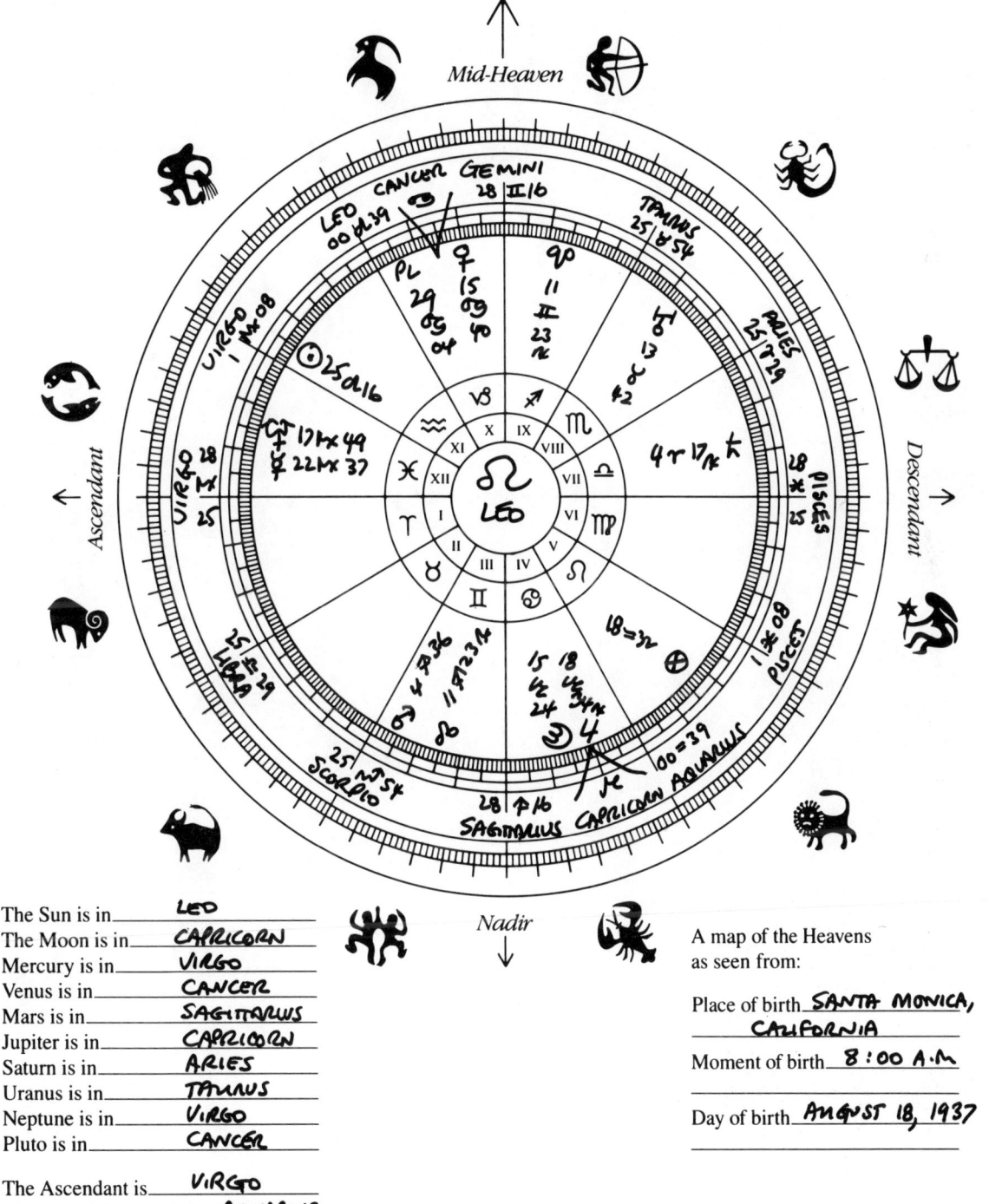

The Sun is in — LEO
The Moon is in — CAPRICORN
Mercury is in — VIRGO
Venus is in — CANCER
Mars is in — SAGITTARIUS
Jupiter is in — CAPRICORN
Saturn is in — ARIES
Uranus is in — TAURUS
Neptune is in — VIRGO
Pluto is in — CANCER

The Ascendant is — VIRGO
The Part of Fortune is in — AQUARIUS

A map of the Heavens as seen from:

Place of birth — SANTA MONICA, CALIFORNIA
Moment of birth — 8:00 A.M.
Day of birth — AUGUST 18, 1937

VIRGO
Teacher of the Zodiac

SUN IN VIRGO, RULED BY MERCURY
August 23–September 22

Virgo is the hardest worker in the zodiac, a sign that just loves to keep busy, and is most content when faced with numerous chores and chaotic schedules and gradually seeing order develop. Mercurial in every way, people born under this sign have a hard time keeping to just one project or interest, because they're always adding to their list of important items and plans, grabbing onto every offer or suggestion as if it were a drug. They are ruled by Mercury, the planet of communication and travel, and therefore have this innate need to search out information, often out of curiosity, and to keep on the move, traveling from house to house, city to city, and country to country as well as on the intellectual and spiritual planes.

Virgos have an insatiable appetite for knowledge, combined with the industriousness of the researcher and the analytical ability of the scientist or technician. Teachers and improvers by nature, they sometimes strike others as fussy and critical, often hurtful in their blunt and accurate observations or their mania for cleanliness and neatness (in the personal as well as professional sphere). Yet they are not by nature cruel or insensitive. They only want their loved ones and coworkers to be the best possible in whatever they tackle.

Nothing ever seems right to Virgos, but they are as strict and critical of themselves as of those around them. Strangely, they make better servants than bosses even though many reach great heights in the executive fields, in public and government offices, and in the performing arts. They feel that while they may be the president of a company or even a country, they are still doing service for others, helping them to have better lives and generally improve their lot. While they may appear to be scolding or nagging, they inspire great enthusiasm and confidence in others by their cool, optimistic attitude toward obstacles and disappointments.

There is a tendency to think of Virgo as the sign of the Virgin and thus as very cold, or devoid of sexual interest. Nothing is further from the truth; Virgos, while they may appear to be discriminating and naïve, feel it is their role in life to make sure all the people they encounter are getting enough attention, affection, or sexual activity. In love they are practical and direct.

Virgo is the sixth house of the zodiac, the house that rules work and servants, the necessities of life, food and clothing, and personal health. And it is the combination of these things that make up the material essence of Virgo—practical, honest, and wise.

So many are attracted to the teaching profession as they can help masses of eager minds at a time. Others find their way into hospitals and institutions where their devotion to duty can be applied without being resented or misunderstood as ambition. Nevertheless, they are calculating and quietly ambitious, often having reward cast upon them in favor of their more aggressive competitors. The analytical ability makes them good at accounts and keeping schedules (they invented lists!), but lack of human contact can make them nervous, so they should gear their office work and financial wheeling and dealing into areas where there are many people around—especially the general public in shops, banks, and libraries. When in the media, they tend toward the commentator or talk-show role, though they can be charismatic performers. They can make a success of any work, but that doesn't mean that they love it. They will continue doing service until boredom takes over, then they will quit. As long as they know that their efforts are making someone happy or getting them organized, they will struggle on, occasionally grumbling and complaining about being overworked for they have a touch of the martyr in them.

They are obsessed with stationery as well as with work. Very rarely can they walk by an office supply shop without feeling compelled to walk in and buy some more stationery, pens, or special recording books and ledgers. Their rooms and cupboards are stacked with enough office material to last ten years, yet this need to surround themselves with these items, valuable to fulfilling their roles as communicators or messengers of the gods, is important to their well-being—almost as important as the rows of unread books they buy on impulse and their wide selection of reference books and encyclopedias, which would make a crossword puzzle fanatic envious.

Traveling Professors

VIRGO DECANATE, RULED BY MERCURY
August 23–September 1

These Virgos get a double portion of the energy and movement necessary for the planet Mercury to be fulfilled, not only in the areas of verbal and written communication but also in travel. These are the writers and the teachers, the salesmen and the preachers. They entertain on cruise ships and they guide other people through foreign cities as well as through life's adventures. Like indefatigable Lily Tomlin, touring the country in *The Search for Signs of Intelligent Life in the Universe,* Mercury never stops with these Virgos.

Nothing is boring to them; they will read and study avidly everything that they set their eyes on. They will store this knowledge and material, ready to pass it on at the vital time. Surrounding themselves with the printed word, papers, magazines, and books, they will collect and organize information into a palatable arrangement in order to feed the hungry, seeking minds of their students and followers.

Hard working yet loving every minute of it, they are strict with themselves and angry when they do not keep to their work schedules. Lacking the fun and imagination to go to a nightclub or social function unless there is some career benefit involved, they work into the night and, even with their extensive desire for learning, can find themselves in a terrible rut, narrow minded and without too many social friends outside their business circle.

At gatherings they appear timid when they are only being polite and considerate. Sensitive to the crass, aggressive behavior of others around them, they will often crawl into their shells and become voyeurs—the eye of a camera. Still, if a gathering starts to fade, they will suddenly become the life of the party, organizing games and events that delight both young and old. Word games, charades, Scrabble, and entertaining skits and sketches—these Virgos have them all up their sleeves, just waiting for the moment to rescue the host or hostess.

Like all Virgos they tend to be overfussy and critical even with their dearest loved ones and colleagues at school or work. They want everything to be done to perfection, feeling that if they can do it so can others, forgetting human weaknesses and frailties or the limits that time itself imposes on various situations. That is why many are drawn to becoming teachers and professors. Some train others at work or volunteer their time to coach sports teams, lead youth groups, and even to provide medical care in far-off places.

It is their longing for travel that gives these Virgos the missionary spirit, even though many are so practical and scientific minded that they cannot really accept religion and philosophy in its abstract forms. They love the law of nature, of the natural cycles of things; the law of the jungle they respect, the service and duty that one is expected to show to one's parents and country they understand, but they find it hard to have faith in the unseen, the unproven, and the supernatural.

Finding it hard to stay in one spot for long, they spread their message along the path they cut out for themselves, but they always want to return and see how well their flock has grown or to revitalize some withering plants whose seeds they planted.

In romance these Virgos' mercurial natures backfire. They are so curious and critical that they either get fed up with the other person's lack of initiative and ideas or they wonder what it would be like with someone else even though they don't want to give much time to the relationship. They often seem to love their work more than their partners, and relationships prosper if their loved ones are willing to participate in their careers or interests.

SIR RICHARD ATTENBOROUGH

Virgo-like, Richard traveled thousands of miles and directed thousands of actors, actresses, and extras to make his epic movie. *Gandhi,* which is about the social history of India, renewed interest in that country and in the passive resistance movement as a whole, from Henry David Thoreau (author of the essay "Civil Disobedience"), to Mahatma Gandhi and the Reverend Martin Luther King, Jr.

It took twenty years before Richard Attenborough produced the Academy-Award-winning film (it won for best film, best director, and best actor). Ben Kingsley, who played Gandhi, is a Capricorn born on December 31, 1943. Gandhi himself was born under the peaceful sign of Libra on October 2, 1869.

Richard was born on August 29, 1923, in Cambridge, England, and was always one of Britain's most popular stars, acting in many popular films, such as *Seance on a Wet Afternoon, Doctor Dolittle,* and *The Great Escape,* but gaining just as much respect as a director of many box-office successes.

He is a Virgo who likes to teach and he has his Venus, the planet of good looks, in Virgo too, giving him his early handsomeness and charm. His Moon in warlike Aries brought him in contact with the more military works—he directed *A Bridge Too Far, Oh What a Lovely War, Young Winston,* and, more recently, the musical *A Chorus Line* with its precision dancing routines.

With his Virgoan love of research and detail, he has taught audiences a lot about history, and his Mars and Neptune, both in Leo, have given him the talent to entertain at the same time.

RICHARD GERE

Though a major box-office star, Richard Gere prefers to be footloose and fancy free, but in the most sincere and almost spiritual way. He lives out of a suitcase, not wanting to be tied down by accumulating material property. He loves his old friends, and he happily travels to see them, not being restricted by traditional Hollywood trappings of wealth.

A Virgo born in Philadelphia, on August 29, 1949, he has his Moon in the sexy sign of Scorpio (it also rules the hustlers and sexual deviants he often portrays), and his private life is most important to him.

It was his Venus, planet of music, and Neptune, the moviemaker, that first attracted him to study various instruments. He learned to play the piano, guitar, trumpet, and banjo. In addition to composing music for student productions, he also joined a band, again traveling with his talents from place to place.

Whether in *American Gigolo, Looking for Mr. Goodbar, An Officer and a Gentleman, Cotton Club, Power,* or any other of his movies, he brings back the traditional type of intensely handsome Hollywood leading man, adding his own touch of individuality.

To prove that he was an accomplished serious actor, and not "just another pretty face," he appeared on Broadway in *Bent.* His performance was acclaimed by critics, colleagues, and audiences alike.

MICHAEL JACKSON

Michael Jackson is one of the most influential stars of the last decade. Born on August 29, 1958, in Gary, Indiana, he is a Virgo with his Moon in Aquarius, the electronic media sign of television, videos, and recordings.

A former child performer with the Jackson Five, as a soloist he is a vibrant force in the music industry with a Pied Piper–like hypnotic power over his fans. The double energy, double-Mercury influence has moved him forward to break music industry records. In 1984 he won a total of seven awards at the American Music Awards and was given a special place in the *Guinness Book of World Records* for that. He then won eight Grammys the same year. His best selling LP, *Thriller,* was number one on *Billboard's* chart for over thirty weeks.

Venus, which rules beauty, art, and music, and Uranus, which rules records and television, are together in the show business sign of Leo within one degree of each other, giving him the brilliant, gentle, and romantic sound that sells his records.

Pluto, the planet of big business, is located next to his Sun, making him a major money-making business in himself. And the creative planet Neptune in Scorpio, which is ruled by Pluto, the god of the underworld, may have inspired the tombstone-ghoulish choreography of his *Thriller* video.

When he has free time he is an active minister for his church, knocking on doors and helping members with problems. Like many Virgos he doesn't drink or smoke and wants others to lead happier, healthier, and more fulfilled lives. He prefers to spend his time by himself and is very uncomfortable around other people: "I'm really only at home onstage."

LILY TOMLIN

Born: September 1, 1939, at 1:45 A.M. in Detroit, Michigan

Lily Tomlin is quoted as saying, in true Virgo fashion, both reticent and vigorous, "Sometimes I worry about being a success in a mediocre world."

To a Virgo nothing is perfect, and Lily has devoted her life to developing the comic characters for which she has become so famous, perfecting and detailing their nuances, foibles, and humor until she becomes a whole world, a whole zodiac, unto herself. In her *Search for Signs of Intelligent Life in the Universe,* her hit one-woman show, she *is* the universe, and a perceptive critic of it as well.

Lily has Cancer ascending and her Moon in Aries. This combination gives her the pioneering spirit of Aries to go alone into "uncharted" areas of show business, and the Cancerian vulnerability of her roles, which other women can identify with, seeing them through the perceptive eyes of Virgo.

She came to fame in 1969 in the hit television series "Laugh-In," when she introduced us to the love-starved telephone operator, Ernestine, a classic to this day.

Having her Moon next to Jupiter in Aries at the top of her chart, both in her tenth house, gave her the luck and the sensitivity to become and remain one of our most endearing stars, one who, in her own words, "always loved to watch people, even as a child."

But it is this same Moon in Aries that makes her independent where love and commitment are concerned, and her Virgo Sun adds yet another strong discriminating aspect regarding her romantic life. Her ascendant Cancer brings her into close intimate relationships that may remain with her throughout her life, and she enjoys the privacy and the comfort of her home, from which she gets the peace of mind and attractive surroundings she missed as a child.

Pluto in the show business sign, Leo, in her first house, gave her the ability and personality to become successful in a very competitive profession.

Her Sun, Venus, and Neptune in the third house of communication give her the talent to write, to entertain, and to mimic, while Mars in Capricorn, the sign that rules clocks, gives her the perfect timing necessary for a successful and brilliant one-woman comedy show.

A winner in everything she puts her mind and talents to, Lily has won a Grammy for her LP, Emmys for her comedy specials on television, and was nominated for a supporting actress Oscar for her performance in *Nashville* in 1975. She was awarded a special Tony for her one-woman show, *Appearing Nightly,* in 1977, as well as the Tony as best actress for *Search for Signs of Intelligent Life* in 1986.

So independent and confident about the way her career was going was she that she recently turned down an offer of half a million dollars from Bell Telephone to acquire Ernestine for their television commercials. Perhaps she should have considered some special deal with the telephone company, though, as her Part of

Fortune is in the sign of Aquarius in the eighth house of money, and Aquarius is the sign that rules the telephone system. But perhaps she has already made her fortune through Ernestine and her famous switchboard calls.

Like other stars, Lily had the strength and conviction to turn down big money offers that would have made her worry more about "being a success in a mediocre world." At least she knows her success comes from living in an idealistic, exceptional, altruistic, and disciplined world, even if that "world" happens to be her own creation.

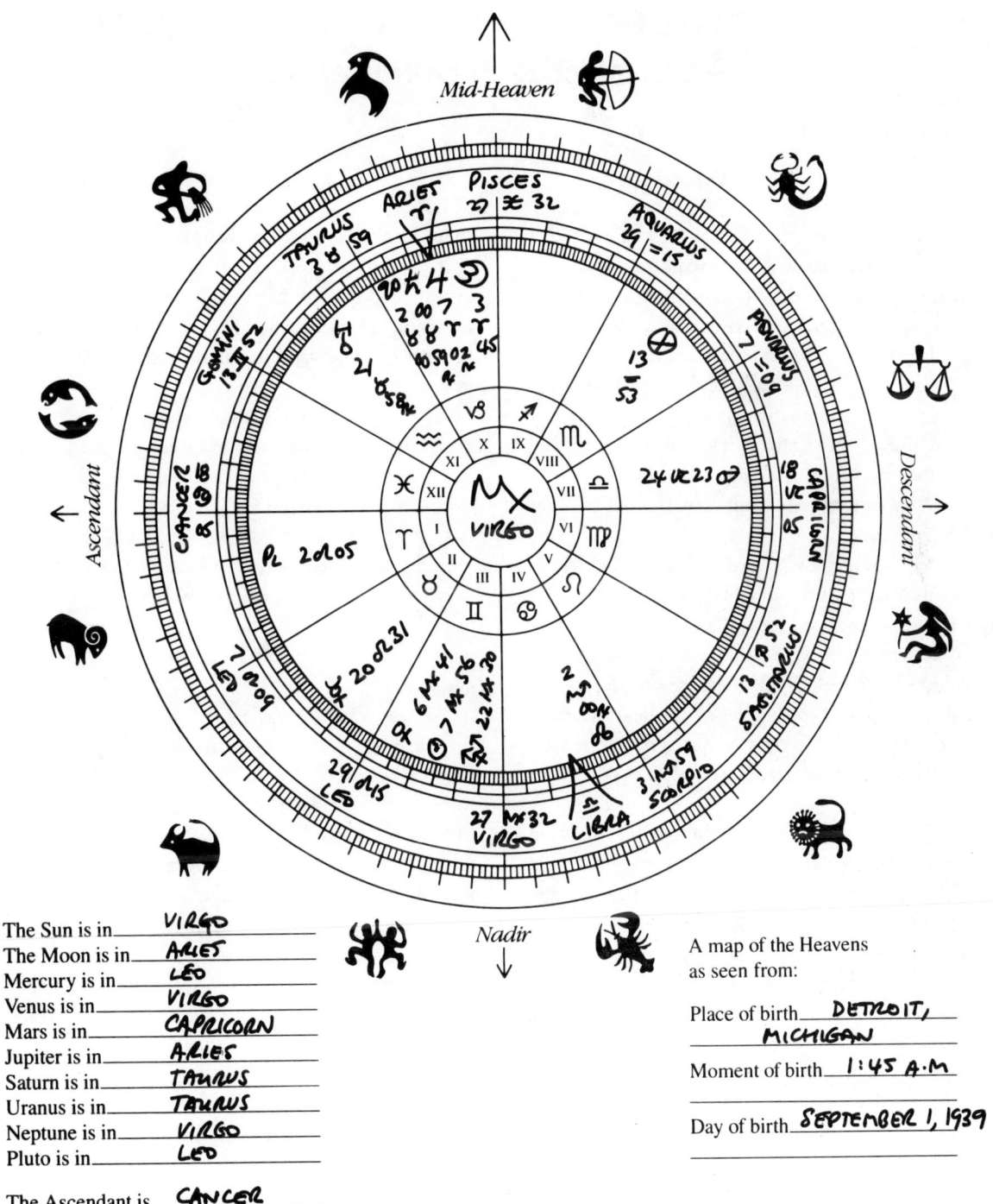

The Sun is in __VIRGO__
The Moon is in __ARIES__
Mercury is in __LEO__
Venus is in __VIRGO__
Mars is in __CAPRICORN__
Jupiter is in __ARIES__
Saturn is in __TAURUS__
Uranus is in __TAURUS__
Neptune is in __VIRGO__
Pluto is in __LEO__

The Ascendant is __CANCER__
The Part of Fortune is in __AQUARIUS__

A map of the Heavens as seen from:

Place of birth __DETROIT, MICHIGAN__

Moment of birth __1:45 A.M__

Day of birth __SEPTEMBER 1, 1939__

Disciplined Workers and Timekeepers
CAPRICORN DECANATE, RULED BY SATURN
September 2–September 11

It is the Saturnian influence on these Virgos that makes them appear such hard workers and critical bosses. It is very hard for them to communicate without scolding their loved ones and coworkers. They expect perfection from themselves and therefore cannot tolerate anything less in others, especially if they are paying for their services. The combination of the planets Mercury and Saturn makes them affable task masters, wanting only the best for those working under them but not having the compassion to see the human frailties of other signs of the zodiac.

They are parental by nature, taking every person they meet into their lives and trying to rule them even though the other person doesn't expect or want this personal attention. These Virgos lack enthusiasm and fun; thanks to their stick-to-itiveness they reach most of their goals but miss out on the joys of personal life. Like other Virgos their work is their hobby and love as well as profession, and this saturated devotion makes them very successful.

Totally tactless and far from diplomatic, they are outspoken to an aggravating degree. While most people will put up with a fair amount of advice, whether they take it or not, these Virgos bring an intolerable amount of pressure to bear, so that nothing can ever be done correctly in their opinion. Yet when the shoe is on the other foot and they are in the servant role, working for others, they are the best of employees, capable of long hours of labor, far above and beyond the call of duty.

Others quickly recognize this workhorse personality and talent, their loyalty and reliability, as well as their total devotion to their employers and country. Some have had great success in matters of government, as ambassadors, politicians, and economists. As commentators on the social conditions of the times, many have become journalists, historians, and advisers to world leaders.

Even as children they may have shown rebellious traits. At college they would be among the first to rally to a cause, whether to stop cruelty to animals, protest the war, or collect signatures against ecology-ruining factories and manufacturers. As children, their patience would make them seem withdrawn, when they were only enthralled in coloring a complicated picture, determinedly finishing off the giant-size jigsaw puzzle, or waiting for their plants to grow in their own private garden.

These Virgos, while not wanting to spend more time than necessary on the rituals and joys of lovemaking, are sexually very skillful and, as in their work, try to be perfectionists. The desire to satisfy and serve their loved ones helps them give their all, each encounter surpassing the previous one. Most ideal is a partner who is willing to double as playmate and workmate. This would save a lot of time, and these Virgos would be able to take love breaks when they felt moved to do so. It is important that they don't feel that those they love hate, resent, or try to sabotage their work projects or force them to give up the valuable time that is necessary to meet deadlines and schedules. Children will be burdensome to them, but they may feel that a large family is a strength as well as a work force for the future to help carry on their business and to look after them in old age. They will expect more than average from their offspring and will encourage them to take an important place in the community.

VALERIE PERRINE

I was invited to come early for coffee. I arrived at the friend's house where Valerie was staying in Chelsea just before 9:00 A.M. It seemed that she had every minute of the day allocated, and she intended to do everything on her list.

A beauty, even at that time of day, Valerie knew that as soon as we had finished looking at her future, she could put on her makeup and be ready to go off to her next appointment in less than ten minutes. And as I recall, she did, looking the most radiant and glamorous woman in London.

Born at 9:20 A.M. on September 3, 1943, in Galveston, Texas, she is a Virgo with her Moon in the beautiful sign of Libra, and her Ascendant is the dynamic Aries.

With the military sign of Aries ascending, it was appropriate that the environment she grew up in would be military—her father was posted to Japan and other overseas bases. Her mother was a former showgirl and this spirit and creative desire came through in Valerie. Giving up her idea of becoming a psychologist, she became a topless showgirl in Las Vegas.

Having Pluto, the god of the underworld, and Jupiter the planet of good luck, both in Leo—the show off, the actor—gave her the talent, looks, and guts to keep working on her first love of show business. She was nominated for an Academy Award for her performance as Honey, the stripper and junkie wife of Lenny Bruce in the movie, *Lenny*.

Her roles have been as varied as her life, and she has delighted audiences in *The Last American Hero, Superman II, Can't Stop the Music,* and *W. C. Fields and Me,* having broken into the movies in *Slaughterhouse Five,* as an outer-space sex siren.

At precisely 10:20 she called out to her friend and hostess, "It's almost ten-thirty! It's time to leave!" With that she threw herself together with the discipline and precision of a computerized timekeeper, and we left the house. "Perfect," she commented as the clock struck 10:30, and we all marched up the Kings Road.

ARNOLD PALMER

It takes a disciplined athlete and perfect timekeeper to win four prestigious Masters Tournaments and to be voted the Associated Press Award in 1969 as Athlete of the Decade. But Arnold Palmer's fans have watched this eagle-eyed golf pro win first prize in the U.S. Open, the British Open, the Australian Open, and in every other major world and national tournament.

Arnold is a Virgo born September 10, 1929, in Youngstown, Pennsylvania, with his Moon (the public) and the planet Saturn (work and rewards), in the sign of Sagittarius, the sportsman, depicted as an archer. It is with the same precision that the archer fires his arrow that Arnold hits the ball. (In 1960 he dropped a twenty-seven-foot uphill putt to win by one slim stroke.)

But it is the hard-working sign of Virgo that makes him continue to be one of golf's all time money-makers. He still attends national meets, chatting with both fans and rivals.

Jupiter in Gemini, which rules the hands, arms, and shoulders, has given him that lucky golf swing. And luck combined with his practical approach to his talent turned him into a prosperous businessman.

Mars and Mercury are both in the well-balanced sign of Libra and bestowed on him his good looks and patient disposition, although his Uranus in Aries has been responsible for sudden losses of the concentration that is so important to him.

This Uranian (television) influence on his looks (Aries rules the face) has him endorsing many products on television.

As Arnold's fellow golfer Bob Hope says about the game, "If you watch a game, it's fun. If you play at it, it's recreation. If you work at it, it's golf."

RAQUEL WELCH

Born: September 5, 1940, at 2:04 P.M. in Chicago, Illinois

I knew I could do it, and I set out to prove to those timid producers that I could do musical comedy." Within the year Raquel Welch had launched her own nightclub act and packed them in from Paris to Rio de Janeiro to Las Vegas. She broke the box office record (held by Frank Sinatra) at the famed Palais des Congés in Paris.

When Raquel replaced fellow Virgo Lauren Bacall in *Woman of the Year* on Broadway in 1982, she received raves from all the critics.

Doing it herself, and not relying on the show business experts who had pigeonholed her into the T & A category, she was willing to spend three grueling months and $200,000 of her own money developing her act. The hardworking determined Virgo character came through.

Raquel has Sagittarius rising over the horizon, which gives her the very healthy physique of an athlete, the long legs of the Sagittarian horse (and she loves to add to them by wearing seven-inch heels), and the willingness to gamble with her life, to take chances, and to be prepared to lose as well as win.

Like many Virgos, she is a nonsmoker, and she loves to read, finally combining her concern for fitness and literature in her book *Raquel—The Raquel Welch Total Beauty and Fitness Program*.

With so many of her Virgo planets in the ninth house of places far from birth, she has become an international star, but only after she ran away from her first marriage to set up life in Hollywood. The choice of cities was perfect; Los Angeles is traditionally a Virgo city, where she would fit in well, and the Sagittarius Ascendant took her into the world of filmmaking.

The Moon in Scorpio made her a sex symbol and gave her the extraordinary figure that towered over audiences at the movie houses. Though obviously delighted at the attention she received, her Virgo personality wanted more intellectual and creative accolades. And it was her three Virgo planets, Mars, Mercury, and Neptune—plus the Sun in Virgo—that combined to help her accomplish that feat. It was after her world-wide success of her night club act that American producers and her public recognized this multifaceted talent she had kept hidden during the making of her early films.

Although happily married now in good Virgo fashion to a fellow professional, French filmmaker André Weinfeld, Raquel found it difficult to find the perfect partner, a weakness in most Virgos. She also had the Sagittarius Ascendant's need for freedom in love and romance, but finally her Moon in Scorpio, wanting more domestic security, and the need for a strong home base took over.

Her beautiful daughter Tahnee, the image of her mother, made her film debut in 1985 in *Cocoon*.

Raquel has learned and proved that others of lesser talent and perception cannot be allowed to take over one's life—that it takes work and the willingness to do much of that work oneself. It is easy to hand over the reins of life to another, as if to say, "Go ahead. I will sit back and wait until the rewards are brought to me on a silver platter." It takes a particular brand of courage to tell those in a position of power that they can be wrong.

Human beings have only one life; what they do with it is up to them. Those who are convinced, as Raquel was, that they can do something that others may ridicule them for even suggesting, and who go ahead and prove the others wrong, are their own champions.

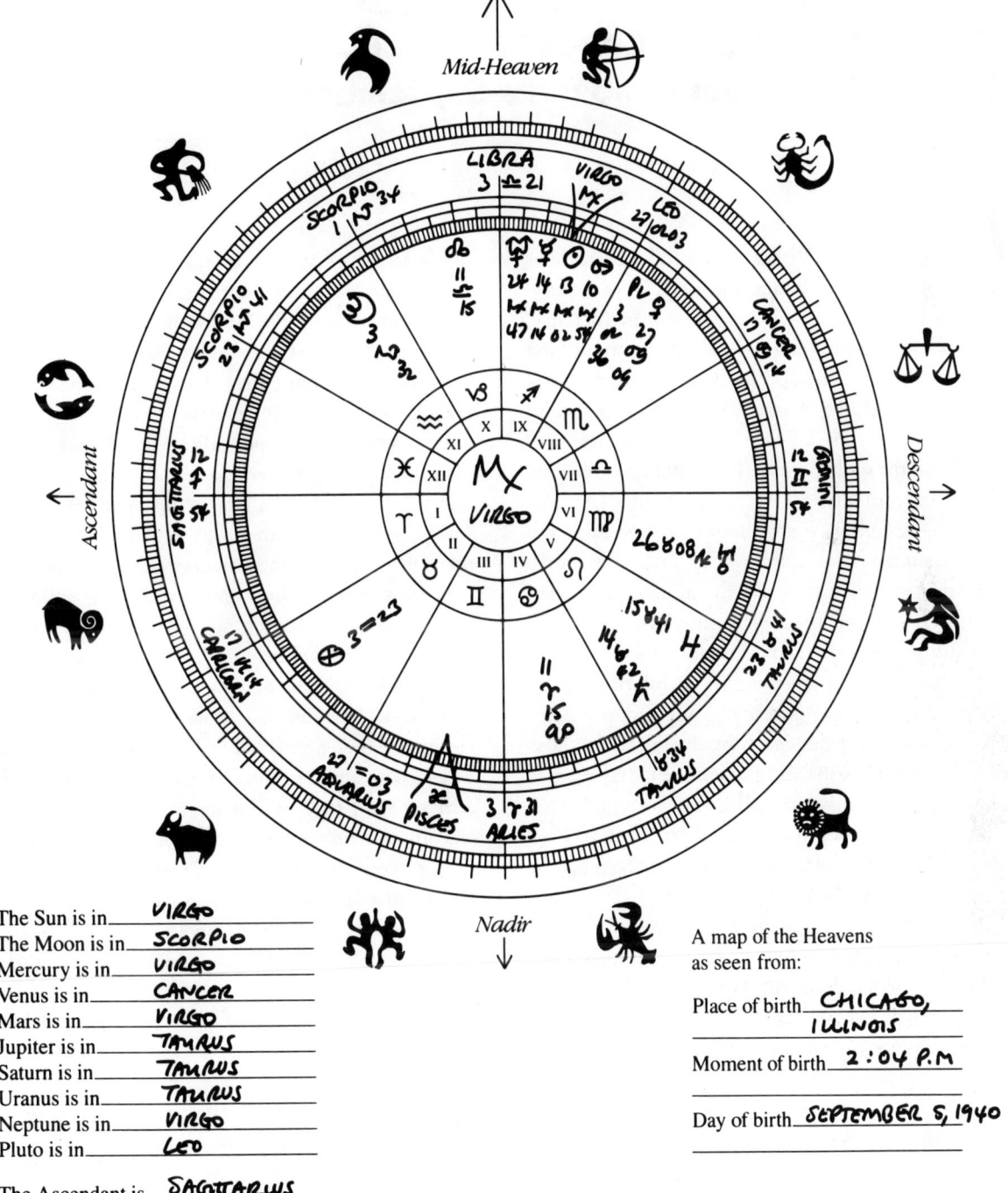

The Sun is in __VIRGO__
The Moon is in __SCORPIO__
Mercury is in __VIRGO__
Venus is in __CANCER__
Mars is in __VIRGO__
Jupiter is in __TAURUS__
Saturn is in __TAURUS__
Uranus is in __TAURUS__
Neptune is in __VIRGO__
Pluto is in __LEO__

The Ascendant is __SAGITTARIUS__
The Part of Fortune is in __AQUARIUS__

A map of the Heavens as seen from:

Place of birth __CHICAGO, ILLINOIS__

Moment of birth __2:04 P.M__

Day of birth __SEPTEMBER 5, 1940__

Artistic Analysts

TAURUS DECANATE, RULED BY VENUS
September 12–September 22

These beautiful Virgos have combined in their horoscopes of Venus, the goddess of beauty, youth, and love, and the wit and wisdom of Mercury. Drawn to the fine arts and to fashionable trends and ideas, they can show them off in the most exquisite and delicate manner, giving another dimension of beauty to whatever they touch. Lauren Bacall the actress and Lauren Bacall the spokeswomen for Fortunoff both epitomize this lustrous Virgo. Owners of art galleries, fashion models, designers, and promoters—they have the magic to catch the public eye as well as the connoisseur's.

The thoughts they bring to a situation or project are idealistic and may be financially unrealistic, but their style of living adds the right amount of flourish and dignity to any occasion. Their homes are full of the most beautiful works of art—paintings, sculpture, porcelain and china, Oriental jades and silks. Even those whose economic bracket doesn't allow them the extravagances of life somehow manage to collect lovely objects that give joy to themselves and to their guests. They are also able to rescue family heirlooms and restore them before others throw them out.

These Virgos really hate dirty work, and while they will work long hours and can be relied upon totally for their loyalty and steadfastness, they work best in pleasant, harmonious surroundings and have extreme reactions to grubby or messy ones. Should they suddenly find themselves in a setting that lacks personality and decor, they soon put it right with a touch of paint, flowers, plants, and some tasteful prints or posters.

They just love to be the center of attention, especially at parties and clubs—they are first on the dance floor when the after-dinner music begins—and usually wear something in the latest fashion, with some outrageous accessory that gets everyone talking.

Music is a must; these Virgos surround their lives with it, and many belong to the local orchestra or operatic society, either as performers or patrons, appearing snobbish to those whose interests are more inclined toward the local football team or disco. But they are sincerely involved with the classics and the arts, and they want to encourage these interests in the young.

Those who go into industry and big business love to do research and have filing systems and offices that are works of art in themselves. Their flair for design ranges from fashion and the home to the style and shape of the latest cars, furniture for offices and factories, and architectural inventions using glass, metal, and marble. Their acute and perceptive minds make them excellent analysts with figures, systems, and budgets, and many end up reorganizing their companies to save personnel power, stock, and overheads. Even in the home they are always making the place easier to live in—the den or kitchen prettier and more efficient to work in—and a haven where their friends can escape from the hustle and bustle of modern life.

Conversation is one of their great talents—helping to balance the debate or discussion, and soothing wounded feelings with just the right phrase that makes everyone feel better and leaves no one embarrassed.

They prefer traditional vacations but are just as happy following their loved ones to exotic islands or resorts. While they are capable of fitting in at a commune or on a camping expedition, they feel much more at ease in a genteel setting where they can wear the beautiful clothes bought for the holiday and gracefully lean against a bar overlooking the ocean or add vitality and wit to a cocktail party.

These Virgo always have to be in love, especially with the Venus qualities they bring to it. They look particularly for a gentle, loving relationship and a partner with many mutual interests, especially in the theater and the other arts. A nice home and family are very important to them. Theirs is usually the prettiest house on the block or the most redecorated apartment, perhaps lifted from the pages of *House and Garden* yet still practical and efficient to work in. These Virgos demand a studio, den, or office in the home, giving them the feeling that when they are in the mood they can get on with their writing, planning, or painting, as they must be able to do it when they want to rather than when forced into it.

GRETA GARBO

If ever Venus showed her influence in Virgo, it was in famous beauty and recluse Greta Garbo, who totally revolutionized the concepts of feminine beauty, hairstyles, and dress in the late twenties and early thirties.

Today it would seem impossible that this great Hollywood legend has not made a film since 1941 *(Two Faced Woman)*. Forty-five years is a long time to keep her public curious about her life-style, still considering her the greatest Hollywood beauty. And she has a cult following that is as discreet as it is inquisitive.

Greta was born in Stockholm, Sweden, on September 18, 1905, at 10:30 P.M., the daughter of an unskilled laborer who died when she was only thirteen. In true Virgo fashion, Greta started work the following year as a lather girl in a barber shop to help her family. When she was sixteen and working in a department store as a salesgirl, she was asked to appear in a short publicity film sponsored by the store, titled *How Not to Dress*. She did other promotional films, which led her to study at the Royal Theater school. Here she was discovered by her mentor, movie director Mauritz Stiller (Cancer, born July 17, 1883).

She came to the United States with Stiller as part of the deal he made with MGM in 1925. Starring in the studio's production of *The Torrent* in 1926, she was an instant superstar and the Garbo myth was born.

Her Virgo Sun and Mercury make her very self-critical and analytical of her artistry, wanting perfection, to be remembered for her early looks, performances, and delicate, Virgo-like mystique, which somehow she has kept intact. Despite being a recluse, she has been discovered by new fans on television and at film festivals, and her old fans still keep her memory in their hearts.

TWIGGY (LESLEY HORNBY)

One of the most interesting Virgos born under this Mercury-Venus influence is actress-model Twiggy. Born Lesley Hornby in London on September 19, 1949, at 12:45 A.M., she chose the name Twiggy for her professional career as a model, mainly for her very slim, twig-like body and the clothes she presented. Her delicate frame and large eyes made her one of the icons of the sixties, but this hard-working Virgo went on to singing, dancing, and acting in films like Ken Russell's *The Boy Friend* and Broadway musicals like *My One and Only* with Tommy Tune. She takes each assignment very seriously and analyzes her performances in great detail—a Virgo's Virgo.

Being born close to the end of Virgo, she has lots of Libran traits, the sign mostly associated with women's fashion, art directors, and glossy women's magazines, traits intensified by having Neptune and Mercury in Libra too. But it was the Moon in Leo, the sign of show business, theater, and the stage, that took her out of the area of modeling, where she was already a star, and thrust her, without much experience, into a starring role in a major motion picture. Only her Virgo Sun sign enabled her to handle this sudden giant step from one profession to another and keep the dignity, poise, and personality the whole world had grown to love. The successful career change was effected by Uranus, the planet of sudden happenings, which was in her house of career at the time of her birth. And it was the planet

Pluto, which was located close to the Moon in Leo, that made her big business for all who were involved with her. Mars in Leo, a location for that planet that seems to be in the charts of many famous celebrities, gave her the stamina to put up with all the work and schedule changes and travels.

She may have had troubles early in life with men who loved her, but having got her career sorted out, she now lives a happy and romantic life. Saturn shows trouble at an early age with men—father, teachers, husband, or boyfriends. As she has such an innocent, naïve look, they wanted to protect her, and tended to restrict her personal growth, not realizing how strong a character she had through learning life's lessons, sometimes the hard way. (I am reminded of how intrigued I was when I met both Twiggy and "Mama Cass" Elliot at the London home of writer Jack Martin. Though Mama Cass was eight years older (born in 1941), these two seemingly very different women were born on the same day. Their physical disparity, which covered a similar vulnerability, had suggested the possibility of a sitcom, for which they were in negotiations. It was July 29, 1974—two hours before Mama Cass died in her hotel room. Patience and interests that can fill in hiatus time between films and television specials are all part of the character that will heap rewards on her in the future as it has in the past.

LARRY HAGMAN

No other television character can be as analytical, critical, irritating, charming, and commanding to watch than J. R. Ewing, played on "Dallas" by Larry Hagman.

Larry was born on September 21, 1931, in Weatherford, Texas, and is a hard-working Virgo with his Moon in the sign of the business tycoon (on and off the television screen), Capricorn.

It is interesting to note that his Mercury (communications) and his Neptune (oil) are both in his sign of Virgo, and that it was his oil-rich character that finally made him an international star.

He also took part in that Neptunian musical, *South Pacific,* which starred his mother, Mary Martin (Sagittarius, born December 1). (Neptune is the god of the sea.)

Naturally, with his Venus in the beautifully artistic sign of Libra, he has a good singing as well as a speaking voice.

Always working in the theater, films, and television, Larry has chosen his roles carefully. His movies include *Fail Safe, The Group,* and *Harry and Tonto,* and he delighted television audiences as the friendly astronaut visited by Barbara Eden on *I Dream of Jeannie,* on which he appeared for five years.

Married to former actress Maj Axelsson, he lives quietly with her and their two children in their home in Malibu when not taping the series on location in Dallas.

He has said, "The time is right for a real bad guy, and, well, I guess I'm it."

LAUREN BACALL

Born: September 16, 1924, at 3:00 A.M. in New York City

I was sitting waiting for my next client, a "Mrs. Partridge," to arrive in my cozy Smith Terrace home in Chelsea. Right on time the doorbell rang. I opened the door, and instead of greeting her I laughed.

"Excuse me laughing," I said. "Please come in."

"I used a different name so that you wouldn't look anything up," she said in that unmistakable, sultry, magnificent voice.

Without too many pleasantries, Lauren was eager to get on with the reading. There were so many questions in her mind. At the time she was starring in the musical hit *Applause* in London's West End.

"Now. When am I going to stop working so hard?"

I couldn't have chosen a more appropriate request for a Virgo. It is the sign of work, of service, of the workaholic.

"Knowing your strong Virgo personality, I would expect that you will never stop. You will carry on working all your life."

My reply rather pleased her, though at that time in her life I am sure she would have loved to take time out of her busy schedule to have a personal, private, and romantic time, even if only for a short while.

Since that meeting, it has occurred to me that she is always on the move, rehearsing new Broadway plays and musicals, touring the United States and the world, always rushing to the theater to put on her makeup and costumes, re-rehearsing scenes with new costars and understudies, and trying to fit in a few television commercial tapings in during her time off.

Lauren has both her Sun and Mercury in Virgo. This makes her very hard working, discriminating, and gives her the appearance of being rather critical and analytical when she is actually more curious and desirous of perfection. Her Leo Ascendant obviously attracted her to the world of show business, and in the first house of her horoscope chart she has the planet Neptune (ruler of film), and her North Node, the point of destiny's rewards in this life, giving her the beautiful, photogenic qualities that have lit up movie and TV screens.

The Moon in Aries is at the top of her chart in the tenth house of career, honors, and fame. This is a placement in the chart of many famous stars, celebrities, sportsmen and -women, and politicians. And with that Aries independent spirit she has been able to take control of her life at times of crisis in which others not so strong would have given up.

The Aries energy and Virgo precision are reflected in every performance she gives.

In her seventh house of marriage, Lauren has the strong, masculine planet Mars in the sign of Aquarius. It was destiny that brought her and costar Humphrey Bogart together as one of the most romantic and idealistic couples on or off the screen. Bogie was born January 23, an Aquarius, a perfect partner for Lauren's Leo Ascendant. (As a historical note, the publicity department of Bogie's Hollywood studio changed his birthdate to December 25, as they thought this would add some magical public relations charisma to his career.)

Her second marriage, to Jason Robards, Jr. (Leo, born July 26), was reflected in her Venus, the planet of

SIGNS OF THE STARS

love, being located in the difficult twelfth house in the sign of Leo. The marriage lasted eight years.

Good fortune and success will continue to shine on her as she has Jupiter, the planet of great luck, in her fifth house of show business and love relationships, a combination that seems to follow her career and personal life. Like fellow Virgos, Lauren is happiest when loving and working with the same man.

Whatever she does—whether starring in the Tony Award winning Broadway shows *Applause* (1970) and *Woman of the Year* (1980); writing her best-selling autobiography, *By Myself;* or advertising Blackgama coats, jewelry, or coffee—she is the ultimate of chic. Lauren once said, "Good taste is a difficulty commodity to find in Hollywood," but wherever you find Virgo Lauren Bacall, you will always be aware of her good taste.

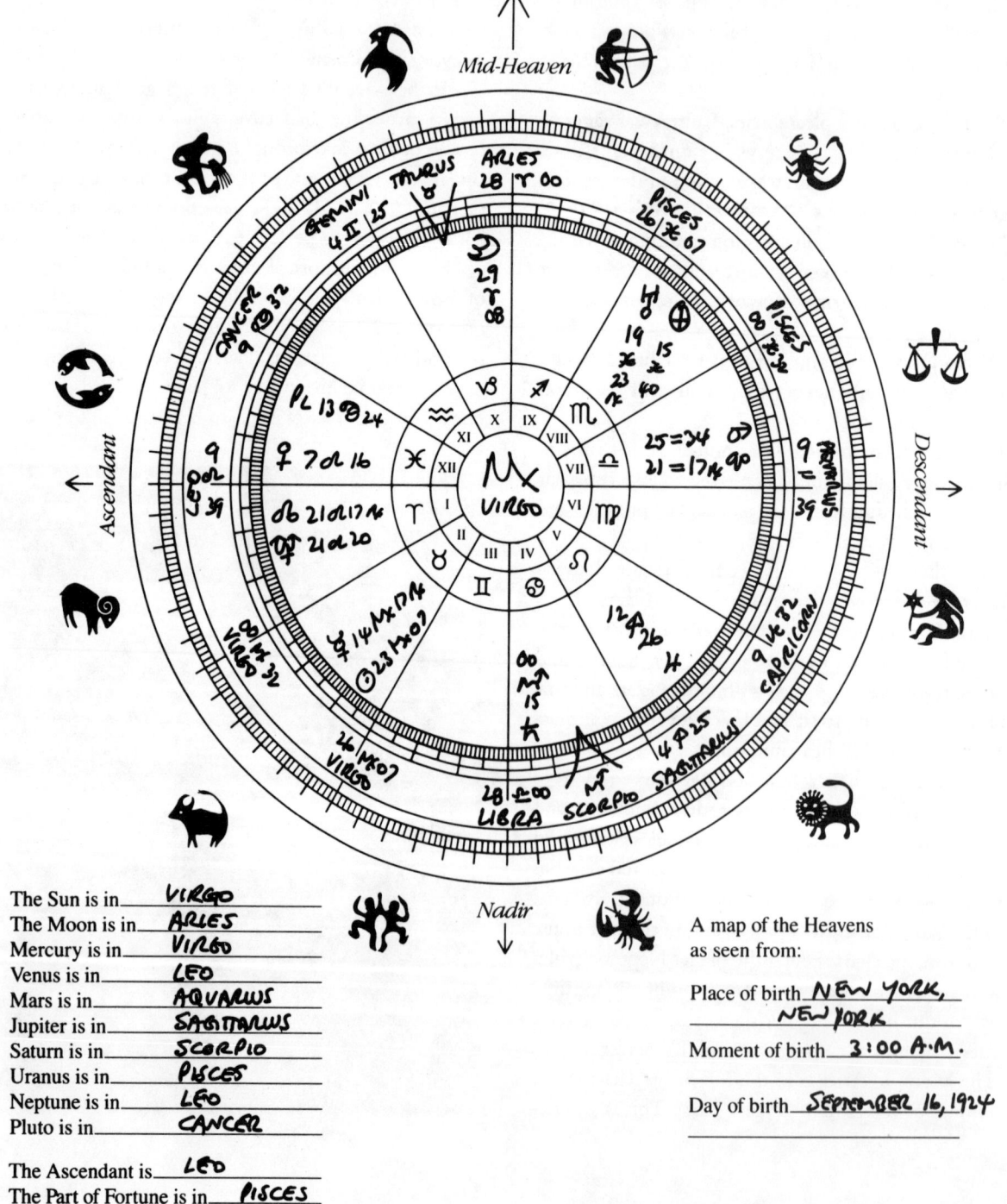

The Sun is in _VIRGO_
The Moon is in _ARIES_
Mercury is in _VIRGO_
Venus is in _LEO_
Mars is in _AQUARIUS_
Jupiter is in _SAGITTARIUS_
Saturn is in _SCORPIO_
Uranus is in _PISCES_
Neptune is in _LEO_
Pluto is in _CANCER_

The Ascendant is _LEO_
The Part of Fortune is in _PISCES_

A map of the Heavens as seen from:

Place of birth _NEW YORK, NEW YORK_

Moment of birth _3:00 A.M._

Day of birth _SEPTEMBER 16, 1924_

LIBRA
Artisan of the Zodiac

SUN IN LIBRA, RULED BY VENUS
September 23–October 22

GLORIA

It is hard to believe that anyone can ever be too nice, too sweet, too charming, or too beautiful in looks and in manner. But all those endearing and admirable qualities exist in Libra, and they can be hard for others less tolerant, diplomatic, and tactful to take. Having always had the knack of saying the right thing at the right moment and saving many awkward situations, they have earned the name "diplomat" in business and political circles. Many actually become international representatives for their company or country, and there are probably more ambassadors and envoys born under the sign of Libra than under any other sign. To add to their gracious and persuasive wit and charm, they are usually blessed with good looks—after all, they are ruled by the goddess of beauty and love, Venus—and so they go through life talking themselves out of tricky situations (often having used their sex appeal to get into the mess in the first place).

Their ability to see both sides of a problem or argument may make them good referees, but when it comes to making an important decision themselves, they are racked with self-doubt, unwilling to make a single move that would destroy their image or interfere with others' plans and virtually having no real point of view of their own. Thus, the world of international diplomacy attracts them, agreeing with one group at one moment and another at another moment, sharing the limelight and glory of one elected official and, without blinking an eye, nodding and helping the person's opponent so that neither feels hoodwinked or victimized.

Fun loving and very flirtatious, Librans always maintain a sense of dignity and decorum and are very scornful of vulgarity. Hiding their displeasure, they will instantly reject aggressive and bullying behavior but will try to excuse it by inventing logical reasons for other critics. Their even-tempered attitudes make them welcome guests at any party or meeting. Their desire to be loved and love others shows in the care they take in buying gifts for their loved ones and generally trying to make the world a better and more beautiful place.

Drawn toward the artistic life, many become famous writers, painters, musicians, and designers. The fashion world is a great attraction to them, and in their young adulthood many become successful models, adorning the glossy pages of popular magazines. The more serious ones may join the symphony orchestra or help rebuild historical landmarks, and they are always discovering treasures for the local museum. Their own homes are full of the most exquisite works of art; the decor is tasteful, usually pastel shaded, and there is much space to move in.

Libra is the seventh sign of the zodiac, and this is the house that rules love partnerships as well as business associates and contracts. Marriage or a permanent relationship is vital to their well-being, but it must be well balanced and free from pressures and anxieties, otherwise they will panic and feel that their whole world is falling apart, seeing crises that don't actually exist. They are the sign of harmony at work and at play, and in this special rose-tinted environment they excel. Those who become lawyers or social workers prefer to work in calm surroundings rather than doing battle in the courthouse, yet their presence adds a touch of class to a case and their choice of words and timing, as in a classical ballet, can win points those less charming and good looking may lose. After all, they got away with murder themselves as children and through their teenage years playing on their attractive personality traits. All they have to do is apply them to the everyday adult world of commerce and reality. Spoiled as children, they will be equally spoiled all through their grown-up years, and their selfishness will be forgiven over and over again—their charm and beauty encourage it.

Excellent at organizing and keeping systems going, Librans have much success with offices, publishing, and efficiency, as they love to make everything work well, whether machinery, relationships, or work schedules. If they could only help themselves the same way that they assist other people with their goals, they would have happier lives. They need others to make up their minds.

Career minded as well as home lovers, they must

watch that they do not spend too much time fanatically on one area of their lives thus ignoring the other equally important areas. Librans need a happy romantic and love life. In both work and romance they are cooperative and willing to make the project work but can neglect other things without realizing it. Creativity is vital, and they are expert craftspersons in many fields of artistic endeavor (and successful, as they are not satisfied with second best). Time and space must be allowed for their hobbies, be they painting, music, silkscreen printing, or sewing. They may be dependent on others in their romantic and social lives but very capable in work. To get the best out of them means praising their accomplishments to date—they will outdo themselves in their next enterprise.

Because of their gracefulness and dignity they are often thought aloof and vain. And their dislike of pushiness in others makes them timid and vacillating, yet underneath they are impatient and temperamental. They are the yin and yang of the Chinese dualist philosophy—the female and the male, the passive and the active. And through their ability to integrate their feelings, ideas, and thoughts, they can be and are much more powerful and influential than their outward appearance and behavior would indicate.

Their total helplessness in the face of romance, love, and mysticism makes them collectors of hearts—both the real ones and the ornate imitations that decorate their homes. Their loving, gentle natures make them fall in love with anyone who shows the slightest civility and concern or who does a good turn for them. But they find it hard just to smile and say "thank you." And each person they fall in love with believes that he or she is the only one, so great are the attention, sympathy, and affection lavished on them, but this Venus-ruled sign has love for all. Unlike Professor Henry Higgins in *My Fair Lady* whose attitude was, "It isn't that I treat you badly, have you ever seen me treat anyone better?" Librans treat all fairly—rich, poor; handsome, ugly; allies and enemies.

Cultural Mediators

LIBRA DECANATE, RULED BY VENUS
September 23–October 1

What could be better than having twice the luck, the capacity for love, the beauty, and the ability to make a fortune than those born under any other sign? These Librans have a double shot of the planetary influence of Venus and are capable of all these wonderful traits. It is luck more than intellect and skill that gets them to where they are. Obviously, they need the talent once they get there, but providence in all its goodness graced these individuals with so much luck and happiness that their personalities alone cover a multitude of mistakes and blunders. As with all Librans, their charm and good looks get them through the worst storms and over the greatest obstacles.

Their love of humanity and their desire to see all people, particularly those around them, happy and in a beautiful environment sometimes makes them overlook the more somber realities of life. Humanitarian and idealist Jimmy Carter had a difficult presidency because of this. These Librans like to think that, in the words of Mary Poppins, "a spoonful of sugar helps the medicine go down." Maybe it does, and if anyone is going to give life its "medicine" in the most appetizing way, it will be these Librans.

Their homes are places of great comfort, and the welcome mat is forever bright and shining, beckoning friends and strangers alike to the safety and warmth of their hearth. Collectors of verses and ditties, which they frame and have on every vacant wall space or dresser top, they still have the first love letters they received as teenagers, the first postcards from the children on their holidays at camp, perhaps little mementos of their early lives, and at least one souvenir for each momentous occasion, operation, family event, or trip abroad. But the place never looks cluttered, for they arrange everything to look like an artist's still life, beautifully balanced and easy on the eye.

Beautiful voices for singing and speaking push them way up front in the arts, especially as performers, actors, musicians, and lecturers. They also have the talent to write poetry and lyrics as well as music, and with it the luck to get it accepted by the publishers, the radio stations, and other singers and musicians.

This Pied Piper ability to get large followings to support them and to cater to their whims can be blamed on the Mona Lisa–like allure that Venus has given them. With a nod of the head, a smile, or an insignificant gesture, they have the world at their finger tips.

They are exceptionally conscious of people around them and their reactions and behavior. Yet it is this sensitivity, compassion, and awareness that makes them so well loved in return. Only through love can the world around them have the harmony, cooperation, and human dignity so vital to their own existence.

In love and courtship these Librans are infinitely variable and so finely tuned emotionally that they seem to sway with every wind. They are avid seekers of affection and sometimes smother others with it, but few signs offer this wonderful combination of love, looks, and affection. Physically, they are amiably vain.

BRUCE SPRINGSTEEN

This dynamic and well-loved performer is truly a cultural mediator, one who has reached out from the glamorous world of rock and roll to the working man he celebrates in his shows. There is an uncanny bond of trust between him and his fans, and his Virgo humanitarianism has inspired him to give up some of his box office receipts, donate the proceeds of a show, and persuade his adoring fans to help those workers not so well off as they are.

Bruce was born September 23, 1949, at 10:50 P.M. in Freehold, New Jersey, a Libra (the sign of the diplomat) with his Moon in Libra (the musician) and his Ascendant Gemini (the great communicator). All these ingredients came together to create this energetic star who really *was* "Born in the USA." This hit became the unofficial anthem of the suffering blue-collar workers of America. Bruce could identify with them and mediate for them with the powers that be.

Perhaps his Saturn (work) in Virgo (the sign of the worker) made him recall his own working-class childhood, and led him to share whatever rewards he had with others—the no-glitter, no-jacket, no-costume hero of the masses.

Uranus in Cancer is his rising planet, and this influenced his recordings and few television appearances and identified him with the American (Cancer) public. Like many people with a Cancerian influence, he has always been insecure about his newly acquired image. His Part of Fortune is also in Cancer, in the exact degree of the United States. No wonder presidential candidates feel that Bruce has political clout.

Believing in self-made dreams coming true, Bruce adds, "Maybe you can't dream the same dreams when you are thirty-four that you did when you were twenty-four, you know, but you can still dream something."

Listen to the words of "the Boss."

CHRISTOPHER REEVE

There is no better symbol, image, or character that conjures up the personality traits of the cultural mediator than "Superman." It seems that somewhere in individuals' charts, especially performers, they live out the predictions and the characteristics originally given to them.

After all Superman is just one of the many wonderful roles that Christopher Reeve has portrayed on stage, screen, and television, but all of them—very much like his off-camera persona—are slightly laid back, gently passionate, disarming, and "cool," whether in the movies *Gray Lady Down, Somewhere in Time, The Bostonians, Death Trap,* or *Monsignor* or on Broadway in *The Irregular Verb to Love, A Matter of Gravity,* and *The Fifth of July,* or on TV's "Love of Life," "I Love Liberty," and "Anna Karenina."

Born in New York City on September 25, 1952, at 3:14 A.M., Christopher is a Super-Libra, with his Sun, Mercury, Saturn, Neptune, and Venus all in his Sun sign Libra, the great diplomat and politician of the zodiac.

Naturally his Ascendant is Leo, the actor, and exactly on it is his Pluto, the planet of transformation (Clark Kent into Superman). Christopher was able to use this strong planetary influence to create his other roles too. It also made him successful in big business.

His longtime sweetheart Gae Exton (Capricorn) is the mother of his two children Matthew and Alexandra. Coming from a broken home, Christopher weighs the decision about marrying very carefully, like other Librans. He's happy as he is.

PRESIDENT JIMMY CARTER

If you think how much luck, love, and charm there had to be around Jimmy Carter in the year prior to his election as the thirty-ninth president of the United States, you can envision the power of this double Venus influence.

Few people had ever heard of him, even up to the time of the Democratic Convention. Many didn't even know what he looked like or anything about his background. But once he decided to use his charm, looks, and love on the nation there was no stopping him. His continual toothy grin was more recognizable than his political philosophy. He tried to win over everyone he met with his love and God's love, too. For never in recent history has a back-to-religion campaign been so strong and the number of born-again Christians so great.

Jimmy Carter, a much more affectionate name than the James with which he was baptized, was born in Plains, Georgia, at 7:00 A.M. on October 1, 1924. The sun was in Libra, but so was the Ascendant in the chart, giving him a double-double share of the lovable Libran qualities. But underneath it shows a strong committed man who can be ruthless when necessary and who likes to keep his true personality and personal life secret from the outside world. The planet Saturn (which rules Capricorn, the sign of government) is in his first house of attitudes and environment in the sign of Scorpio, and his Moon is in Scorpio giving him tremendous influence over the public, in a strange secret way that only history will reveal. His critics may argue that he is too nice and indecisive, but that is his public image—a safe one when men with strong outward convictions are regularly bumped off. He knows where he is going and what he is doing and secretly works toward the end result, as with his instant presidential campaign. No one would ever have suspected his desires; he wasn't even on a long list of probables twelve months earlier. Luck played a great part, but his underlying strategy of Scorpio did the rest.

Pluto, the planet of big business and power, is in 13:29 degrees of Cancer, which is the exact degree of the birth date of the United States, July 4, 1776, the thirteenth day or degree of the sign of Cancer. As it is placed at the top of his chart, the midheaven being 14:30 degrees of Cancer, this influences both the ninth house of higher mind, foreign affairs, and international matters and the tenth house of government, honors, and fame. Had he remained just governor of Georgia he could have fulfilled these indications in his chart, but the luck and ambitions of the Libra-Scorpio combination made him try for the top.

His planet Venus, which influences his love life, is in the sign of Leo; his mother Lillian and his wife Rosalynn are both Leos. Both share his public affection, and both are in the limelight as all Leos tend to be.

As a cultural mediator, he was very successful in the Camp David summit meeting, a political and a personal coup at a time when his political image was wavering. Begin, a Leo represented by the Sun that rules Leo on one side of Carter's Ascendant, and Sadat, a Capricorn represented by Saturn exactly on the other side of the Ascendant, were balanced diplomatically by Carter, the Libran, showing his affinity to both sides. He was able to bring about the beginnings of an important peace treaty in the Middle East. Librans desire an environment of peace more than anything else. But Carter's Scorpio traits are ruled by the Planet Mars, god of war, and Pluto, god of the underworld, both of which had a devastating effect in starting World War II.

Past Carter's charm and loving nature there is an amazing figure of a world leader, easily misunderstood from his moments of indecision and bad timing, but who will be remembered historically as one of the leaders who changed the world for the better.

OLIVIA NEWTON JOHN

Born: September 26, 1948, at 6:00 A.M. in Cambridge, England

Olivia, a true "cultural mediator," has been able to bring her special brand of culture and stardom to every continent of the world and to span the oceans as easily as she sings.

I sat with her and Elton John (no relative) and other invited stars at the opening of her hit musical movie *Grease,* in which she starred opposite John Travolta, in New York. Afterward, at the party at Studio 54, she told me her date, time, and place of birth, but we didn't have a chance to go over her horoscope until we met later in London.

Olivia had just arrived to do a concert in London, and I was costarring in the BBC-TV series "Star Signs." We met at her suite at the Inn on the Park, overlooking Buckingham Palace.

Unlike our first meeting, when she attended her premiere with her hair done outrageously in fifties' period style, she appeared in the traditional style I was more accustomed to—the country-fresh, girl-next-door image that her recording and television career had promoted until her role in *Grease*—her long blond hair falling gently to her shoulders.

At that time she was going through an up-and-down love relationship with her manager, Lee Kramer, a Scorpio, but as her horoscope chart indicated, a new love was in the offing.

Her Ascendant Virgo gives her the ability to work hard, yet she is happiest spending time in happy home surroundings with her husband and other loved ones, listening to classical music or enjoying the countryside and the beauties of nature.

Though her Mars in Scorpio attracted her to her former manager, Kramer, it was his tremendous drive and encouragement that helped her make her mark in Hollywood in the early days of her career. With Mars located in her third house of communication and travel, she was destined to travel a great deal with his energy behind her.

Now happily married, she doesn't feel the need to be on the road all the time. Jupiter in Sagittarius in the fourth house of home and property gives her tremendous pleasure, joy, and profit from any real estate matters she gets involved with, and she will enjoy redecorating and creating the perfect environment for herself, her husband, her baby, and, of course, her animals.

A well-balanced, peaceful, and love-filled life is very important for Olivia (and for all Librans), and once she has found it she won't let it go.

"I don't have the desire I think a lot of performers feel to get the applause. It's not life and death to me. I like to sing, and I love doing what I'm doing, but it's not a dire need."

While making the movie *Xanadu,* she met and fell in love with her husband Matt Lattanzi, ten years her junior. But then Librans themselves often look ten to twenty years younger than their real age, so Librans Olivia and Matt are ideally suited both physically and emotionally.

Olivia Newton John was born in Cambridge, England, on September 26, 1948, at 6:00 A.M., and when she was five years of age her family moved to Australia.

Like many stars she has her Moon in Cancer, placed high in her chart in the tenth house of career

and fame. It is located next to the planet Uranus, the ruling planet of electronic recordings. With both in the sign of Cancer, she has been able to make a big name for herself in the United States, it being a Cancer country (July 4).

Librans are naturally attracted to the fine arts, music, singing, and everything that is beautiful, and Olivia looks and behaves in the true, gentle, loving manner that makes her feel most comfortable. She is home loving, a lover of animals, and makes friends easily.

In 1973, Olivia, already an international name, won the Country Vocalist Grammy. Her records have sold in the millions. It must have been her planet Mars (energy and physical activity) in the sexy sign of Scorpio that transformed her goody-goody image into the sex goddess of the video "Let's Get Physical."

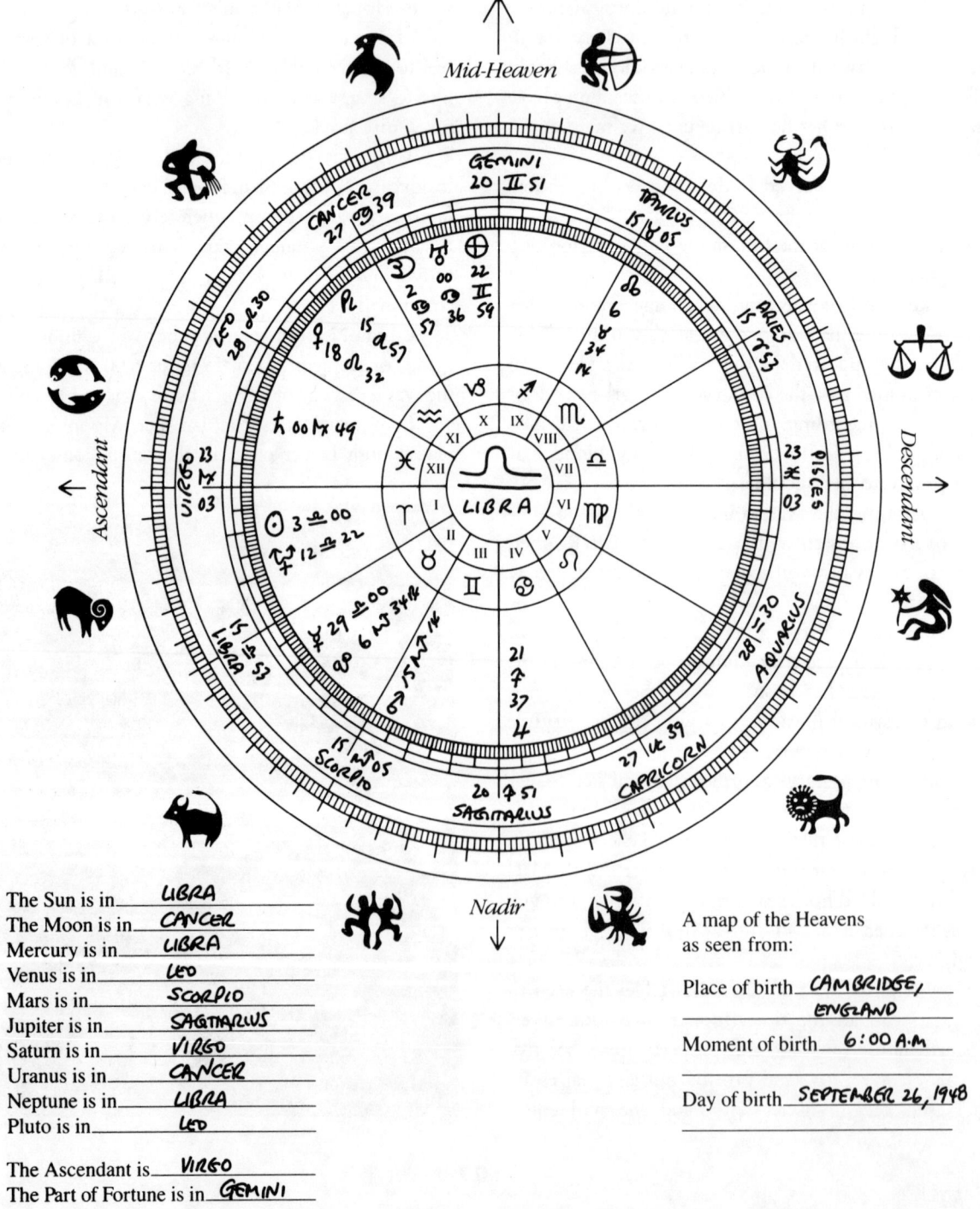

The Sun is in __LIBRA__
The Moon is in __CANCER__
Mercury is in __LIBRA__
Venus is in __LEO__
Mars is in __SCORPIO__
Jupiter is in __SAGITTARIUS__
Saturn is in __VIRGO__
Uranus is in __CANCER__
Neptune is in __LIBRA__
Pluto is in __LEO__

The Ascendant is __VIRGO__
The Part of Fortune is in __GEMINI__

A map of the Heavens as seen from:

Place of birth __CAMBRIDGE, ENGLAND__

Moment of birth __6:00 A.M__

Day of birth __SEPTEMBER 26, 1948__

Friendly Reporters

AQUARIUS DECANATE, RULED BY URANUS
October 2–October 11

These are the people at parties who have all the up-to-date gossip, know all the latest sports scores, report to all within listening range the news almost before it happens, and somehow have an uncanny knowledge of the future. Television's show business reporter Rona Barrett is a classic example of these charming know-it-alls. They are a wonderful mixture of love, charm, and entertaining personality given to them by the planet Venus and the curious and exciting minds of the planet Uranus. Whether in the public eye or just happy in their own home, they love gadgets and spend much of their time working and playing with televisions, telephones, Telex machines, CB radios, and other electrical gadgetry.

Radio and television commentators who look and sound good while telling all to a news-hungry public, pop singers whose words and music put all in a loving mood, writers who explore the future through science fiction, and filmmakers like Steven Spielberg (Taurus, May 14, 1944) and George Lucas (Sagittarius, December 18, 1947), who put our space fantasies on celluloid, all have this influence of Venus and Uranus.

After all, Uranus is the ruling planet of the Aquarian Age; in the very short time since its discovery in 1781 it has brought us into a very exciting period of the world's history, including the inventions associated with electricity, flying, and space travel. Now, in this age of computers, we are speeding into the future not only in thought but also in material plans and predictions. Suddenly everyone, from politicians and economists to fashion and home designers, is in the prediction business.

Always wanting to improve the status of those around them, many seek work in public health or politics. Social workers and therapists encouraging the recreation and occupations of those who are handicapped or injured try to use the latest inventions and theories to help their patients. Politicians no longer keep looking back at history but ahead into the future for their town, city, and country. Many successfully plan the rebuilding of their city's depressed areas by utilizing electrical railroad and communication links and radio and television surveillance, thus encouraging residents' pride and the restoration of their own homes.

When young these Librans would always be in love with radio and television stars, always collecting autographs or offering to help celebrities in whatever way they could. They would organize their own concerts and pop shows in the schoolyard or in their gardens. They were winners of all sorts of artistic competitions and successful in getting their letters to the editor published (as they had the wisdom to write about something that was important at the time), being rational rather than ascribing their success to luck.

At school their brilliance surprised teachers and other students alike, and their ability to retain and recall information gave them points over others less gifted, making them walking encyclopedias who were always willing to share their knowledge and help others with their homework and problems.

These Librans tend to marry late, for they love their independence and their freedom to travel whenever they have the whim to do so. However, when they do marry it is out of great love and respect for their loved one and also the promise of what such a relationship will bring. They are working pals; they will not only help each other and share the joys and sorrows of success and failure but inspire each other to go further than they could have on their own. These Librans exhibit a balance between independence and dependence. On the distaff side, they tend to put their lovers through an intricate web of tests, to evaluate their worthiness and potency. Love seems to trigger off other talents not thought possible before. They want romantic environments always, whether at work or at home, but full of superefficient gadgets such as telephones in every room, microwave ovens, videotape security controls, and buzzer systems. Flowers and beautiful works of art decorate every nook and cranny, and beautiful smells from perfume to cooking fill the air.

SUSAN SARANDON

Susan visited me in my West Side office in 1976, and when I looked at her horoscope chart it was easy to see why she had just "lucked into acting." With Venus in Scorpio right at the top of her chart in the tenth house of career and fame, she would have success in whatever she decided to do.

It was through love (Venus) of her husband that she met his agent while she was at college, and he signed her up. At the time she was married to actor Chris Sarandon (Leo, born July 24, 1942). Until then she had not considered acting and had taken no classes. She was a natural from the beginning.

Born Susan Tomaling on October 4, 1946, in New York City, at 2:25 P.M., she is a Libra with both her Moon and Ascendant in the photogenic sign of Capricorn, which gives her her beautiful luminous eyes and a vulnerability that makes others feel they have to protect her.

Since she had her Sun and Neptune (film) close together in Libra, the motion picture industry was the best outlet for her talents, even though she appeared onstage in New York in *The Rocky Horror Picture Show* and *Extremities,* she is best remembered for her roles in the movies *Compromising Positions, Atlantic City, King of the Gypsies, The Great Waldo Pepper,* and *Pretty Baby,* in which she played Brooke Shields's prostitute mother. In many, she displays the pixieish charm of these Librans.

Her Capricorn Moon has attracted her to politics, and she is very outspoken about her liberal views and is active in the nuclear freeze movement.

SIGOURNEY WEAVER

What actress would enjoy oozing her way through messy extraterrestrial goo and slime, fighting off big-teethed aliens, and making love in the most uncomfortable places on this planet or another? Sigourney Weaver, star of *Ghostbusters* and *Alien* does, and she has the sense of humor to go with it. Her flair for dry humor and her "almost intimidating beauty" make her a force to be reckoned with socially as well as professionally.

Born Susan Weaver, on October 8, 1949, in Los Angeles, she later took the name of a character in F. Scott Fitzgerald's *The Great Gatsby,* Sigourney. She is a beautiful, Botticelli Venus-like Libra with her Moon in the warlike sign of Aries, which explains her skill with martial arts and dexterity with fifty-caliber heavy machine guns.

Her Sun in Libra is in exactly the same location as Neptune, god of the sea (and all that goo [oil]), establishing a kind of intimate sensuality between her and her environment, an ambience aided by her Venus in the sexual sign of Scorpio.

Pluto, god of the underworld, in Leo, conjunct with her Mars, god of war, also in Leo, explains the trend in her roles of conflict, survival, and victory. She actually attended a radical guerrilla-theater, activist group in Stanford early in her training.

LUCIANO PAVAROTTI

Luciano Pavarotti enjoys appearing on talk shows, reporting on his latest adventures, and occasionally preparing a favorite recipe. This Libra's impulse to talk—as well as sing—gets him out there.

He was born in Modena, Italy, on October 12, 1935 at 1:30 A.M., a Libra with his Moon in Aries (which rules the head and therefore the resonant voice) and his Ascendant Leo, the showman.

The location of his Moon (public) in the ninth house of foreign places far from birth has made him popular all over the world, and he has very little time with his wife and three children in their home in Rimini, where he spends one month every year. His destiny was to be always on the move.

His Venus in Virgo in the first house gave him his beautiful singing voice, and the discipline necessary to learn all the roles for his repertoire.

Uranus in Taurus at the top of his chart also indicated fame using his voice, especially through the media and recordings, as Taurus rules the throat.

He loves singing, and genuinely loves people, and is as happy reaching his legendary high Cs and thrilling his fans as he is sitting entertaining his audiences with stories and anecdotes.

RONA BARRETT

Born: October 8 at 4:15 A.M. in New York City

Voted one of the ten best-known Americans, Rona Barrett is one of the greatest television personalities of all time. With her fortitude, vision, luck, good looks, and charm she has been able to manipulate the electronic medium and many of the people whose livelihoods depend on it. Rona, Hollywood's reporter supreme, is probably also the friendliest reporter, passing on the latest tantalizing snippets of news about our favorite personalities or delving into the most sensitive, intimate, and moving details of the lives of some of the most important world figures of our era.

While I was her house guest over Christmas and New Year's, we were having breakfast when a bouquet of three dozen roses was delivered. They were from a producer, an associate of long standing, whose movie she had criticized on her network television program the day before. Attached to the bouquet was a note: "Dear Rona, I love your integrity. With love, . . ."

Whether in business, romance, financial deals, or reportage, Rona is honest and sincere. She has an impact that at times has made some of the most powerful men and women in show business nervous. More than anyone, she may have kept Hollywood moguls honest, for no one could ever restrain her from telling the truth.

Born in New York, Rona is a Libra with Virgo ascending and a Moon in Cancer. This Libra-Virgo combination makes her a perfectionist. Rona started in public relations, helping stars create the right image. Applying the same discipline and hard working to herself and her own career, Rona zoomed into American homes within a very short time of deciding what she wanted to do with her life.

Youthful and slim, she appears younger than her years, and her charm and diplomacy get her guests and interviewees to relax, whereby she obtains very frank comments and intimate disclosures, for they feel safe in her tasteful and sensitive hands.

Her Virgo Ascendant has given her the ability to organize her own life, career, and staff, and not only is she the star of her own creation but also produces, writes, and raises money for her enterprises that range from radio and television syndication and magazine publications to records and many fringe promotions.

But her Part of Fortune in the sign of Cancer, next to her Moon and Pluto in Cancer, has brought her to the American public. Rona is a household name, and for years fans have waited with excitement to hear her tell the latest about their favorite stars.

This same planetary combination in Cancer has given her a magic wand with real estate matters and, using her artistic talents and her incredible taste, she has been able to transform her various homes into works of art and make profit from them. Recently she built from scratch a magnificent home in Beverly Hills that could be described as a palace of the Aquarian Age—a kinesthetic delight as one sensually runs one's fingers over the marble and the soft, padded luxury of high style, with all the electronic accoutrements necessary to a lady involved in high-power media, yet comfortable enough to be the home that Rona dreamed and created, overlooking a romantic, misty lagoon.

But it was her Uranus in Taurus, in the eighth house of money, that brought her to television. Uranus—the space age planet of electronics, video, and computers—was a natural money-maker for Rona and made her a superstar in her own right. Together with the Part of Fortune and the Moon giving her fame and success with the public, by using her initiative and style, she was able to take advantage of everything that that area of show business had to offer her.

It must have been the Virgo rising that made it difficult for Rona to find the perfect partner for marriage, for Libras are great romantics and are always in

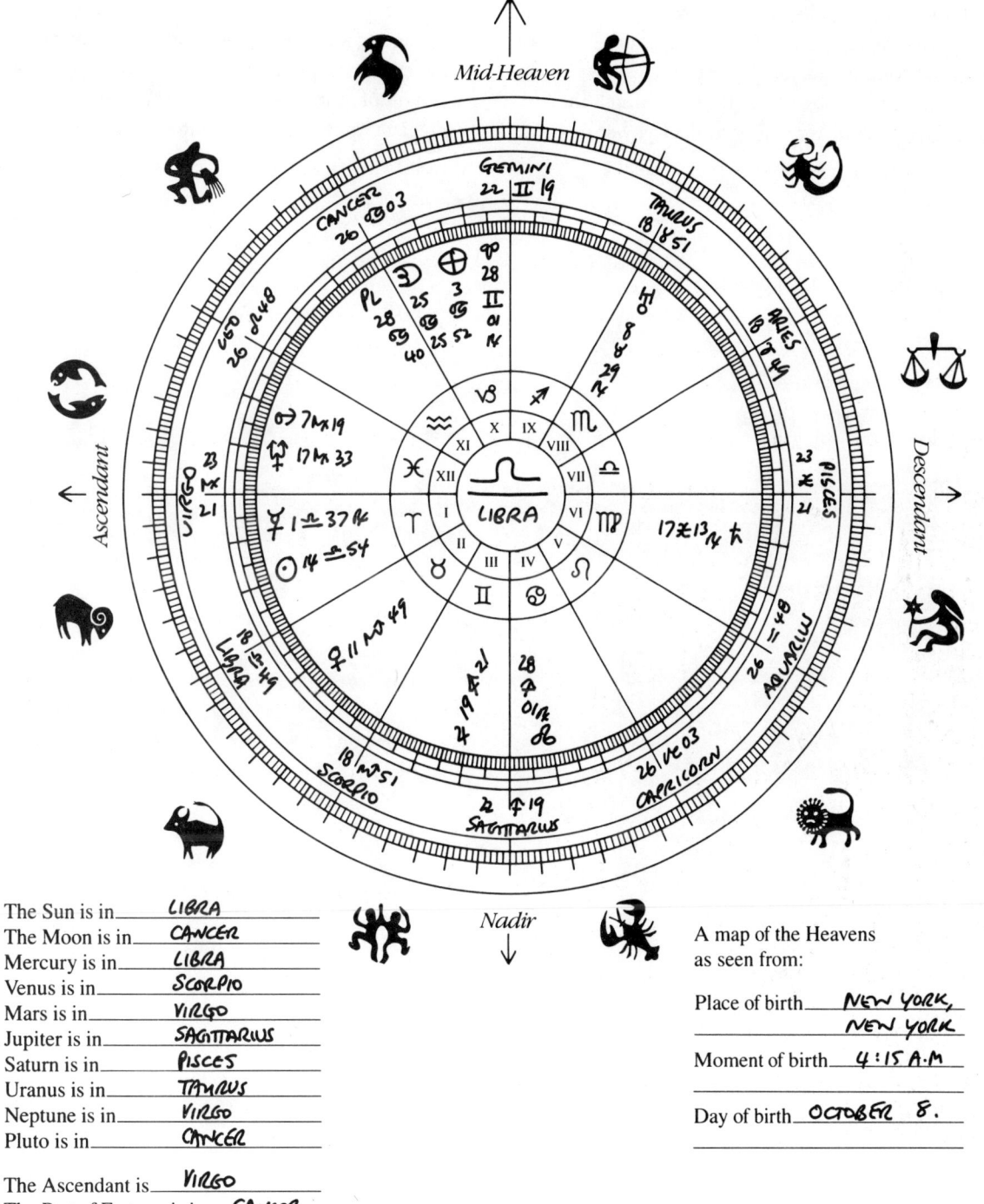

The Sun is in LIBRA
The Moon is in CANCER
Mercury is in LIBRA
Venus is in SCORPIO
Mars is in VIRGO
Jupiter is in SAGITTARIUS
Saturn is in PISCES
Uranus is in TAURUS
Neptune is in VIRGO
Pluto is in CANCER

The Ascendant is VIRGO
The Part of Fortune is in CANCER

A map of the Heavens as seen from:

Place of birth NEW YORK, NEW YORK

Moment of birth 4:15 A.M

Day of birth OCTOBER 8.

love. Yet this Virgo influence affected her choice of husband until she was in her late thirties. It was important to find someone who could share and help in the empire she had established and bring her the fun and romance she needed.

Having looked at her chart earlier in the year, I had predicted that she would marry in June. I was close. In June she met William Trowbridge, who proposed to her almost immediately. Remembering my words, she agreed and married him in September.

Her Jupiter in Sagittarius in the third house of writing and communications has expanded all her speaking, writing, and publishing skills, from which she will make a fortune. And her ability to manage her own life gives her the experience and the knowledge to manage others'.

With this determination, courage, hard work, and the ability to see clearly what she wanted, Rona worked methodically and carefully toward her goals, from syndication to the networks.

Admired by her peers, she has had to be very cautious in her choice of friends. "I'm not friends with the stars because if I was I couldn't tell the truth about them."

We await with bated breath the next friendly reportings from Rona, knowing that they will be fair minded, principled, moral and have just the right amount of outrageousness to entertain and enlighten. We can't wait another minute to find out.

Romantic Gumshoes

GEMINI DECANATE, RULED BY MERCURY
October 12–October 22

The investigative curiosity of the planet Mercury makes these Librans excellent detectives and analysts; they find symbolic or real details and clues in everything they read or see. They are great readers of thrillers and mysteries, crossword puzzle wizards, and chess champions, with the luck of Venus thrown in. This touch of the romantic makes every conquest involve a love relationship, real or imaginary, for these Venus-Mercury adventurers.

They are the modern-day heroes, like princes from the past charging into battle hell-bent on some cause, or like *Star Wars* heroine Carrie Fisher, princesses of the future. Some are international spies who woo their way into secret premises and seduce their victims as they pass on top-secret information. It's not surprising that debonair "gumshoe" Roger Moore should have played two of contemporary literature's most famous spies, the Saint and James Bond. Their looks and beauty attract and weaken all potential enemies and help them overcome obstacles.

Their manner of speech is usually precise, distinct, and dignified. To some it may appear snobbish or overeducated, but they seek perfection and beauty from the language they speak just as they do from their works of art and their loved ones. In their writings they are optimistic and concerned about the philosophical effect on those reading their words. Their lyrics and music are always bright and uplifting, and their performances or lectures leave audiences wanting more.

As children they would read voraciously, collecting books and information to help them quickly through their studies and on to more professional work. Some would become child actors and actresses; others, writers for a local newspaper's juvenile column and winners in music and art festivals and competitions. Those less artistically talented—and there wouldn't be many—would use their other talents and instincts to help run family businesses, to paint and decorate, and to earn money delivering newspapers and magazines and working in local stores.

Because of their years of investigating, they tend toward negativism, being skeptical of people they meet and the accomplishments they claim. They tend to grow to trust others rather than trusting them at first sight, but once their faith has been proved nothing will ever destroy the love they bestow.

As they like action and immediate results in all things, they get bored very easily, they often resort to impractical methods to resolve situations—methods that somehow happen to work. Among their main concerns is access to transportation that will get them to their destinations in the shortest time and by the most direct route—a fast sports car or a helicopter for those who can afford it. Frequent travelers on the Concorde across the Atlantic, they appear to love a jet-set life, and they endure the nervous ills that go with that existence.

Traveling lovers, these Librans appear frivolous and fickle, but they need sexual stimulation more than most. Most will find an outlet in books and magazines and be only mentally disloyal to loved ones back home. Some will insist that the loved one travel with them, thus making a great business as well as a romantic team. Their vanity attracts short-lived relationships en route, and their dearest loved ones have to get used to their flirtatious behavior—often right in front of their eyes—all part of the person they love. They tend to want a fantastical love life, too, as full of drama and intrigue as the pages of a gothic novel. They often make better lovers than husbands or wives, but their air of romance and adventure can be charming.

ROGER MOORE

One of the most exciting and adventurous actors since Errol Flynn, Roger Moore is a true "romantic gumshoe" with his portrayals of both the Saint and James Bond.

Born in Stockwell, London, on October 14, 1927, at 1:00 A.M., Roger is the son of a London policeman. His early years were full of stories of crime, escaped prisoners, and—as his father remained a policeman in London throughout World War II—international spies. These provided an ideal background for this investigative Libra.

Both the Sun and Mars were located in Libra at the time of his birth, and both were in the third house of communications and activity with the hands. He excelled in art and drawing at school, and his first job was with a company that specialized in animated cartoons. However, it didn't last long, and since he was out of work someone suggested that he could make money working as an extra on a film being made at Denham Studios *(Caesar and Cleopatra)*. With his Leo Ascendant, common to many show business people, he was destined to agree.

As Roger tells it, "I did this highly pleasurable job for a few days, and on the third day, as I walked through the gates, a car stopped alongside me." The codirector on the film was Brian Desmond Hurst, who asked him if he was interested in becoming an actor. "It didn't occur to me *not* to be interested in becoming an actor! From that moment it seemed that I [had] always wanted to be an actor." Hurst told him that if his family would support him for a while, he would personally pay his fees at the Royal Academy of Dramatic Arts (RADA).

Roger looks very Libran—slim, blessed by the planet of beauty, Venus, and appearing much younger than his actual age. He is very even tempered most of the time, and he loves congenial surroundings. But, he confesses, he is "ugly in the mornings," adding, "I can be rotten. Luisa has seen me throw a whole plate [full of food] across the room," expressing the Libran hint of temperament.

His moon in Gemini attracted him to more than one marriage, and Luisa Mattioli, a former Italian actress, is his third wife. It is a very clever and witty Moon position, too, and as it is well placed in the tenth house of career and fame, it has given him much satisfaction, success, and publicity. Nevertheless, many of his astrological traits come out in his performances rather than in his personal life, as is the case with many actors.

Roger's Mercury in Scorpio makes him very suspicious, curious, and critical and gives him a somewhat obstinate, forceful, but reckless nature, plus a tendency toward sarcasm or verbal one-upmanship, at which Roger is a master. But the fun-loving Leo Ascendant always comes to his rescue. Roger was once asked what he would do if he ran into a problem. "Telephone three people," he replied. "My agent, my bank manager, and my astrologer."

ANGELA LANSBURY

Angela Lansbury is a "romantic gumshoe"—especially in her current television series, "Murder, She Wrote"—and the viewers enjoy her every antic as she goes about solving the crimes.

She was nominated for an Academy Award for her very first motion picture role in *Gaslight* (1944) and again for *The Picture of Dorian Gray* and *The Manchurian Candidate*.

Born in London on October 16, 1925, Angela is a refined, beautiful, artistic, and gentle Libra, with the Sun, Moon, Mercury, and Mars located in that sign. She has been able to woo audiences as Cockney maidservants and as hussies and heavies, and her singing and dancing in the second phase of her career, when she attacked Broadway—with *Anyone Can Whistle, Mame, Gypsy,* and *Sweeney Todd*—won her four Tony Awards (one for each show).

Saturn in Scorpio (work and investigation) played a vital part in many of her roles, as she has worked in more than seventy films and is now particularly known for her starring role as mystery writer Jessica Fletcher of "Murder, She Wrote."

Having seen Angela in *Gypsy* in London, one year before she opened in it on Broadway, I predicted publicly that she would win a Tony for the role when it came to New York. Her manager at the time, Barry Krost, told me that this production wasn't scheduled for the United States. Later he called me up to tell me of the New York offer, and she did win a Tony for *Gypsy*. Peter Shaw, her husband, now manages her career.

JOHNNY CARSON

Charming, friendly, and one of the most famous—and richest—faces on television today, Johnny Carson is the king of the talk show, entertaining late-night America, changing the mood of his stress-filled viewers and turning them into relaxed, laughing, romantic couples.

He was born on October 23, 1925, at 6:15 A.M. in Corning, Iowa. Being born on the last day of Libra, he has some Scorpio traits, too, especially as his Mercury (communication) and Saturn (work), are both in Scorpio. Underneath Johnny's charm he's a very in-depth, investigative interviewer (Scorpios are the detectives of the zodiac).

His Ascendant, Mars, and the Sun both being in Libra keeps him looking young and slim and lets him handle the most difficult guest with the skill of an international diplomat. He also has the daring, energy, and talent to do most of the outrageous comic stunts himself and to make the Libran's precision of speech into a comic tool.

"The Tonight Show" is a perfect vehicle for Johnny's particular brand of genius. His Uranus in Pisces is in the area of show business, especially the media, and he has had a great influence on the lives and careers of many new entertainers and stars.

His Moon and Jupiter are together in Capricorn, and this adds the brilliant comic timing to his monologues and to conversations with his guests. In practical business terms, too, the hour his show airs gives him much more flexibility with his rather adult humor.

CARRIE FISHER

Born: October 21, 1956, at 12:49 A.M. in Burbank, California

Arriving at the hospital on Pico Boulevard in Los Angeles, I asked the nurse in charge for directions to Carrie Fisher's private room. Carrie had just had her tonsils removed, and her friend and mentor, actress Joan Hackett (who died in 1983), had asked me to do her horoscope chart to cheer her up.

"While you are going to her room, would you mind taking these extra towels?" asked the nurse.

"I'll be happy to take them," I replied and continued down the hallway to her room. Dressed in my best California white slacks and shirt and a pale yellow golf jacket, I couldn't have looked less like the traditional notion of an astrologer.

I knocked gently on her door. It was opened by a very friendly nurse's aide who asked me in and told me to put the towels in the bathroom. As soon as I had done this, there was a slight pause—the aide obviously thought I would leave until I announced that I was Fredrick Davies and had an appointment with Carrie. All this time she had been lying prone and seemingly unconscious, with her eyes closed, trying to ignore all the commotion.

At the mention of my name, she leaped from the bed, grunting a few sounds (she couldn't yet speak), and ran into the bathroom. I could hear the water running and a lot of hustle and bustle of dressing. Suddenly there appeared the future Princess Leia of *Star Wars* in a pretty antique dressing gown and crocheted lace bonnet. Graciously she gestured for me to sit down, offered me some hot tea, and sat down to listen to what was in the horoscope chart I had prepared for her.

It was full of exciting news and prospects, and we arranged to travel to Las Vegas together as soon as she was feeling better and could talk to visit her mother, Debbie Reynolds, appearing at the Desert Inn. (Her father is singer Eddie Fisher).

If her parents weren't influence enough, her Leo Ascendant guided her to show business, and with her Moon in Taurus, at the top of her chart in the tenth house of fame and career, it was obvious that she would succeed. When we next met, backstage at the London Palladium, where she was appearing with her mother in the Debbie Reynolds Show, she did in fact have her own spot and sang to the critical raves of all the London newspapers.

Pluto, the planet of big business, in her first house made her a major box office attraction by the age of twenty-one. In 1977, when *Star Wars* hit the big screen, she became an instant star. The sequels, *The Empire Strikes Back* (1980) and *Return of the Jedi* (1984), gave her a permanent place in the annals of Hollywood. The series revolutionized the movie business.

Saturn in her fourth house of home and family indicated the early separation of her parents (when Carrie was only two). Eddie ran off to marry Liz Taylor. Carrie says, "It's hard to believe she was my stepmother for a while; we only met a couple of times."

Although the planet of restrictions may have given her the unsettled home life she was to experience all through her growing-up period, it also gave her karmic lessons—the result of the North Node being located next to Saturn. Her rewards in this life were because of her parents, for better or for worse.

Even marriage was not destined to be easy for Carrie. Mars in Pisces in her seventh house of partners and marriage brought her a stormy marriage to Scorpio Paul Simon (born November 19, 1942), whom she wed in August 1983 and split from in 1984. But with the Part of Fortune also located there, Carrie could have a wonderful, rewarding, and fulfilling life with someone who not only becomes her romantic partner but a business partner too.

The Sun and Neptune in the third house of writing

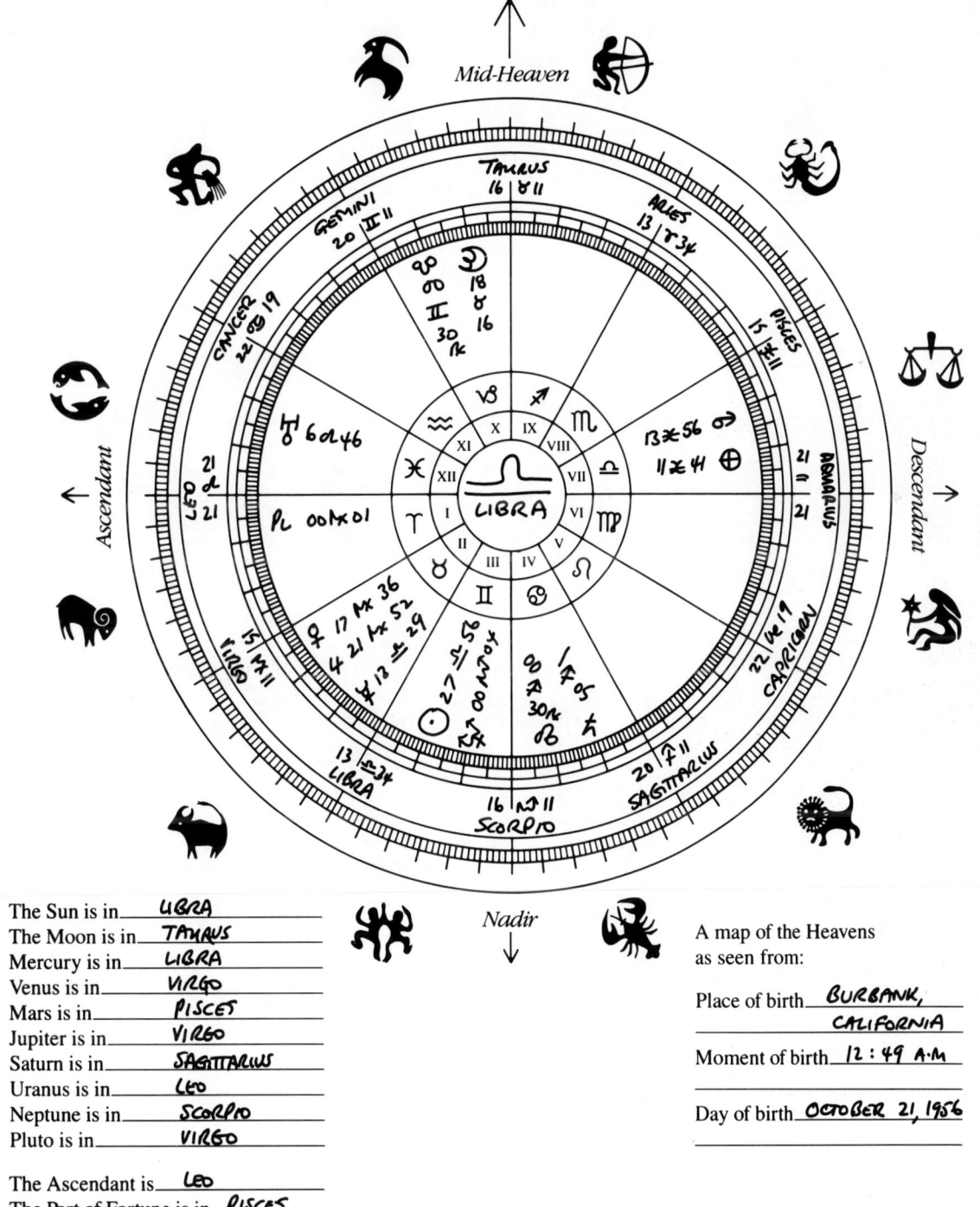

The Sun is in LIBRA
The Moon is in TAURUS
Mercury is in LIBRA
Venus is in VIRGO
Mars is in PISCES
Jupiter is in VIRGO
Saturn is in SAGITTARIUS
Uranus is in LEO
Neptune is in SCORPIO
Pluto is in VIRGO

The Ascendant is LEO
The Part of Fortune is in PISCES

A map of the Heavens as seen from:

Place of birth BURBANK, CALIFORNIA

Moment of birth 12:49 A.M

Day of birth OCTOBER 21, 1956

and communications show that she will be able to make a great success through writing as well as acting, and she might well write a novel or screenplay.

Carrie's relationship with her mother, also a client of mine, is a very good one. "We talk about most things, and we argue. I'm not very political, but I did rebel against her once—the only time I ever refused to do something she asked. Well, we were invited to go to chapel with President Nixon and in no way did I want to go. 'No, I won't go!' I shouted. 'I refuse ab-so-lutely. I'd feel like such a hypocrite!' I yelled. So I went. My mother said I would have to because it was in the papers that I was going. Anyway, I refused to join in the service."

To her credit, Carrie admits that this act of defiance was known only to herself and her conscience. "Afterward he sent me *that* picture with 'May all your dreams come true' written across it."

Princess Leia is indeed a space-age "romantic gumshoe" as she cavorts through space shooting people and shouting, "Got you!" This twenty-first-century detective brings out the sense of adventure in everyone, putting viewers in a kind of intergalactic fairy tale—a cross between *Buck Rogers* and *2001*.

SCORPIO
Detective of the Zodiac

SUN IN SCORPIO, RULED BY
PLUTO AND MARS
October 23–November 22

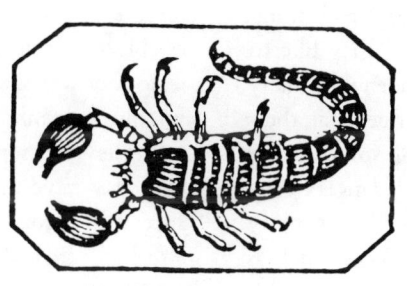

No other sign of the zodiac has this wonderful combination of sensuality and ambition, for Scorpio is ruled by the fiery and energizing planet Mars as well as the mysterious and sexy planet Pluto, god of the underworld. It is no wonder that Scorpios themselves say they are the "worst sign," the most "evil sign," and the most "dangerous sign," for they like to give that wicked impression—it is all part of their illusion. Exotic in all they do, from their makeup and dress to their achievements and desires, they have the ability to accomplish anything they want in life. On many occasions they discard their goals once they have reached them, for they enjoy getting there more than staying at the top, both in their professional and their love lives.

Sexy and very temperamental, they create terrible anxieties for themselves by being overambitious, critical, and unnecessarily secretive. This need to be very baffling to those close to them is part of the cloak they like to wear over their real selves. It is no wonder that many men and women with a heavy Scorpio influence in their charts would volunteer as international spies during wartime and enjoy all the intrigue and dangers they would have to face. Even in peacetime they happily engage in jobs that need the cover of darkness, such as credit investigation, police work—especially plainclothes detective work—secret government missions, and confidential jobs for political figures.

But often this obscure side of them is kept hidden, too, and outwardly they give the impression of frankness, and support, while they secretly and cunningly work against those whose fate is in their hands. Always on the go, their ambitions are numerous and they can easily take over the work of their employers as well as their control and position. Their shrewdness in reaching the top is both admirable and distasteful, for one cannot help being amazed at their daring and courage at one moment and being horror-struck at the methods used in the next. But somehow they seem to get there and win the support and loyalty of enthusiasts and critics alike.

Basically, they are more philanthropic than first impressions would indicate, and they are just as excited and enthusiastic about other people's plans and ambitions as they are about their own, especially if they love them. They will go out of their way to help others achieve their goals, supply them with the necessary funds and physical labor, and enjoy their success as if it were their own. But should there be feelings of envy and competition instead of true affection, they will help get the other person to the top only to take over the power once they are there. Regardless of their fantastic drive, they are not selfish, for they see their role as that of the power behind the throne. They feel that with this strength in a business or personal relationship, they can use their position or their friends and loved ones to change the world for the better, even though the majority would not approve or want it that way. This can work for a situation or against it, can help overcome obstacles or create new ones, impose less pressure and fewer rules on a group or establish a dictatorship. They truly believe that this mysterious power should control all with whom they come in touch, openly or secretly.

They are sometimes mysteries even to themselves and may have difficulty setting goals. But the driven, successful Scorpios burn with a dark light and are streaked across the pages of history.

There are no limits to the kinds of work they will apply themselves to and make a great success; the end result each time represents a major challenge, and they will not stop till this is attained. Love of luxury gives them added financial drive, and if they could control their somewhat sarcastic speech, no relationship would be impossible and no one could resist them.

As they are daring and enterprising, they are attracted to jobs that are nonroutine and need a lot of initiative. Apart from the obvious involvement in secret organizations, many have great talent in the entertainment fields and mix their underworld activities with their art by working the nightclub circuits and with the big business moguls who control show business all over the world. Some enter the medical profession, especially as surgeons and anesthesiologists, and others become fine researchers or pharmacists. They are perfectly suited to working as sheriffs or detectives in the local community and, conversely, dealing in shady, under-the-counter business that may have to be kept secret from the police. Big-business affairs attract them, and they have a knack for getting experts to work for them, so work as contractors and engineers is lucrative and gives them the control they seek and need.

Schemers and dreamers all of them—subject to the same magic that inspired many adventurers and explorers to go off and discover new continents, new oil wells, or new medicinal cures. Scorpios will open up new doors and vistas for everyone.

Their methods may vary but their goals are the same—the highest position in whatever profession they enter, for themselves and for those they love. It is impossible ever to know what side they are really on, and one must use one's intuition and gut feelings to sense when they are rivals rather than close friends.

Patriotic Sorcerers

SCORPIO DECANATE, RULED BY PLUTO AND MARS
October 23–November 2

The power of these Scorpios, having the double influence of Pluto and Mars, makes them heroes both on the battlefield of life and in the ministries of peacetime. This excess of creative energy is like a volcano, ever exploding and sending off its ideas from the depth of its soul. Their imagination brings forth ideas and inventions that no other brain could think of, let alone develop, for they have help—some secret, spiritual help from the gods—whether of the underworld or the universe.

Magical personalities, they can with a wave of their wands turn defeat into victory, failure into success, enemies into allies. They experience no repressions so they know no fears, and they exhibit a fertile imagination that boggles the mind and exhausts the viewer.

Victory, no matter what or how or when, is the ultimate goal. There are no thoughts of losing, and their characters are of such determination and commitment that they will "hang in there" until no opposition or competitor remains a threat.

Everyone is immediately aware when these Scorpios enter a home or business establishment, for they radiate a charisma that ranks on stardom as in the case of magnetic Burt Lancaster. They have no doubt that they will be accepted, and they hold hypnotic control over those in their presence. Blunt and immediate in their demands, they want to know all the details, all the contacts and associations, while they themselves remain totally uncommitted and mysterious. Nothing would please these Scorpios more than to use information innocently obtained to force others to follow their lead, like the Pied Piper, leading the rats out of the village of Hamelin, leaving the total population in awe and fascination of him. When they tried to doublecross him, his anger was directed against them, and he took his revenge by leading their children away, never to be seen again.

Scorpios love war but not necessarily destruction. Often blamed for their self-destructive qualities, they never actually seek to harm themselves. It is part of the risk—to build something, something must be destroyed, whether an ideal, a structure, or, if needed to fulfill their aims, themselves.

While it may appear that they are always at combat somewhere in their lives, they can be considerate and overly generous when their sensitive heartstrings are touched. They will raise funds for charity and for the destitute and will wage holy war on city hall to help minorities, but unless this impulse is triggered off in them, they can become lazy and vacillating. They need a battle somewhere in their lives.

This is the most sexually oriented sign of the zodiac but not always the happiest, for many of their partners will not be able to appreciate their sexual energy. Many couples will end up talking and evaluating their psychological needs rather than just getting on with it. Through this analysis, emotional hang-ups and blocks can develop. In some couples frigidity that is foreign to both is brought upon them by performance standards demanded by this Scorpio. Physically both males and females are strong and like strong partners most of the time, but in the soul mates they choose for life they move toward more sensitive and passive spouses.

While they may be called the most sexually active sign of the zodiac, they are not necessarily the most sexually happy, or have the most fun in their sex life. So much depends on the partner, for this Scorpio can achieve a high level of sexual gratification with anyone, unless opposition is felt.

HELEN REDDY

Helen's recording of "I Am Woman" not only sold millions of copies but was immediately accepted as a feminist anthem by women in all walks of life.

"I don't think of myself as a feminist. I'm a singer who has had my woman's consciousness raised," she states.

She was born in Melbourne, Australia, on October 25, 1941, at 5:50 P.M., to show business parents, and she started to perform when she was four. By the time she was nineteen she had her own weekly television show in Australia, called "Helen Reddy Sings."

Her Sun and Mercury, the planet of the writer and speaker, were together in Scorpio, but her Venus (singing) was in the crusading sign of Sagittarius, which probably explains her success with "I Am Woman." Her Moon in Capricorn, in the ninth house of places far from birth, only added another political thrust to her image.

Helen has Aries as her Ascendant, making her strong and determined, an achiever. She won the pop vocal Grammy in 1972, appeared in the movie *Airport 1975*, and still packs them in at concerts all over the world.

HENRY WINKLER

Henry Winkler's popular character "the Fonz," which he played for ten years in "Happy Days," *was* charisma. Winkler has always felt a tremendous empathy with, and responsibility for helping, his young audiences and children in general. An advocate for children's welfare, he produced a video on child abuse called *Strong Kids, Safe Kids*. And as Fonzie he was always coming to the rescue of any of his friends in trouble.

Born in New York on October 30, 1945, at 12:51 P.M., he is a Scorpio with the Sun and Mercury in that sign, and his Moon is in the sign of the teacher, Virgo.

Through his character he has been able to influence his fans, as they identify with Fonzie's sensitive side and realize that he understands them. Even his choice of wardrobe for "Happy Days"—he always wore a black leather jacket (Scorpios normally like leather and metal)—reflected this.

His Ascendant, the area in which he most excels, is Aquarius, the sign of television, and he is made for the medium. He has a winning personality and goes right into the homes of his followers. "Fonzie fever" made him one of the most popular and memorable personalities in television history, and his inventiveness and desire for control led him to producing and directing.

As a director he has done several television shows, including "All the Kids Do It," about teenage drunk driving, which ties in with his love for American youth. He hopes that they will listen to him. He is a true humanitarian, a patriot, and a big brother to millions of fans out there.

DAN RATHER

This renowned newsman reflects the potent heroism of these Scorpios with courage in their tails. While he was working with a CBS radio affiliate in Texas, his management of the CBS's round-the-clock reports of President Kennedy's assassination brought him to the attention of the powers that be in the network. His cool professionalism and his intense search for facts and truth gave the listeners and viewers faith in the information he conveyed.

Dan was born in Wharton, Texas, on October 31, 1931, at 6:13 P.M., and he has his Sun, Mercury, and Venus in Scorpio, the sign of the investigator. His aggressive planet Mars is in Sagittarius, the hunter, aiming at his prey.

He had wanted to be a reporter for as long as he could remember, and now as CBS Evening News anchorman and also its managing editor, his love of uncovering a story, of getting to the truth, still gives him his greatest excitement and feeling of achievement.

His Ascendant is the loyal, patriotic, and stubborn sign of Taurus, and his attitude and stick-to-itiveness approach to a subject have developed a whole army of right-wing enemies who tried to buy up CBS stock so they could have some control over Dan's reporting, which they considered biased against them.

Pluto in Cancer, the planet of big business in the sign of the United States, destined him for a major role in U.S. history. In his strong position with CBS television, Dan can wave his magic wand and do what he considers proper and honest for the American public.

BURT LANCASTER

Born: November 2, 1913, at 9:12 A.M. in East Harlem, New York

Being in the right place at the right time certainly was the magic that changed Burt Lancaster's life. The story of Burt's meeting Hollywood agent Harold Hecht in an elevator and Hecht's making him an instant star is one of show business's favorite legends.

Burt was born in Manhattan's East Harlem to a large Irish family. A Scorpio ruled by the two planets of battle, Mars and Pluto, he learned about life on the city streets, becoming an accomplished street fighter and scrapper. But it was his Sagittarius Ascendant that attracted him to the glamorous life of the acrobat and, later, to the movies. He dropped out of New York University, to which he had won a scholarship, to join a circus as a trapeze artist (source of his firsthand experience when he later starred in the movie *Trapeze*). But, not achieving great success in that profession, he gave it up to work in a department store.

It was when he returned from action in World War II that he was discovered by Hecht, who thought he was an actor and asked him to read for a part in a Broadway play he was producing called *The Sound of Hunting*. It closed after three weeks. But Burt was noticed by Hollywood scouts, and the following year he starred in *The Killers*.

Burt and Hecht formed their own production company and were later joined by another producer John Hill. They produced several big Oscar-winning successes, including *Marty*. In 1960 he received an Oscar for his role in *Elmer Gantry,* and in 1962 he won the Venice Film Festival award for his sensitive performance in *Birdman of Alcatraz*.

His Moon is located in the practical sign of Capricorn, which makes him successful in business as well as one of the world's most hardworking stars. It also attracts him to politics and to theology, especially with his Jupiter, the guru planet, also in Capricorn in his first house of disposition and personality. When signed by CBS to star in the six-part television series "Moses, The Lawgiver," he studied Jewish philosophy to prepare himself for the role.

Burt's Sagittarius love of travel has been satisfied by working on location for his movies and also by entertaining the U.S. armed forces on USO tours. And sports and athletics have been highlighted in many of the roles he has played, notably *Jim Thorpe All-American*. Thorpe (Gemini, born on May 28, 1888) was the U.S. athlete who won the pentathlon and decathlon at the 1912 Olympics, and was one of America's greatest baseball and football stars.

It must have been Burt's Venus, the planet of good looks, in the romantic sign of Libra in his tenth house of career and fame, that caught the eye of Hecht and his early directors. As it is also the planet of good luck, Burt was destined for success.

His Sun in Scorpio has made him very ambitious, daring, and philanthropic. But as it is a very temperamental sign, he is likely to lose his temper easily. He once walked off a Mike Wallace interview in anger. In addition, the location of Mercury, his planet of communication, in Sagittarius in his twelfth house brings on a lot of self-undoing, due in part to the frank, honest, and impulsive reactions he learned on the streets as a child.

Saturn and Pluto in his seventh house of marriage have given him two marriages connected with his work. His first wife (a very brief marriage) was a trapeze artist.

He then met his second wife, Norma Anderson, while overseas on a USO tour in World War II. Their marriage ended in divorce in 1969, having produced five children.

He loves all animals; his Ascendant sign is the man on the horse, Sagittarius the centaur. It was appropriate that his *Birdman of Alcatraz* was so well received.

Scorpio is the great detective of the zodiac, Sagittarius is the seeker of truth, and Capricorn brings law and order. With this astrological combination, it is no wonder that Burt has made so many wonderful, diverse films, bringing his characters, their professions, their talents, their personalities, and their magic to the screen.

His secret for remaining mentally and physically young and healthy: "As long as you are curious, you defeat age!"

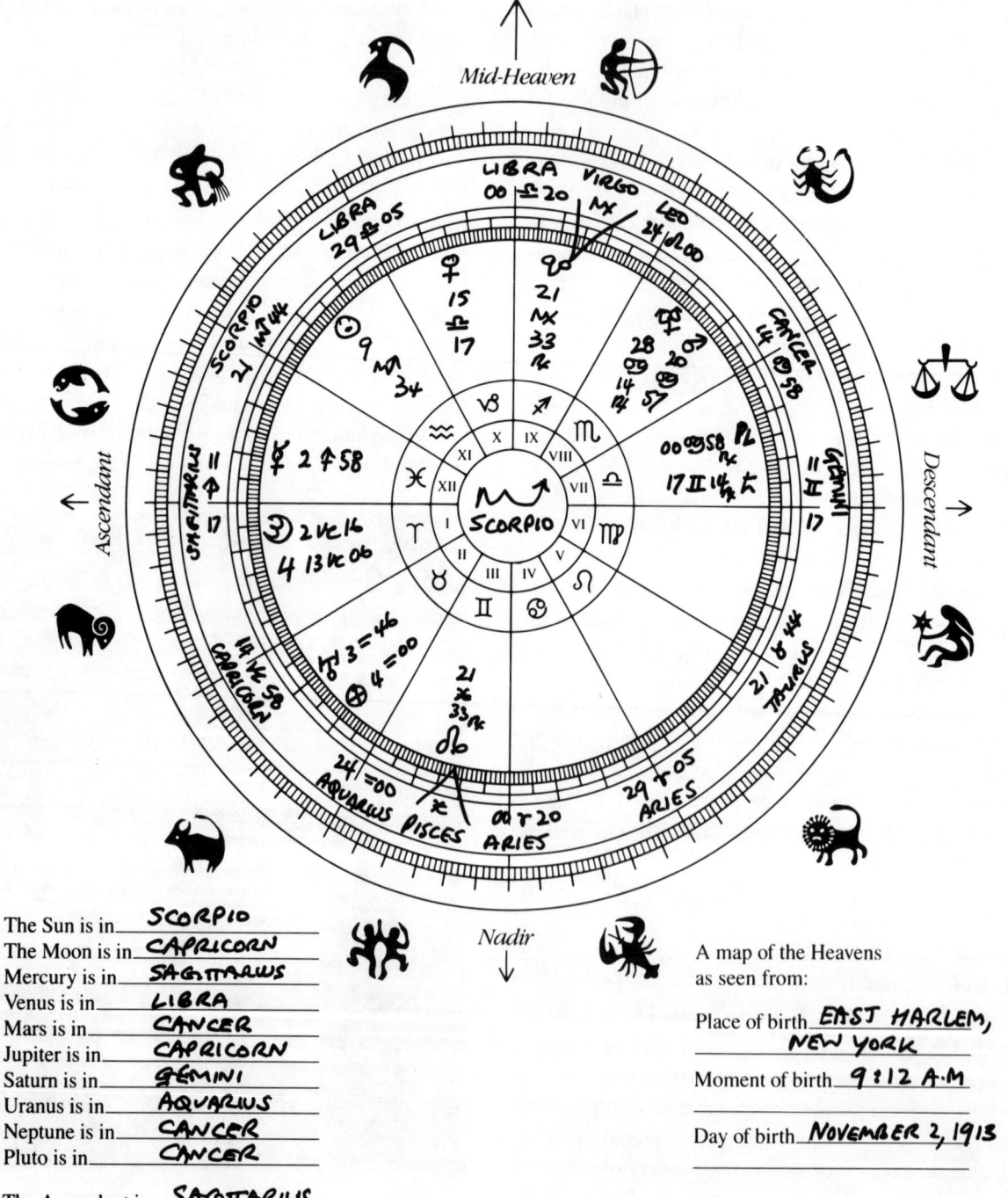

The Sun is in _SCORPIO_
The Moon is in _CAPRICORN_
Mercury is in _SAGITTARIUS_
Venus is in _LIBRA_
Mars is in _CANCER_
Jupiter is in _CAPRICORN_
Saturn is in _GEMINI_
Uranus is in _AQUARIUS_
Neptune is in _CANCER_
Pluto is in _CANCER_

The Ascendant is _SAGITTARIUS_
The Part of Fortune is in _AQUARIUS_

A map of the Heavens as seen from:

Place of birth _EAST HARLEM, NEW YORK_

Moment of birth _9:12 A.M_

Day of birth _NOVEMBER 2, 1913_

Seductive Vigilantes and Watchdogs
PISCES DECANATE, RULED BY NEPTUNE
November 3–November 12

These Scorpios have the strongest character in the zodiac—one that can affect the world for good or ill. They are influenced by a combination of the planets Pluto and Mars plus the mysterious devotion and sacrifice of the planet Neptune, god of the sea, who could raise the sea to fury with his trident. They are rarely frivolous, always dedicating their lives and careers to some cause in the service of mankind. They were both victims and perpetrators during the Crusades, the Spanish Inquisition, and the witch-hunting trials of Salem. They can suffer for what they believe, and they are also willing to kill for what they believe is the right path, the will of God. Sally Field, a two-time Oscar winner for playing strong, crusading characters, is a good example of this determined sign. Scorpios consider themselves very spiritual and would refuse to believe that there is any other force pushing them than that of God. Their warlike Mars approach plus the devastating effect they have on the world at large, their families, or the community due to the influence of Pluto, the god of the underworld, make them heroes or tyrants.

Whether in politics, religion, trade unions, or business, they want to have responsibility and take on the mantle that the job entails. Their passions are vivid, therefore they live in a world of total drama and never let up for a moment, finding peace only when they are asleep or dead! Some escape into the Neptunian state of drunkenness, while others become great painters, writers, and musicians, expressing themselves through the tormented characters portrayed in their works.

As children they would be the ones who would gain most pleasure from frightening others or giving their nurses or nannies a shock by jumping out of closets or pretending to drown or hang themselves. They would have had academic success both scientifically and artistically, being able to use their creative Neptunian traits and analytical Plutonic traits. They would lie awake at night waiting for their parents or brothers and sisters to come home, curious about the ways of adults. And they would often escape to visit friends, returning by climbing through the bedroom window. Their hypnotic air would even affect other schoolchildren, who would be at their mercy.

Romantically, as has been implied, they are rather unusual and very, very attractive sexually. They have a sensuality that appeals to most people, but it can also frighten them. This fear of danger in their expression and behavior is usually unfounded; basically, they want a gentle, loving partner to share their life with. Their appearance and habits, however, tend to attract those who are not looking for this kind of life, and so it is the situation that creates the character of these Scorpios rather than the other way around. Romantic to a fault, they will spend lavishly on their loved ones and enjoy their martyred feelings if jilted or let down at any time.

These Scorpios aren't totally saturated in romance and sex. It is generally their looks and stature as well as their style and behavior that turn others on. It could be the farthest thought from their minds, yet they are forced to face the fact that in every situation—be it business or pleasure, with male or female—the impression they give is that of the great seducer. Perhaps their secretive Scorpio natures hide the real people underneath, and what is really going on in their minds when we speak to them, we may never truly know.

CHARLES BRONSON

This potent star of *Death Wish*, vengefully ridding the streets of criminals, became synonymous with "vigilante" and has a rough-hewn quality that is seductive. As a Scorpio he was destined to succeed in whatever he decided to do, but it wasn't until after he had been in the army and worked as a construction worker, short-order cook, truck driver, baker, and even a Bingo spieler on the Atlantic City boardwalk, that he discovered the theater.

A friend persuaded him to attend a performance of *Anna Lucasta*. It was the first time that he had been in a theater to see a play, and he was extremely bored by the whole thing until he learned that the leading actor actually got paid seventy-five dollars per week for only two hours' work each night.

In true Scorpio fashion, the next day he was auditioning for a Philadelphia little theater group, and he got the part. He has been an actor ever since.

Born in Ehrenfeld, Pennsylvania, November 3, 1921, at 8:45 P.M., he is a Scorpio with Cancer Ascendant. It was the combination of these two sensitive, moody, and sensual signs that brought him immediately to the attention of the reviewers in his first movie *You're in the Navy*. (Lee Marvin, Pisces, born February 19, 1924, also made his debut in this movie.)

At the time he was still using his baptismal name, Charles Buchinsky. His brooding, mysterious, magnetic Scorpio personality wooed critics and directors alike, but his rugged looks prevented him from being cast as a leading man in the United States. It wasn't until he went to Europe to play the lead in a film, which immediately became the highest-grossing picture of the year in France, that the American producers saw his box office potential. His next film, for an Italian company, *Once Upon a Time Again in the West*, broke attendance records all over Europe. It was then that he became a box office draw of phenomenal proportions, one of the most unusual in the history of the cinema.

Neptune, the planet that rules the cinema, is in Leo, the sign of the showman, in his second house of money-making. But his Pluto, sitting on his Ascendant, both in the sign of Cancer, showed that eventually he would have the same incredible success back home.

His *Death Wish* role combined his Scorpio rulers, Pluto, god of the underworld; Mars, god of war; and the mysterious planet of intrigue and illusion, Neptune.

KATE CAPSHAW

Hers may be one of those exciting careers that Hollywood legends are made of, yet behind all the glamor and the publicity there is still a lot of struggle and hard work. Kate had just given up her career working with the handicapped and, with her daughter, left Los Angeles for New York. A change of life, a change of career, and Kate decided to do some modeling. Her photos were seen by Steven Spielberg (Sagittarius, born December 18, 1947), and he signed her up for *Indiana Jones and the Temple of Doom*. This led to other movies, including *Windy City* with John Shea (Aries) and *Power* with Richard Gere (Virgo).

Born in Fort Worth, Texas, on November 3, at 10 P.M., she is a Scorpio with her Moon in Libra, the sign of beauty, and her Ascendant is Cancer.

Perhaps having Uranus, the planet of sudden changes, sitting on her Ascendant brought about such good fortune. And having Mars, Venus, and Neptune together with her Moon in Scorpio gave her striking photogenic looks that she had not thought about during her early marriage. The Cancer influence took her into the more nurturing, caring professions.

Mercury, the planet of travel and communication, in Sagittarius, the filmmaker's sign, took her to many exotic locations to film her movies. It is fascinating, too, to realize that it was Spielberg, a Sagittarius, who launched her into the movies.

A very seductive actress and a very spiritual person, Kate is also idealistic, wanting only the best for everyone.

SALLY FIELD

Born: November 6, 1946, at 4:23 A.M. in Pasadena, California

I actually met the real Norma Rae when we were both appearing on *To Tell the Truth* in New York City. Her name is Crystal Lee Sutton, and the movie had been made about her as a valiant young woman (played by Sally Field) struggling with work, love, and family for her rights and those of fellow Southern textile workers. During a break in the taping, I discovered that Crystal Lee's birthday was May 14, 1956, appropriately under the sign of labor leaders, Taurus. She also confided that she had not received a cent from the movie.

Like Norma Rae, Sally would not allow her industry to hold her back, to keep her locked away in the Hollywood pigeonhole labeled "cute." She was grateful for the wonderful success she had had with *Gidget* and later as Sister Bertrille in *The Flying Nun,* which established her as a household name, but she wanted more than ever to be treated as a serious actress.

Winning an Emmy for her multipersonality character in the television movie *Sybil* led her to her major motion picture role as the "seductive vigilante and watchdog" Norma Rae, for which she won her first Academy Award in 1979. She won a second Oscar for *Places in the Heart* in 1984.

A Scorpio with Libra ascending and her Moon in Aries, Sally hides that very strong and determined combination behind her soft, gentle, and ageless Libran exterior. The Scorpio Sun and the Aries Moon are both fighters. Scorpio gives her the personal ambition and courage to go after her goals; Aries makes her feel like a crusader, on screen and off; and Libra, the sign of the scales of justice, wants fairness for all.

Librans, ruled by the loving planet Venus, desperately want love and affection. It is the sign of hearts, and many Librans will collect hearts, romantic souvenirs, and love letters, almost making their homes into shrines.

Perhaps it was Sally's Jupiter in the first house that gave her the wonderful, bubbly, giggling sense of fun associated with Gidget, and the religious significance of Jupiter (the sign of the traveling guru) may also have had something to do with her "flying nun."

Nevertheless, Sally was destined to have to work hard for her rewards, for in the tenth house of career and honors she has the planets Saturn, disciplinarian and restrictor, and Pluto, ruler of big business. Through her own discipline and planning, she created her own big-time career in show business, as both planets are in the sign of Leo.

Her Part of Fortune, located in the fifth house of film, television, and theater in the sign of Pisces, helped her with her movie career and also with "causes" (an important need for Pisces) and success with her two children, Peter and Elijah.

Sally was willing to give up her fame and television stardom to prove that she was serious about her acting career, and she took three years off to study and to do summer stock. "Nobody took me seriously. Nobody had any respect for me. I felt like a joke in the profession. So I decided to change my whole life—and I gave up my business manager, my agent, and my husband. And started again!" She succeeded in shedding the Gidget–Flying Nun image, becoming the Academy Award winning performer we know today.

Her Libran Ascendant is attracted to all that is beautiful and creative. She loves the piano, enjoys literature, and sewing, and quilting.

But her Moon in Aries, which has a strong influence on her love life, tends to be rather independent, impulsive, and needs a certain amount of freedom. She must have a very special man who can understand that this very sensitive and feminine woman on the outside is very strong, opinionated, and ambitious inside.

To appreciate Sally means looking past her public image into her heart. "I've felt bitter because the people who laughed at me were laughing at the deepest part of me, and yet they'd never seen it."

In 1985 she married Allan Griesman, her second husband, finally fitting all the parts of her life together to give her the happiness and emotional security she worked for so long. She has won the love, affection, and respect of those most important in her life—her husband, her children, her family, and her peers.

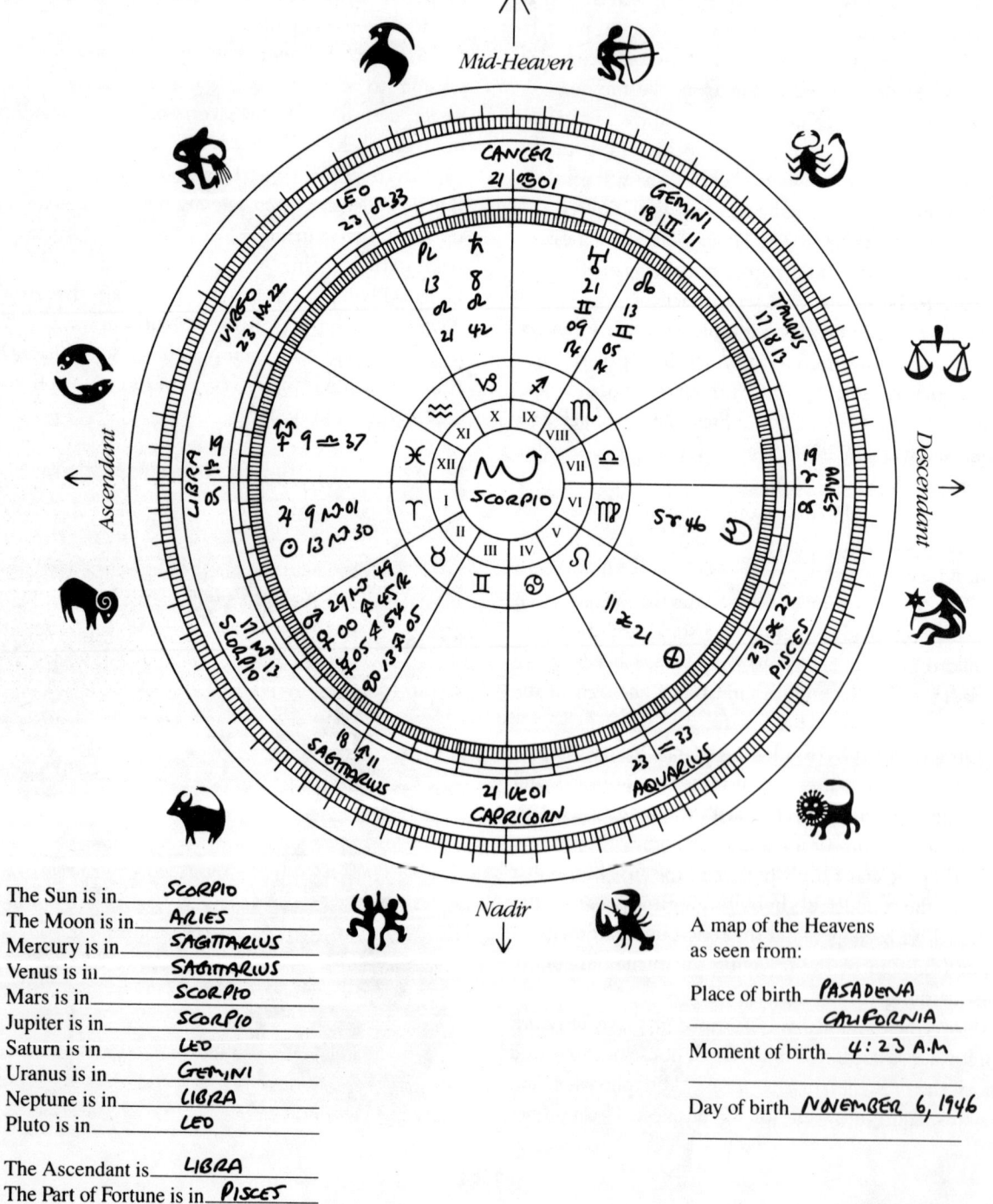

The Sun is in _SCORPIO_
The Moon is in _ARIES_
Mercury is in _SAGITTARIUS_
Venus is in _SAGITTARIUS_
Mars is in _SCORPIO_
Jupiter is in _SCORPIO_
Saturn is in _LEO_
Uranus is in _GEMINI_
Neptune is in _LIBRA_
Pluto is in _LEO_

The Ascendant is _LIBRA_
The Part of Fortune is in _PISCES_

A map of the Heavens as seen from:

Place of birth _PASADENA CALIFORNIA_

Moment of birth _4:23 A.M_

Day of birth _NOVEMBER 6, 1946_

Inquisitive Humanitarians
CANCER DECANATE, RULED BY THE MOON
November 13–November 22

These are the most gentle and compassionate of the Scorpios, for they have the powerful influence of the Moon to balance the devastating effects of Pluto and Mars. Kindness and generosity are strong traits behind a somewhat stern and serious exterior. Candid, determined, radiant Goldie Hawn is one of these transmuted Scorpios. When they allow themselves to relax they are fun loving. They enjoy playing games with the children, getting involved with big business plans, protecting the neighbors, or leading a march on city hall to save the parks. They can be warlike in their approach to their careers and the desires of their families. Their intense psychic faculties sense danger just as acutely as they sense the opportunities for themselves or their loved ones. Their hunches are accurate, but they keep their doubts hidden (like the dark side of the Moon) for fear of losing what they love most.

These Scorpios are always the upstanding members of any community and are often in service-oriented jobs. They also feel they want to protect everyone and everything around them. They will walk the dog, check the locks, and water the plants if someone is sick or away on vacation. Not only will they volunteer themselves, but they give their employees orders to help whoever needs assistance. In politics they become the friendly mayor or the busy senator who flies home to award prizes at the local fair or flower show.

Even as children, they would knock on the doors of elderly people in the neighborhood, asking if they needed a job done (hoping for a little reward, of course!). Some of them would set up stands in front of their homes and sell fresh lemonade during the hot summer days, making enough money to take themselves and their friends to the latest space film.

Their need to feel loved and part of the family would tend to make them stay home and travel mentally through reading or watching television. They would develop uncanny feelings about when to get out of a dangerous or tricky situation that could get them into trouble. Brilliant in their studies, they would ask their close friends over to help them with difficult homework, and their parents would always be prepared to add another setting at the dinner table.

While they may not appear as ambitious as the other Scorpios, they have the same determination to succeed. They must reach the top, but they will not hurt anyone on the way up and they do it in a quieter way, beating any competitors so subtly that they don't know it's happening. Once in a position of power they become friendly dictators, capable of destroying their enemies but preferring to manipulate them and win them over.

In romance they are ardent and passionate, but they look for a marriage partner rather than just a love affair. The need to have a home and children is very vital, and they therefore take their courting habits and their reputations seriously. They are not afraid to take their loved ones home and introduce them to the family. Sometimes this family-get-together atmosphere may make the other person feel boxed in, but these Scorpios like to share every experience with all their loved ones. They are among the most ideal people for a long and happy marriage—with all its ups and downs, its dramas and joys—for once committed they would rather put up with a bad decision than lose the person to whom they have given their love and their word.

The way to this Scorpio's heart is through the family, through entertaining in the home, through cooking for the local football team, or taking the whole family out to celebrate at the favorite restaurant around the corner. They can be calculating and cunning, they won't show their hard side, but remember they have the capabilities to crush you emotionally, just as they can make you exceptionally happy.

CHARLES, PRINCE OF WALES

The future king of England—a role that also brings with it leadership of the Church of England—Charles has been well versed in all subjects—social, artistic, scientific, and metaphysical. Though he is cautious about his feelings and beliefs, he is open and inquisitive enough to search for answers to many of the world's great mysteries and unexplained phenomena.

Born in London, November 14, 1948, at 9:14 P.M., this Scorpio has his Sun and Mercury in that sign as well. His Ascendant is the royal sign of Leo, and his Moon at the top of his horoscope is in exactly the same degree as his mother's Sun sign in Taurus.

It is his Mars (action) and Jupiter (luck and sports) in the sign of Sagittarius that gave him skills and success with riding and his favorite sport, polo. Sagittarius is the sign of the man on the horse.

When Charles was asked to comment on the ups and downs of wedded bliss, he wisely pointed out, "Marriage isn't an up or down issue. . . . It's a side-by-side one."

If he rules as wisely, he will indeed be a humanitarian king.

DICK CAVETT

I attended a dinner at the St. Regis Hotel in New York City for the Museum of Broadcasting and talking to Dick afterward, I told him I was working on a project about the late Truman Capote (Libra, born September 30, 1924). The next morning five video cassette tapes of Dick's interviews with Truman were on my desk. Dick is one of the kindest, most sincere, and most considerate professionals in the television industry today.

Dick Cavett was born in Gibbon, Nebraska, on November 19, 1936, at 1:24 A.M. He has his Sun and Mercury in the investigative sign of Scorpio, his Moon in serious Capricorn, and Virgo, the teacher, is his Ascendant. No wonder he takes his time with his guests, never pressures or hurries them, and always entertains and enlightens his audiences with his "Dick Cavett Show."

Neptune in Virgo on his Ascendant attracted him to the world of illusion, and he became well known in his community as a teenage magician. The active planet Mars in Libra (the balance) gave him the physical skills needed to be a gymnast.

But the combination of his Sun and Mercury in Scorpio in his third house of communications really drew him to comedy writing. He was one of the writers for Johnny Carson's "Tonight Show," and he wrote for "The Jerry Lewis Show" and Jack Paar.

The humorous planet Jupiter in Sagittarius gives him the intellect, skill, and timing to aim well-intentioned barbs at his guests. He has a brilliant, quick mind, full of memorable one-liners just waiting for an opportunity to be used. He has won three Emmys for his show.

He is married to actress Carrie Nye. When asked about children, Dick wryly remarked, "We haven't ruled the possibility of children out [but] I figure I'm the blessed event in our family."

TED TURNER

A man who starts his own Olympics to help world peace is indeed a humanitarian on a grand scale. Ted Turner is a winner in whatever he does. He doesn't stop until he succeeds, and he won't let go once he has the treasure in his hands, whatever it is. He is a true ambitious, philanthropic Scorpio, with great inquisitiveness and curiosity about life. His international activities and projects have been decidedly humanitarian.

Ted was born in Cincinnati, Ohio, on November 19, 1938, at 8:50 A.M., with both his Sun and Venus (good luck) together in the sign of Scorpio. His Ascendant is the sporty sign of Sagittarius, the traveler, the gambler, and the crusader.

Winner of the 1977 America's Cup yacht race and owner of the Atlanta Braves, he also loves to hunt and owns the Cable News Network (CNN), which now reaches 22 million homes.

Mercury, the planet of communications, is exactly on his Ascendant in the sign of Sagittarius, and with his Moon and Mars in Libra in the house of great achievement and fame, Ted has been able to attain nearly every goal he has gone after.

His planet of wealth, Jupiter, is in the media sign Aquarius in his second house of money, while Uranus, the television planet, is in Taurus, the money-making sign, in his fifth house of show business. In 1985 he purchased MGM/UA, guaranteeing his movie channel a lifetime of hit movies such as *Gone with the Wind*.

"Whenever there is an opportunity, you take advantage of it. Everybody who is successful does that," reflects Ted Turner.

GOLDIE HAWN

Born: November 21, 1945, at 8:45 A.M. in Washington, D.C.

At first glance you wouldn't think that Goldie was a Scorpio, except for those big, bright, wide eyes taking in everything around her.

She visited me in my little house on Smith Terrace in Chelsea, just off fashionable King's Road, on one of those balmy, sunny afternoons so rare in Britain. She was introduced to me by another actress and friend, Linda Harrison (Leo, born July 26, 1945), whose husband at the time, Richard Zanuck (Sagittarius, born December 13, 1934), was producing the movie *The Girl from Petrovka,* starring Goldie.

She told me she was leaving for Sardinia the next day for a vacation. In the reading I did for her, I said I could see her having a cholera inoculation before she left. She later recalled that after the session with me she had gone to a party and there was the doctor, whom she had been trying to avoid. He was scheduled to give her the dreaded injection. He rushed her immediately to his nearby office and gave it to her. She giggled as she told me about it.

Goldie's romantic life has always been as important as her career, and whenever we meet, whether in Hollywood, London, or New York, we always discuss it.

Goldie grew up in Takoma Park, Maryland. Her father was a violinist and her mother ran a dance school and a gift shop. After high school Goldie taught dancing for a while. She made her professional acting debut at 16, playing Juliet in a production of *Romeo and Juliet* at the Virginia Stage Company, before moving to New York, where she got a job at the 1964 World's Fair. She auditioned for everything in New York and got turned down by some of the biggest directors and was shown the door at the top nightclubs. But she remembers them with a special humor and affection. Especially the time when she was really down and out: "I had a go-go agent who booked me [into] a strip joint in New Jersey. I made twenty dollars for dancing my buns off; he got five dollars of it. I had to dance in sequin pasties on tabletops, with guys exposing themselves. And on top of that I had to hitch a ride back to New York on the back of a truck. I really don't believe the things I went through, but I wanted to be in show business so desperately."

It was this determination and passion that eventually made Goldie a major star. A Scorpio with her Moon in the witty sign of Gemini and the philosophical, good-humored Sagittarius as her Ascendant, she was able to weather the storms and endure the embarrassments of her early show business days.

Through a series of jobs—in Puerto Rico with a rock band, in Las Vegas in a chorus line, and in Los Angeles on an Andy Williams TV special—an agent finally saw her and offered her three segments on *Laugh In*. Director Billy Wilder liked her work so much that he signed her for his movie *Cactus Flower,* for which she won an Oscar in 1969. That was the beginning of Goldie Hawn, superstar.

While her Moon in Gemini has been a major influence—for it brings her humor, good-natured spirit, and wonderful bubbling approach to life into the environment she lives and works in—the Moon also has a strong effect on romance and marriage. Goldie was destined to have more than one important marriage in her life.

Uranus, the planet of talents and television, also in Gemini, enabled her to take her unique comedy talent to television. Sagittarius, her Ascendant, is the sign of the moviemaker, and Goldie has been able to produce as well as to star in some of her films—this once doll-like and dizzy comedienne—the witty Gemini—is now considered one of the most powerful women in Hollywood. Her Mercury, the planet of communication, also in Sagittarius, gives her the ability to write for as well as perform in movies.

The planet of greater good fortune, Jupiter, is in her

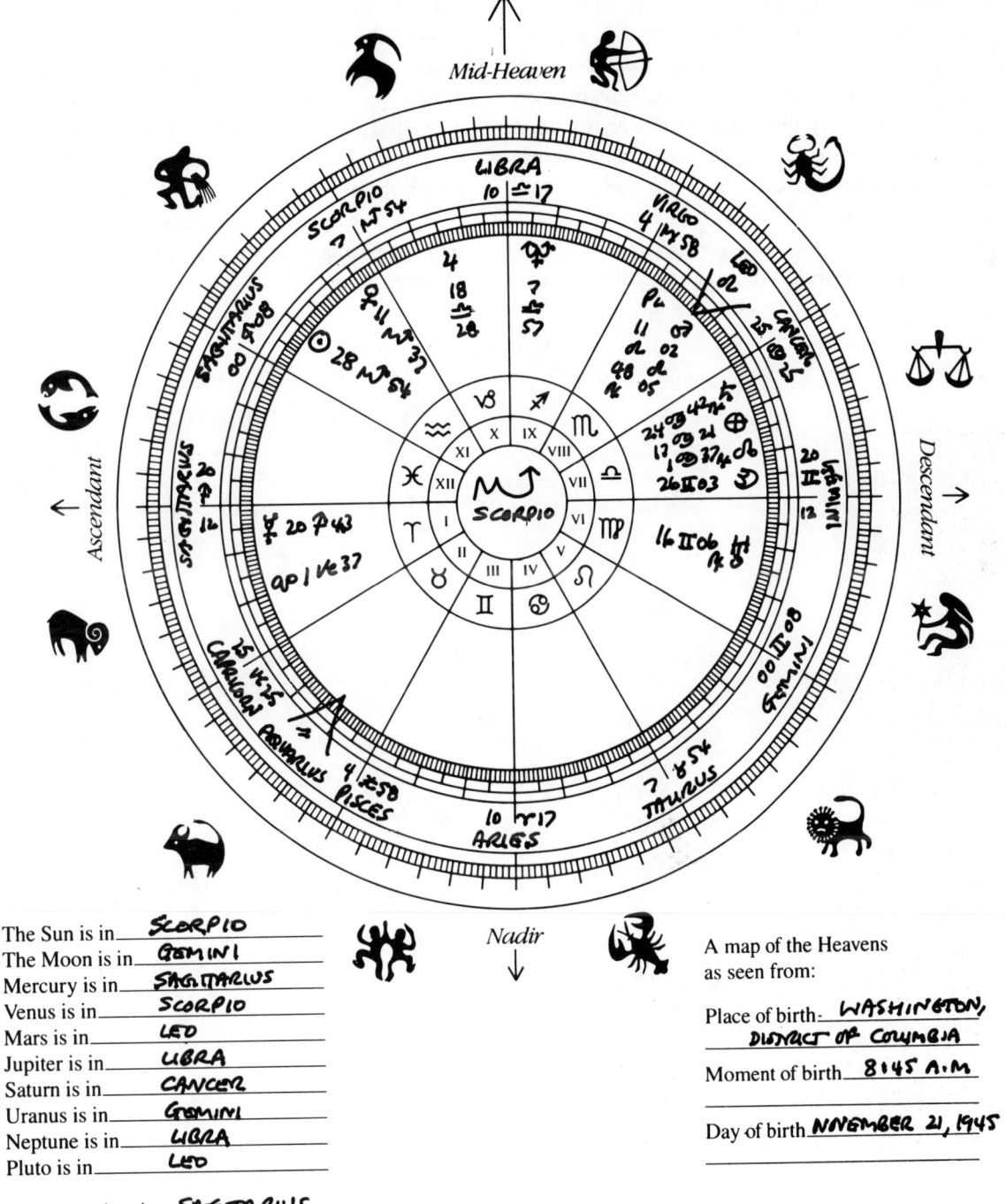

The Sun is in SCORPIO
The Moon is in GEMINI
Mercury is in SAGITTARIUS
Venus is in SCORPIO
Mars is in LEO
Jupiter is in LIBRA
Saturn is in CANCER
Uranus is in GEMINI
Neptune is in LIBRA
Pluto is in LEO

The Ascendant is SAGITTARIUS
The Part of Fortune is in CANCER

A map of the Heavens as seen from:

Place of birth: WASHINGTON, DISTRICT OF COLUMBIA
Moment of birth 8:45 A.M.
Day of birth NOVEMBER 21, 1945

tenth house of career, fame, and honors, located close to Neptune, the creative planet of the movie business, in the sign of Libra, the sign of those who always look young.

Having Saturn in Cancer in her seventh house of marriage has given her a tough time hanging on to a long permanent relationship. Needing someone strong and masculine to help control her life, career, and emotions, she falls in love with equally independent and ambitious lovers (such as current beau Kurt Russell), who either take over or take her for granted when they marry her. Fortunately, she has the North Node in the seventh house of marriage, bringing her rewards, happiness, and fulfillment with her marriage partner. The Moon in that house makes her fruitful, and she was destined to have beautiful and talented children. She has two: Oliver, born in 1976 and Kate, born in 1979.

Her Venus in Scorpio makes her incredibly sexual and sensual in a very innocent and naïve way. She can be temperamental, too, a side she keeps hidden, as many Scorpios do.

Eventually she will have much success, wealth, and good fortune through marriage, as her Part of Fortune is in Cancer in the house of marriage, business partnerships, and contracts.

The warmth she projects, plus the fact that she is so attentive and sincere without any personal vanity or conceit, brings her success in many ways. Would-be rivals and competitors (even other female stars) are easily wooed—in no way threatened by her personality or her achievements. She is ambitious for all those around her, as well as for herself and her loved ones.

Goldie is a true selfless humanitarian in a business in which there is so much cutthroat competition that it is hard to be generous and kind, and she is able to remain impish and inquisitive in a world that sometimes forgets to laugh at itself.

SAGITTARIUS
Philosopher of the Zodiac

SUN IN SAGITTARIUS, RULED BY JUPITER
November 23–December 22

The spiritual idealism and good humor of the planet Jupiter, which rules this adventurous sign, attract all the good things of life—love, wealth, good health, and the abilities to laugh at obstacles and stand up for ideals. The frankness and open nature of Sagittarians could almost be labeled faults, for there are times when the truth should be shielded or tempered to make it more acceptable and less painful. But as their symbol is half-man, half-horse (one half often being wiser than the other), they say things they later regret. Yet they are able to laugh longer and louder than anyone else, particularly about their own failings and troubles.

Believing in their faith, their politics, and their goals so strongly, Sagittarians become leaders who have many worshipful followers and supporters. No one has stronger loyalty to spiritual beliefs, and many become members of the clergy or become involved in religious work as laypersons in their communities. They have a way of making God more palatable—warm and compassionate, not the strict disciplinarian that so many others portray. They love the outdoors, for they are in tune with nature and feel close to the earth, trees, plants, animals, birds, and insects.

Freedom and space are their two biggest requisites for peace of mind. They disappear and roam the fields and mountains, fish in the streams, hunt in the snow, and camp where they can see the sunrise. Although it is hard for them to be tied to any one person or group, they will be loyal if committed to a team or organization as long as they feel that when their commitment has been honored they can escape to their beloved solitude, where they can get into their own thoughts and work on their own philosophy.

Under pressure from others, they have a fortunate way of not really offending by using wit, humor, and the latest jokes to set up their grand exit. They work best on their own, for they hate masters and will not be driven. But if given a free rein, they are the most cheerful and zealous workers, exceptionally honest and optimistic.

Even though they love their sweethearts and admirers to worship them and to be faithful and true, their own behavior and conceit give them the appearance of being flirtatious and unreliable. Once the loved one understands that Sagittarians cannot be tied down, and that their need to be alone is simply that and nothing to do with wanting other affairs or encounters, the possessiveness lifts and feelings of tolerance and devotion replace jealousy and suspicion.

The ninth sign of the zodiac, Sagittarius rules the high mind, spiritual beliefs, logical and judicious thoughts, foreign affairs and international business, travel, and philosophy. Sagittarians can show justice and mercy; they are magnanimous, generous, inspirational, and reverent in all that they do.

In both business and personal relationships with Sagittarians, it is really hard to accept the detachment they display, however affectionate they may try to be. This makes them seem very unromantic and uninvolved, which is not quite the case.

Being so visionary, many Sagittarians are drawn toward a religious or spiritual life, making their marks in higher education and the histories of religion. They aspire to be heads of colleges and universities. Those who worship nature will want a life outdoors, and others will help deprived children in the cities or offer their services to government or community recreational centers. I have met many great film producers and directors born under the sign of Sagittarius. The movies they made were of the highest caliber, often with religious themes or based on biblical stories or Eastern mystical characters. They pass on their vision and interpretation of human beliefs through a light-hearted entertainment medium, still embodying the message and the law.

Their love of travel attracts them to work in the travel business, as tour guides, airline staff, and travel agents, or to jobs that include a lot of travel. The attraction to foreign places makes them ideal candidates for missionaries, ambassadors, teachers in foreign universities, and members of the Peace Corps. They are high on the international lists for athletics, sporting achievements, and other physical competitions. Preferring to be alone, they may choose to ride sharks bareback off the shores of Florida or to track down "Big Foot" in the mountains, with the same sense of determination and success. They are always lucky.

If they end up in routine positions, it won't be for long. If allowed to stay in the job, they would be the most adventurous and speculative bank managers, making millions through their foresight and hunches.

They are horsemen or -women at heart, which—combined with their love of gambling—attracts them to horse racing, betting, and owning stables. I always think of the cowboy and the Indian as symbolic of Sagittarius. After all, the greatest Indian in the tribe was the one who gave the most away, and the second greatest was the one who could steal the most horses from the neighboring tribe.

Gambling Politicians
SAGITTARIUS DECANATE, RULED BY JUPITER
November 23–December 2

With a double helping of good luck and good humor from the planet Jupiter, which rules Sagittarius, these are perhaps the luckiest and most philosophical people of the zodiac. They can laugh at life and see its incongruities in a lighthearted way. These Sagittarians get twice as much help from Jupiter than do the others, and so they are likely to take twice as many chances in life, gamble more than others, and win more prizes and competitions. Rueful visionary Woody Allen is one of these Sagittarian life enhancers.

Adventure and daring enterprise are prerequisites for many. They have no interest in a course of action without risk. Boredom sets in very quickly with them, and they are apt to give up at the slightest hint of conventional methods or a conservative approach to business. They like to create their own style, and because of this they stand out in the world as real characters. They have an undeserved reputation for being frivolous, not to be taken seriously, but when the achievements of the men and women born at this time are listed in the annals of world history, they have done more than many others to establish new and unusual forms of international relations, military strategy, and gambling. Many are athletic and excel in the sports arena, and their mental capacities are equally impressive.

The Confucian proverb "He who doesn't gamble has no luck" was meant for them, but they can even laugh off their rare failures. Whether as children imitating Billy the Kid or as adults changing the political approaches and attitudes of a city or a people, they win more supporters than opponents. Even those who may not approve of the methods used cannot but have some admiration and respect for such daredevils, secretly hoping they will succeed.

As children these Sagittarians would always play jokes on the schoolteacher or sports coach. They would keep the whole class in stitches with elaborate anecdotes about their parents, neighbors, and older brothers and sisters, as well as embellish the way that their team won against great odds in the annual football match with the rival giants from the neighboring town.

Their wit and imagination makes life magical for themselves and others. In love, freedom is vital to these wandering Sagittarians, who are made restless by jealousy. They like equally the euphoria of the best restaurants and hot night spots and contemplative times in a park or garden. They are happiest with signs that can respond to their sense of fun and fantasy, their delight in sumptuousness, and their need to risk all for the possibility of gaining even more. These Sagittarians will promise others a rose garden—and deliver!

SAGITTARIUS

DAVID MERRICK

I sat with David discussing his horoscope chart at Pinewood Studios, during the shooting of *The Great Gatsby*. It was a fascinating meeting, as our paths had crossed several times during my visits to New York, but because of his enormous show business empire there, he never had much time for himself. There were always other people and current productions. A true "gambling politician" of the old school, he was able, by his list of successes, to get angels (Broadway investors) to line up waiting to back his next potential hit.

David Merrick was born in Saint Louis, Missouri, on November 27, 1912, with his Sun, Jupiter, and Mercury all in the optimistic, speculative sign of Sagittarius. With his instinct for hit shows David became known affectionately—and not so affectionately—as the "Abominable Showman." He produced more than eighty major plays, including some of the giants of the American stage. Tony Awards line the shelf of his office for *Fanny; Hello, Dolly; Oliver; Promises, Promises; Gypsy;* and *Child's Play*.

His Venus in Capricorn in the second house of money-making has given him the ability to be practical and frugal, not to inhibit any creative flow but only extravagant overspending. David told me that he had actually brought in *The Great Gatsby* at roughly $6.5 million—a minor miracle considering its opulence and today's movie pricetags. That's gambling for high stakes, as was the phenomenally successful revival of *42nd Street*.

Like a local politician, David was able to get most of Newport society to take part in the party scene for "Gatsby," over 700 of them in their own jewels and finery. David actually negotiated a $1 million loan of jewelry from Cartier to be worn by Mia Farrow in the film. Mrs. Janet Auchincloss (Jackie Onassis's mother) was a frequent visitor to the set, and with her husband, Hugh, threw the elegant start-of-production party for the cast and crew.

His Moon in Cancer makes him rather a recluse, but it also makes him treat his staff like part of an enormous family. Still, he willingly appeared on television to promote his productions.

"I hate all the interview shows, but I do them because I have to become a sort of medicine man, and TV is a great way to do it these days. Easier than standing on a street corner and making a spiel. It sells tickets, and that's part of the job of the producer."

CAROLINE KENNEDY SCHLOSSBERG

An American fairy-tale wedding took place on July 19, 1986, when Caroline Kennedy married Ed Schlossberg, when the Sun was in Cancer, the astrological sign of the United States (July 4, 1776), and all the nation's hearts were with her and her family.

Regardless of her ambitions and dreams, Caroline will always be part of U.S. political history, and her independent spirit is much admired by all those who, along with her, mourned the loss of her father, the late President John Kennedy (Gemini, born on May 29, 1917).

Caroline was born in New York City on November 27, 1957, at 8:15 A.M., and she has her Sun, Mercury, Saturn, and Ascendant in the sign of Sagittarius, the freedom-loving, philanthropic, and philosophical sign of the zodiac.

Her Moon is in Aquarius, the sign of the intellect, and she chose as her husband a man whose personality traits are very much like her late father's.

In her seventh house of marriage partners she has two signs, Gemini and Cancer. Her father was a Gemini, and her husband is a Cancer, born July 19, 1945. They actually married on Ed's forty-first birthday. Ed will help her settle down in peace and quiet in the home she has always wanted so badly.

Despite the public attention given her all her life, Caroline has had the devotion, love, and guidance of her mother Jackie, who had to be both parents for her and her brother John (also a Sagittarius, born November 25, 1960). The two children are a credit to her.

As Jackie once said, "If you bungle raising your children, I don't think whatever else you do well matters very much."

RICHARD PRYOR

Richard Pryor took his explosive, controversial, and satirical comedy and staked his career on it, and he came out a winner. Only he could get away with those sad truths and observations and dramatize them in such a way that comments on social injustice, drug problems, and prejudice could be put over the airwaves. But he hasn't stopped trying to raise people's consciousness of the problems black people still have to face daily.

"Life is great for me. But if I try to get a taxi in New York, they think I want to go to Harlem and go right by me. So what's changed?" Richard observes realistically.

He was born in Peoria, Illinois, on December 1, 1940, at 1:02 P.M. under the sign of the filmmaker and the comedian. His Moon is in the big business sign of Capricorn, in his tenth house of fame and honors. His Ascendant is the mystical, highly romantic, and sensitive sign of Pisces, which also rules drugs and alcohol. He succeeded in overcoming his personal problems with these, turning his whole life around to make himself one of the most fabulously funny film actors in Hollywood. He did it to make money to pay his medical bills, and he was successful.

His big hits include *Stir Crazy, Bustin' Loose,* and *Superman III.*

Richard adds, with his own special humor, "It's been a struggle for me because I had a chance to be white and I refused."

WOODY ALLEN

Born: December 1, 1935, at 6:00 A.M. in Brooklyn, New York

When I arrived in New York in 1964, Woody Allen was appearing at the Bitter End, a most popular comedy spot in Greenwich Village, especially with the students of nearby New York University.

He didn't seem like the traditional vaudeville or nightclub comedian, yet like his other fans I attended his performances as if he were the newfound guru of Manhattan. Perhaps it was his special brand of cynical parody that made him a vocal spokesman of a society soon to be overwhelmed by the Vietnam War—a society that had witnessed the horror of the assassination of President John Kennedy on November 22, 1963.

Woody would use devastating understatement to cut to the core of his subject, whether political or emotional. Before he became a big star, his first wife, Harlene Rosen, sued him when he sniped at her in his first nightclub act.

But it was Woody's destiny to go into the movie industry. He was born Allen Stewart Konigsberg in Brooklyn, New York, on December 1, 1935, at 6:00 A.M. (sunrise), with his Sun, Mercury, and Jupiter all in the sign of Sagittarius, the filmmaker.

Naturally, this combination also gave him his incredible wit and ability to bring humor to situations that could otherwise be tragic, nostalgic, or distressing, without losing human dignity in handling the transcription from idea to vision for the public. And his Sagittarian sense of fantasy has produced such films as the antic, surrealistic *Sleeper,* and the wistfully ironic and romantic *Purple Rose of Cairo.*

His Ascendant, Scorpio, added an intense delving and analytical capacity necessary to get to the root of certain problems and translate them into humorous psychological symbols. Even physically, Woody has the large beak of Scorpio's second symbol, the eagle, and his limbs always look as if they are about to withdraw into his scorpion's shell.

Mercury (the writer and the speaker), his rising planet, in Sagittarius has made him a master of philosophical humor on the screen, onstage, and on records.

But his "groupies" of the sixties (like myself) are still his biggest fans, though he has been able to capture the restless spirit of young people, whether students or yuppies, and transpose his vision of the trials and tribulations of American living onto the screen as entertainment that is sensitive, amusing, and at times outrageous.

Jupiter, the planet of good fortune, is in exactly the same location as his Mercury, and brought him good luck with his writings. His movie *Annie Hall* won three Oscars—best picture, best screenplay, and best director—in 1977. It starred his longtime lover Diane Keaton (Capricorn, born January 5, 1946), whose real name was Diane Hall.

His Moon in Aquarius has given him a strong, independent spirit in his romantic life, even though he has been married twice. (His second wife, Louise Lasser [Aries, born April 11, 1939] starred in the TV series "Mary Hartman, Mary Hartman.") There followed his affair with Diane Keaton, and he is now happily settled with Mia Farrow (Aquarius, born February 2, 1945—a perfect sign and combination for his life-style) and all her children in New York City.

With his Part of Fortune also in Aquarius, he may find his romantic and professional collaboration with Mia a most rewarding partnership in every way. Their association has already produced *A Midsummer Night's Sex Comedy, Zelig, Broadway Danny Rose, Purple Rose of Cairo, Hannah and Her Sisters,* and *Radio Days.*

The planet of music, Venus, is high in his chart in Libra, and his love of playing the clarinet in a jazz group every Monday at Michael's Pub in New York City was his only excuse for not attending the Monday night Academy Awards ceremonies in Hollywood to collect his Oscars.

His Scorpio Ascendant has infused him with the need for self-knowledge, and he visits his analyst at least three times a week. Perhaps this therapy brings out the intimate side of himself that also shows through his brilliant, self-effacing comedy, in which he can joke about the weaknesses and the serious attitudes that others in his profession wear heavily on their shoulders.

Life is unpredictable, but one must make an effort. "After all," as Woody has wisely pointed out, "showing up is 80 percent of life."

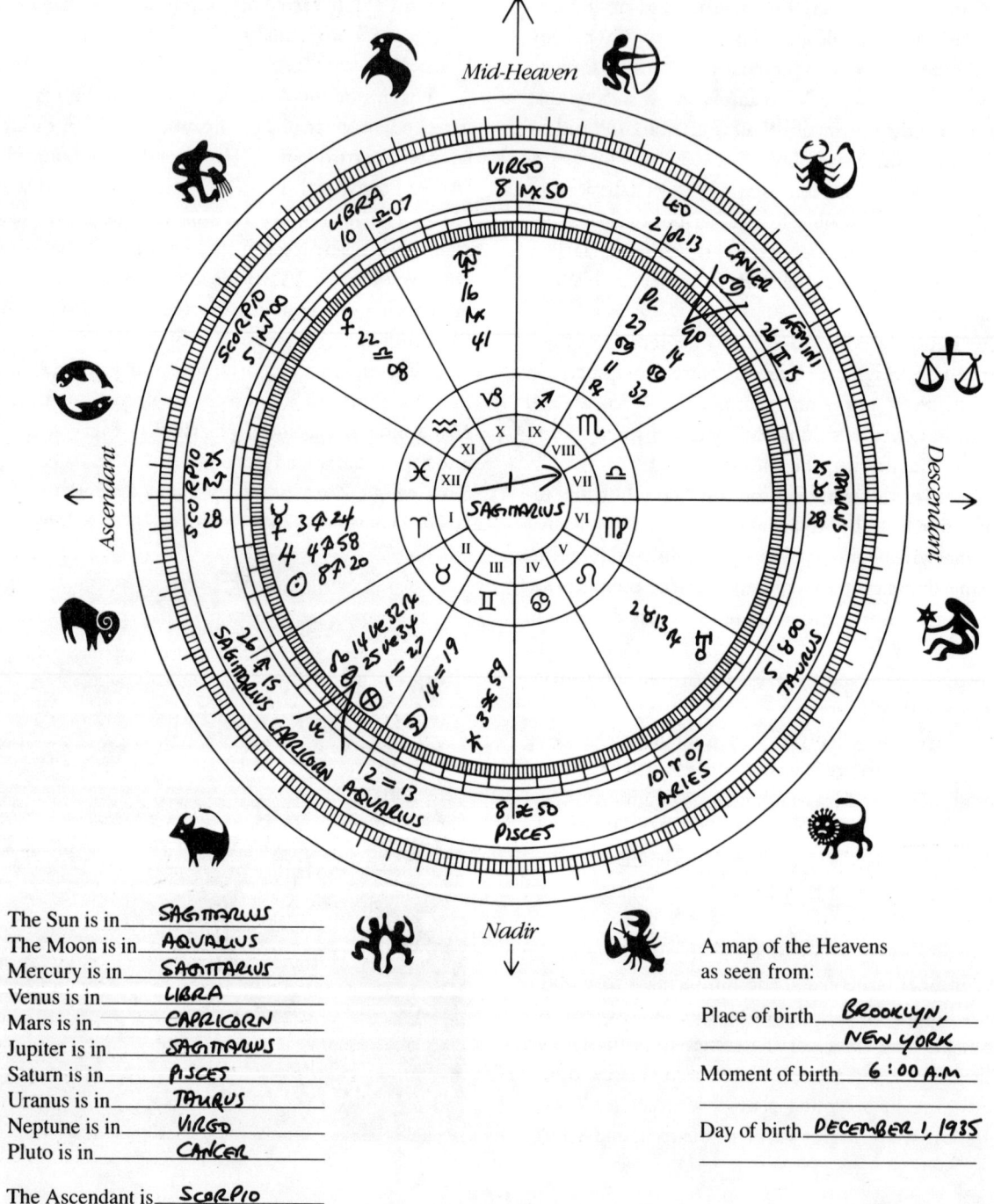

The Sun is in **SAGITTARIUS**
The Moon is in **AQUARIUS**
Mercury is in **SAGITTARIUS**
Venus is in **LIBRA**
Mars is in **CAPRICORN**
Jupiter is in **SAGITTARIUS**
Saturn is in **PISCES**
Uranus is in **TAURUS**
Neptune is in **VIRGO**
Pluto is in **CANCER**

The Ascendant is **SCORPIO**
The Part of Fortune is in **AQUARIUS**

A map of the Heavens as seen from:

Place of birth **BROOKLYN, NEW YORK**
Moment of birth **6:00 A.M**
Day of birth **DECEMBER 1, 1935**

Humorous Missionaries

ARIES DECANATE, RULED BY MARS
December 3–December 12

Bundles of nervous energy bursting with creativity, whose philosophy is that the only way to fight life's battle is to see the funny side of everything, these Sagittarians are a mixture of the idealistic and jolly planet Jupiter and the militant, energizing planet Mars. They have a peculiar wit that will touch the heartstrings one moment and have their audience rolling in the aisles the next. Theirs is the spirit of the clown whose antics and playful tricks have children clapping their hands with glee or weeping when it appears that he has been hit by a well-aimed plank or run over by a carnival car. They cannot keep still in their desire to get their message across, and so they become world travelers, explorers, ceaseless performers (like Frank Sinatra), and street-corner evangelists.

The newscaster reporting from the front lines, the filmmaker making a documentary about starving children in deprived areas of the world, the clown or joker on television reminding us that "the devil" makes us do it, the humorist digging a verbal needle deep into the heart of the matter, or the warrior making a futile last stand (idealistic to the last yet the butt of many jokes in history)—all have the wonderful personality and attitude of these Sagittarians.

Never at a loss for words, never willingly holding back the giving of love and affection, never stepping away from their religious vows, they are more expansive and exploratory than dogmatic. But once they have set their goals and their hearts on a theory or a faith, they are the greatest supporters and financial sponsors. They love to bring joy to the world through their writings, performances, and music. Many great singers, composers, and lyricists who lift the spirits, create an atmosphere, and prepare everyone for the parade were born in this period.

As children they would always fight and play games of strategy, delighting in cowboys and Indians, hide-and-seek, and physical games of skill played indoors on a rainy afternoon. More restless than most children, they would jump from one hobby to another. A game played too long would bring on a practical joke or a temper tantrum. Horses were a big attraction, and those who lived in the country would spend hours caring for their favorites; others would learn to ride with great skill, emulating their fictional Western heroes or winning cups and ribbons at the local horse show annually.

Noisy, they want their message to get across. They have no use for quiet, subtle advertising; they have the glamour and pizzazz to put over even the most blatant and tasteless promotion to smiles, applause, and approval instead of the expected sneers and ridicule. Life is one big rodeo (or stampede) to them, and it doesn't matter how many bodies hit the dust—the spectacle alone warrants the broken bones and bruised pride.

In love these romantic warriors get a fair share of bruises, but mainly to the heart. They are not willing to give the full attention their loved ones need; their projects and plans are far too important to hold up for a quick love affair or reunion. They can live happily independent with numerous lovers on call, but they will strive to find the perfect partner who would be willing to put up with the poor treatment meted out by these exciting but questionable love mates. They need freedom and will kick down the doors if they feel themselves prisoners of love. And they will break down the doors with an ax if they think they have been locked out.

They are fighters in and out of bed, humorists in and out of bed, and lovers in and out of bed. And they must always be the victor, the entertainer, and the adored or they will look for another audience.

ELLEN BURSTYN

Ellen really is an actress with a mission—one who is willing to take on responsibilities to help her profession. From 1982 to 1985 she was the first female president of Actor's Equity, and also in 1982 she was named coartistic director, with actor Al Pacino (Taurus, born April 25, 1940), of the Actor's Studio in New York.

In 1975, Ellen won both a Tony, for *Same Time, Next Year,* and an Oscar for *Alice Doesn't Live Here Anymore.*

Ellen was born Edna Rae Gillooly on December 7, 1932, in Beachwood, Michigan, at 4:00 A.M. The Sun and Mercury were both in the sign of Sagittarius, the filmmaker, and her Moon was in Aries, the sign of the leader, which made her such a good union president for those three years.

Neptune, the planet of film and illusion, and Mars, action and energy, are in exactly the same degree of Virgo, which gives her wonderful organizational abilities and teaching skills.

Her movies include *Resurrection, Harry and Tonto, The Exorcist, The Last Picture Show,* and many others.

A "humorous missionary," Ellen is serious when she says, "I think there's a time in your life when you've got to be of service to other people. I've been very lucky in life and feel I should start giving back."

TERI GARR

We were both appearing on Fox Television's "Midday Show," which was being televised from the furniture department of Bloomingdale's in New York. The hosts were Bill Boggs (Cancer, born July 11) and Lucie Arnaz (also Cancer, born July 17), Teri was promoting her latest movie, and I was making predictions about the Super Bowl.

It was 1978, the Chinese Year of the Horse, so I chose the Dallas Cowboys. There seemed to be a logical tie; after all, the previous season Oakland had won with quarterback Ken Stabler, whose nickname was the Snake, and 1977 had been the Year of the Snake. The Dallas Cowboys won.

Teri was born at 9:30 A.M. on December 11, in Los Angeles, with both the Sun and Mars, the planet of energy, in the sign of Sagittarius, which rules the legs.

Her first career began at thirteen years of age, when she joined the San Francisco Ballet.

With her Moon in Scorpio at the top of her chart, she was destined for a major career, and with her Ascendant Capricorn her special photogenic qualities would soon have Hollywood signing her up. Once she started acting in movies she worked hard. Her more important films have included *Close Encounters of the Third Kind, Tootsie, One from the Heart,* and *Young Frankenstein,* and she has appeared on many TV shows.

Venus is her rising planet in the sign of Aquarius: Teri always looks young, and fresh, and her lighthearted sense of humor compensates for the hardworking individual she is, taking her work and career as seriously as if she were on a mission.

FRANK SINATRA

Born: December 12, 1915, at 3:00 A.M. in Hoboken, New Jersey

Pugnacious, rampant Ol' Blue Eyes has been his own best crusader ever since his earliest days in Hoboken, where his dreams of fame drove him out to sing in roadside cafés and turned him from an awkward boy into a sexy tough. His image as a fighter has followed this Mars-ruled crooner throughout his career. So much has been written about him that he seems like a superpower unto himself, a "missionary" carrying the message of Frank Sinatra to the world. The exploits of Frank Sinatra in love with the world's most beautiful women, doing deals with the world's most powerful underworld figures, eating lunch with the world's greatest politicians and sports figures—whether the gossip that went along with the pictures was true or false, it gave him the glamour and the character that everyone envied. At the edge of the third decanate, there is some of the fighter and lover in him, a man with as many supporters as enemies (who were always looking for a way to damage his reputation). But in true Sagittarian fashion he won every battle and remains the great hero, sex symbol, and star he dreamed of becoming when he leaned against his grandmother's door in Hoboken.

Libra rising whisked him into a world of great art and music and a life-style far above his environment at birth. Like most Libra-influenced people, he was able to surround himself with beautiful things, homes, objects of art, and loving people. Libra rising also gave him the power complex that alludes especially to political circles and adds the diplomatic air that wins through despite all he does to fight it.

His Moon in Pisces gave him his success in movies and also the ability to get the emotions and moods from his songs. One critic wrote, "He really believes those silly words." That is how he was able to hit the hearts of millions, young and old, and stir them into holding hands, kissing, and necking. He was the best ally a boy or girl in love could have—a secret weapon to help melt a rather cold reception.

A Sagittarian with many planets in the houses of travel, he has spent many years traveling the globe. Internationally a superstar of the greatest magnitude, he may still fight when he visits foreign lands, with the press in particular, but that has always been his way. Humphrey Bogart once said: "Frank thinks of paradise as a place with plenty of women and no newspapermen. He doesn't realize he would be better off the other way around."

Married first to Nancy Barbato, with whom he had three children, and later to Ava Gardner and Mia Farrow, he is now happily married to Barbara Marx, a Pisces—which matches his romantic Moon position in Pisces.

His Mercury, planet of communications, is in Sagittarius, making him outspoken but honest. He will often say things he may later regret, but he's proud he said them anyway. With Mars, the planet of war and battles, in his house of career, it was destined he'd have to fight

to get up there and stay up there, but everyone loves a fighter and a sticker with courage. Even his opponents must admit they love to fight a lover. The punches are gentle even if they hit the right places. He still has the image of a sexy tough. Why not? It still packs in the audiences and sells his records.

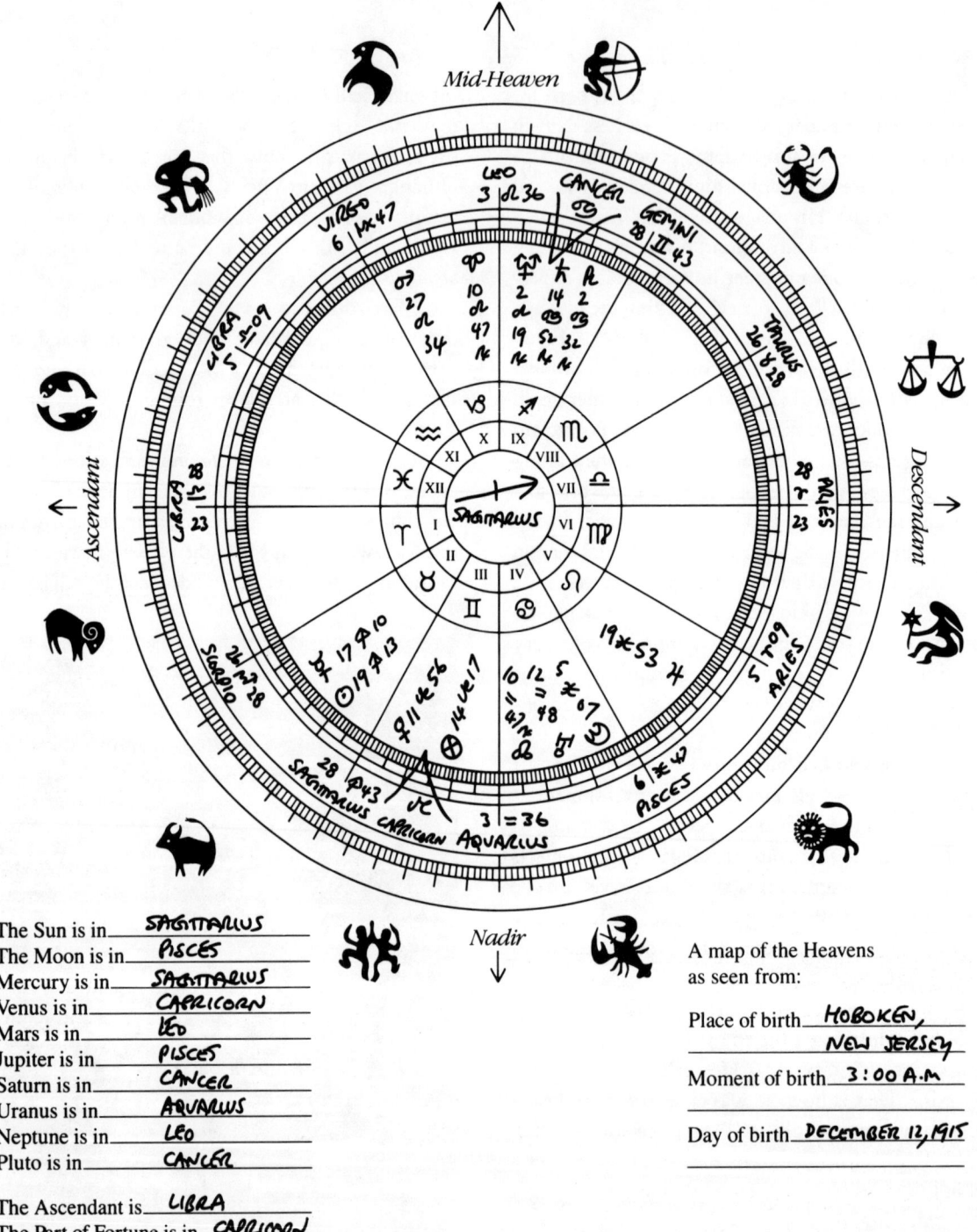

The Sun is in SAGITTARIUS
The Moon is in PISCES
Mercury is in SAGITTARIUS
Venus is in CAPRICORN
Mars is in LEO
Jupiter is in PISCES
Saturn is in CANCER
Uranus is in AQUARIUS
Neptune is in LEO
Pluto is in CANCER

The Ascendant is LIBRA
The Part of Fortune is in CAPRICORN

A map of the Heavens as seen from:

Place of birth HOBOKEN, NEW JERSEY

Moment of birth 3:00 A.M

Day of birth DECEMBER 12, 1915

Fighters and Lovers

LEO DECANATE, RULED BY THE SUN
December 13–December 22

You just can't keep these Sagittarians down. They are so optimistic and magnanimous, yet they have to meet many obstacles and tilt at many windmills, real and imagined, before they get the rewards due them. They have the best of luck from Jupiter combined with the radiance of the Sun. These Sagittarians make good ambassadors and emissaries to foreign lands. They are philosophers who can see at a glance the errors of a whole people and can, with a few lines of poetry or prose, get the message across—creating slogans that become the spirit of the mob and the quotable scenarios of historians. Publisher and producer Bob Guccione is typical of this archer's appetite for effect.

Loving life more than the luxuries and pleasures that it offers, they willingly fight but prefer to live to see another day. They will bargain and placate the foe even when it seems impractical, and they must swallow their pride and appear gullible and tolerant when they would rather be dogmatic and fanatical. Preservation of self and country, of soul and spirit, gives them a strange conceit and a self-righteous approach to final decisions—they are usually out of the palace and on the fastest jet out of the country before the enemy realizes or the time bomb goes off.

In their early years they could be seen charming their competitors on the tennis court, drinking the health of their opponents before a duel, a boxing match, or Indian wrestling. They are great actors and imitators with the perseverance to come back time after time to make farewell speeches when their last movie was not a critical success and they want to win the sympathy of vast audiences. Probably the most popular, if not the most generous people in the class, they could win their way into the most sophisticated dinner parties, secret societies, and exclusive clubs using their charm and dynamic personalities, never allowing anyone to say no.

Lovers with the most sophisticated methods, they have great style and charm. They charm everyone who comes in contact with them and happily fall in love with the person they plan to conquer, for they see no difference between the passions of temper, anger, and hate and the passions of love, loyalty, and idealism. They will win whatever methods they use. They are the double agents who go to bed with both sides, get paid by both sides, and are proudly claimed by both sides as the clever conniver, who gambled, inspired, and won every encounter.

They must always be in love, and they must have a loved one in every town, city, country, and small island that they have to visit. Life and rewards are no good without someone to share them with instantly. They rarely show depth but can be endearingly idiosyncratic and eccentric. Because they are inclined to move around, they tend not to be choosy, not requiring a conversationalist or someone who shares the same sporting or intellectual interest; they are interested in only one thing.

DON JOHNSON

Proclaimed by at least two major celebrity magazines as the sexiest man on television, Don Johnson continues to woo the viewers on the hit prime-time series "Miami Vice," fighting crime in Florida.

Don was born in Flatt Creek, Missouri, on December 15, 1949. His Sun in Sagittarius and his Moon in Libra, with his Neptune in the same sign, gave him the looks that took him into movies and television.

His films include *The Magic Garden of Stanley Sweetheart, The Harrad Experiment, A Boy and his Dog,* and his television appearances include "The Rebels," "Revenge of the Stepford Wives," "Elvis and the Beauty Queen," and "The Two Lives of Carol Letner."

Jupiter (greater good fortune) and Venus (good luck) are both in Aquarius, the sign of television, launching him into a big time television career. Saturn (rewards) and Mars (martial arts) in Virgo (teacher) may help him get through rehearsals and classes in the martial arts. He may take his career too seriously at times and miss all the fun to be had in doing the series. No matter how complicated life is, he can make it seem very simple, but he still feels slightly nervous, knowing how fickle fans and network executives can be.

Determined to establish his popularity, he has negotiated a superstar's salary, knowing that his own self-worth and publicity are just as important as the shows. Don is willing to fight for something he loves, and that includes many more seasons of "Miami Vice."

LIV ULLMAN

The Sun and Leo shine from the serene, strong face of one of the screen's most inspired actresses, a lover of extraordinary philosophical proportions in numerous Ingmar Bergman films such as *Persona, Hour of the Wolf, The Passion of Anna,* and *Cries and Whispers.* As a fighter, Liv's work with the International Rescue Committee has been ceaseless, and she was appointed a UNICEF ambassador of goodwill in 1980, a suitable role for a crusading Sagittarian.

Born in Tokyo to Norwegian parents on December 16 at 7:20 P.M., Liv's Sun and Mercury combination in Sagittarius attracted her to the film industry, while her Pluto and Ascendant in Leo led her later to the stage.

Her Moon is in Libra in the fourth house of home, and it was her work—and characteristically complex love affair—with director Bergman, a Cancer, that led her to stardom. Saturn, the planet of work, in Aries in the ninth house of places far from birth, keeps her traveling, either filming on location or as an ambassador.

A typical life-loving Sagittarius, Liv has told me that her name actually means "life," and she seems almost to overflow at the brim with it. "I think that almost everyone is basically thirteen years old inside," she says.

JANE FONDA

Whether fighting for a cause or for someone she loves, Jane Fonda is both a fighter and a lover. In fact, she married a leader of the antiwar movement, Tom Hayden (Sagittarius, born December 11, 1939), who is currently a member of the California legislature, and all profits from her *Jane Fonda Workout* books, records, videocassette tapes worldwide go to her husband's political organization, the Campaign for Economic Democracy.

Jane was born in New York City on December 21, 1937, at 9:14 A.M. Her father was Henry Fonda (Taurus, born May 16, 1905) and her brother Peter is a Pisces (born February 23, 1940).

She has her Sun and Venus, the planet of beauty, in Sagittarius, the sign of international business, health clubs, and the film industry. Her Ascendant and planet Mercury are both in Capricorn, excellent for business.

Jane's Jupiter, the planet of good fortune, is *on* her Ascendant but *in* Aquarius, bringing her good luck in everything she does. Mars is also in Aquarius, and as the planet rules action and energy, the combination of exercise and video made the workout program the successful and profitable business it is today.

This alignment of planets also brought her success as an actress, and she is the proud winner of two Oscars, one for *Klute* (1971) and the other for *Coming Home* (1978), but she also received Oscar nominations for *They Shoot Horses, Don't They?, Julia, The China Syndrome, On Golden Pond,* and *Agnes of God.*

Jane states, "I am a revolutionary—a revolutionary woman."

BOB GUCCIONE

Born: December 17, 1930, at 2:30 A.M. in Brooklyn, New York

I had written the astrology column for *Penthouse Forum* in London, but it wasn't until I came to New York that Bob and I became friends. Like all Sagittarians, Bob Guccione was destined to have an exciting life, and his crusading spirit, his creative artistic background, and his love of beauty in all its forms made him one of the foremost fighters for the First Amendment's freedom of the press, especially where adult literature was concerned.

It was a big surprise to find that after his long working day, his greatest joy is to entertain at home. He is an accomplished chef, and he would always delight his guests' taste buds with a newly discovered recipe he had created himself. Not wanting to socialize in the popular clubs and restaurants, Bob prefers inviting his business associates and friends to his spectacular home on New York's East Side.

Bob was born in Brooklyn, New York, on December 17, 1930 at 2:30 A.M. His Sun is in Sagittarius and his Ascendant is Libra. His first love was art, and he worked in Rome as an artist, absorbing the great works of art that adorn the city and the Vatican.

His Libra Ascendant attracted him to the fine arts and gave him his visually creative talent, which ranged from oil paints to photography, and he ended up in London where he started his publishing empire.

Because of his Libra rising, his environment would always be one of beauty, and an extensive art collection adorns his walls. Unlike most Sagittarians, Bob prefers to stay at home instead of traveling. Perhaps he got it out of his system in his early years as an artist, and he now concentrates on the worldwide distribution of his publications and the syndication of his television programs.

Many big movie producers and directors are Sagittarians, and Bob moved into the film industry when he produced *Caligula,* about the decadence and depravity of ancient Rome.

Given this, it should come as no surprise to discover that Bob's Moon is in Scorpio, the sign that governs sexual activity and genitals, giving him tremendous ambition and drive. Both in his magazines, *Penthouse, Omni, Viva, Variations,* and *Penthouse Forum,* and in his TV-film production, Bob is daring and adventurous and will fight for his rights to do the things he wants.

His Moon and Venus, the planet of love and beauty, are both in exactly the same degree of the sign Scorpio, making him both attractive to beautiful women and a candid celebrator of them in *Penthouse*. The comparatively new *Omni* magazine offers readers great visual excitement with its twenty-first-century photography and space-age graphics.

Bob's companion and business partner of over twenty years, Kathy Keeton (Aquarius) is responsible for most of *Omni*, always way out in front of other publishers in new formats and presentation; Aquarians are always years ahead of other people with ideas and inventions. Sharing Bob's mansion, Kathy is just as perfect a hostess at dinner parties as she is a dynamic head of a publishing company. They make a loyal, devoted, and loving team.

Jupiter and Pluto, the planets that rule wealth and big business, especially radical businesses like Bob's, are positioned in the ninth house of publishing and legal matters, a combination that has made him rich and fa-

SIGNS OF THE STARS

mous but also brings him occasional court battles. Since both planets are in the sign of Cancer, real estate and property investments can make him much money. As this sign governs the domestic life, Bob is very proud of his five children, especially Bobbie, who has launched himself into a rapidly expanding music, recording, magazine, and book publishing business. This planetary conjunction would also explain Bob's culinary talents.

His Part of Fortune is in the hardworking sign of Virgo. A self-proclaimed workaholic, he works over fifteen hours a day and has honestly earned every penny of his millions.

His enthusiasm for life and his youthful idealism give him the spirit and looks of someone who enjoys every minute of his life, whether he is "fighting" or "loving."

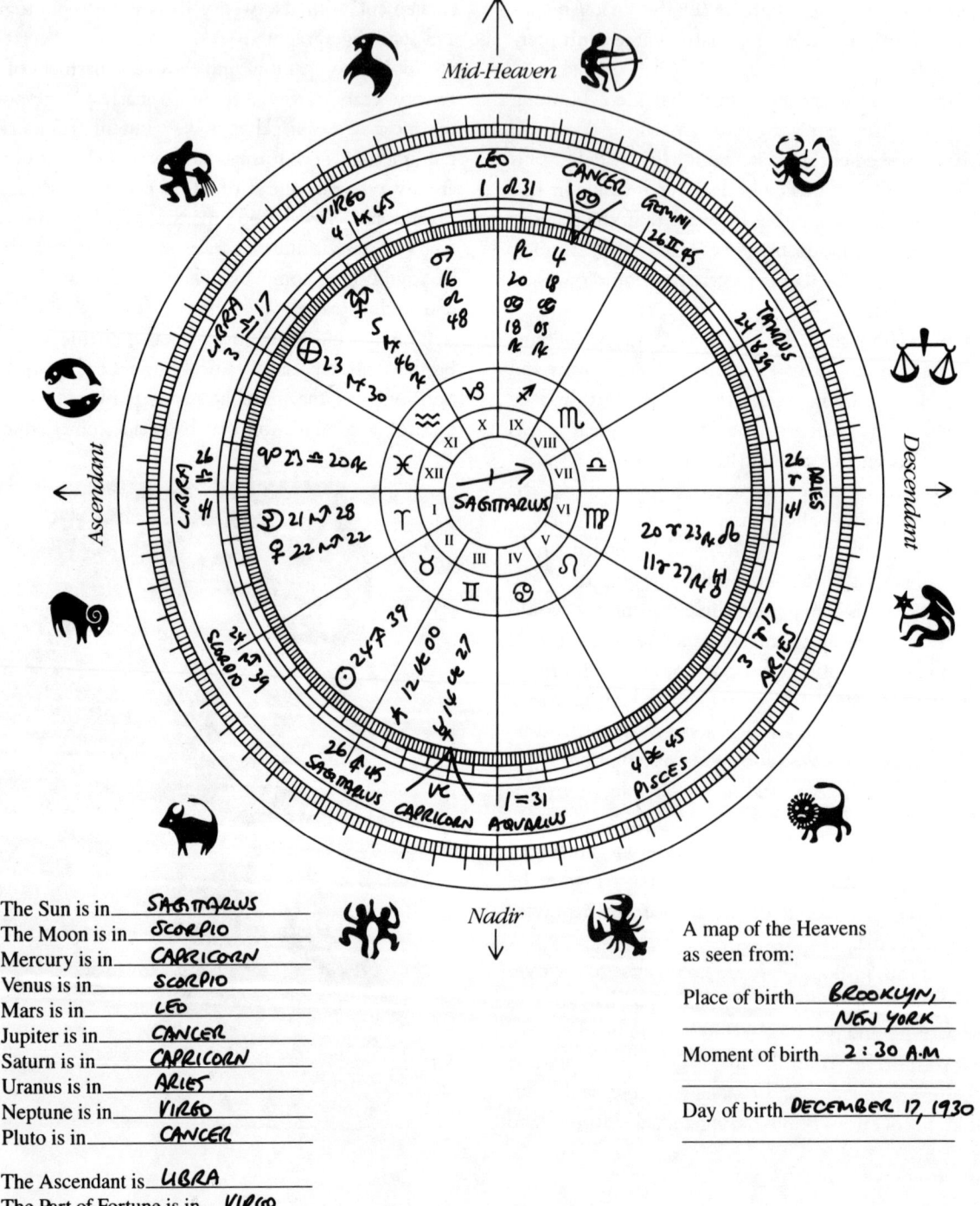

The Sun is in **SAGITTARIUS**
The Moon is in **SCORPIO**
Mercury is in **CAPRICORN**
Venus is in **SCORPIO**
Mars is in **LEO**
Jupiter is in **CANCER**
Saturn is in **CAPRICORN**
Uranus is in **ARIES**
Neptune is in **VIRGO**
Pluto is in **CANCER**

The Ascendant is **LIBRA**
The Part of Fortune is in **VIRGO**

A map of the Heavens as seen from:

Place of birth **BROOKLYN, NEW YORK**

Moment of birth **2:30 A.M**

Day of birth **DECEMBER 17, 1930**

CAPRICORN
Disciplinarian of the Zodiac

SUN IN CAPRICORN, RULED BY SATURN
December 23–January 19

Behind their stern exteriors beat hearts of butter that melt at the slightest injustice, hurt or rejection. Hard to believe, but Capricorns are probably the most sensitive people of the entire zodiac, yet they hate to show their true feelings. That would be a weakness on their part; after all, they demand much from others and won't put up with tears and pleas from those weaker, so how can they allow themselves to show their Achilles' heel? Their serious nature can be boring even to those who love them, and their tendency to criticize and grumble gives them the appearance of being ogres when they are actually hiding from their real selves, projecting a camouflage of words and body language. Their ambitions are their greatest love, and they will be true and honorable to their chosen profession, but once they chose a wife or husband—usually late in life—they are constant, loyal, and loving.

While they discipline others, demanding more than physically or mentally possible, they demand even more from themselves. Seeking perfection and a high level of performance, they will labor over work projects that take others much less time, and for this reason alone they stick to a job or a career and eventually become famous and publicly successful. Both men and women strive for recognition in their field of endeavor, almost to the loss of their marriage at times. They want to be famous, and somehow whatever they do captures the public eye. Whether women's rights leaders, heads of the biggest secret police organizations in the world, producers of some of the greatest motion pictures of all times, or local politicians winning over and over again against all odds, and often against public opinion—they have the great ability to make their losses into assets and their gains appear like victories.

Security is vital to them, and this can turn to miserliness if they are not encouraged by their loved ones to share their rewards. Their systematic accumulation of antiques and heirlooms from other family members who would rather throw these dust collectors out with the rubbish, and their investments in property, cars, and other status symbols, give them the aura and surroundings fit for a top executive, a millionaire, or a capitalist regardless of their political persuasion, which is usually extreme left or extreme right. No perching on the fence for them!

Romantically subdued, they are nonetheless physically skillful in love. They hate to waste time with all the pleasantries and "romantic nonsense" that help to build up confidence and passion in their mates. It is not unknown for them to go for months without telling their loved ones that they really love them. They think their presence is enough, and their spouses can suffer much anxiety through self-evaluation, developing doubts and gradually losing that vital spark. Once this side of them is clearly recognized as normal (for them), the relationship will continue—with sexual pleasures and unromantic dinner conversation.

The feeling of being a scapegoat carries over into much of their work; they are the ones who have to make sacrifices, and they are the ones who must always compromise, both politically and personally. They are the ones who have much sorrow, or so they think, where others have none.

Even with all their success and attainment, they exude a sadness that makes others want to protect them from the hard, cruel world. It is this soft, melancholy character that gives them tremendous public appeal and exceptional photogenic qualities. Their attraction to cameras, tape recorders, and other electronic recording devices makes them excellent photographers, producers, and spokespersons.

Much to the amazement of those who readily come to their rescue when Capricorns are going through outwardly very low periods of their lives, the scheming and plotting that goes on below the surface reaps its rewards in glory. They triumph over all, to the surprise of everyone.

Even in friendship there has to be some element of business—a deal or money-making project that keeps the affection on a well-balanced material and spiritual level. In love there has to be an air of caution, as there is always the underlying fear of losing their loved ones or being rejected for some small weakness or idiosyncracy of behavior.

Perfectionists who would like to rid the world of want, pestilence, and disease, they may also want to impose dictatorial rules and regulations on the masses. They know best. No discussion or argument can sway them from their rock once they have committed themselves. Likewise, no storm can take them off course, and no wave is big enough to swamp their dedication.

Great assets to have on a local football team or save-the-animals committee, they have a determination that will make a success of the project and its goals, and their spirit will be like a rallying flag when they go into the fray. But with others they can be wet blankets, dampers of fiery ideas, especially if they have no true concern or interest. They may show great wisdom and insight into the problems and ambitions of others, but unless their own light is lit they will not be eager to get involved however much they may like or love them.

Unlike the rest of the signs, whose natures depend on a blend of various planetary combinations, the Capricorns' Saturnian influence is so strong that it negates most of the other less severe and serious tendencies, so that all Capricorns are very much alike. They are immediately recognizable through their leadership qualities and political maneuverings; their stubbornness in not giving in to the enemy and refusing to listen to advisers; by their boredom at family get-togethers, weddings, or picnics; and most of all by their ambitious and patient climb up the ladder of success.

Politicians all of them may be, but they are certainly not diplomats. Dictators more than democrats and conservative rather than liberal, they are the upholders of justice and the law—their law, naturally—and they believe what they do is fair and true to thoughts of free people. Their motives are pure, but their methods are something else. If they hate to spend time on all "that romantic nonsense" with the person they love, then their patience won't be long-lived with strangers, enemies, and competitors. Others must ignore and become immune to their blunt and clumsy remarks, even when their sensitivity is hurt. After all, they are great lovers—and through the loyalty of their faithful followers, gained the reputation of great warriors too.

Humble Organizers

CAPRICORN DECANATE, RULED BY SATURN
December 23–January 1

The double Saturn influence in these Capricorns' charts makes them doubly cautious, doubly ambitious, and doubly acquisitive. To those of weaker astrological makeup they become father figures or earth mothers, relieving others of painful decisions, loneliness and fear. While they may create upheaval and sadness in their own lives, they can lift others out of the gutter of despair to float over the garbage and sorrows of living in the modern-day world and see through the mists of idealistic, rose-shaded dreams that with Capricorn's help can become reality. The spunky determination of Mary Tyler Moore, a Pollyanna with personality, has cheered many.

Willing to wage war for their pet cause or loved one, they are like the mountain goat ready to lock horns with the enemy or rival suitor. Their motto is more systematic ambition than practical self-preservation. Their honor is worth more than their bank account, and they are filled to the brim with thoughts of duty and self-sacrifice. Most problems come from their grumbling about all the compromises that they have to make, when it was usually their own idea in the first place.

On meeting anyone, these Capricorns may be turned on and dig into the person's romantic or business life, immediately seeking ways to help one or the other. Should there be a negative reaction, they will immediately appear bored, disinterested, and at worst critical. But the positive, charming, witty, and gay conversationalist in them saves the party should the music stop, the drinks run out, and solemn silence hang like a shroud over the festivities. They are at their best in a crisis.

Timing is very important. Saturn is the timekeeper as well as the disciplinarian of the zodiac, and most of these Capricorns live long lives, for their success tends to come in later years. Meanwhile, they help others make their goals truth and eliminate many of the time-wasting ideas they considered important in their youth. Time and history can change anyone's philosophy. It is the wise Capricorn who learns from the mistakes of other leaders and with this precise and ironclad knowledge brings down the rival warlords, establishing their own brand of "democracy" before the final curtain of life comes down to the accompaniment of cheers, bravos, and encores.

They will falter long before they fall; their limbs will give way years before their brilliant minds. They have the ability to run large empires, to become entrepreneurs in show business, to run gambling casinos like a department store chain, and to head the FBI so securely that no one feels free from the penetrating eye, computer, and files of Big Brother.

In romance they are proficient and exceptionally skilled in all the sexual arts, from Eastern to Western. However, they resent spending too much time at it and may keep an eye on the clock even at the height of passion. Like many earth signs, they are practical. They are just as likely to take a sex break as someone else a coffee or lunch break, and as they are always ready to satisfy their loved ones there is no waiting for a sexual high. In a quick one-night sexual encounter they respond quickly and with rare abandon, giving an Academy Award performance. But should they be interested in a long-term affair or romance with future marriage in view, they are much more cautious and discreet. Then, fearing rejection from the one true love that means everything to them at the time, it will be several meetings before they will show real affection or emotion. Naturally reticent and serious about matters of the heart, they will not express words of love in a flippant or offhand way. Often blamed for their seemingly cruel or unkind behavior for not expressing their feelings, they are nevertheless extremely loyal, devoted, and faithful in marriage. Very few of these Capricorns ever consider separation, let alone divorce.

These Capricorns are better for marriage than for love affairs and flirting. Even with their ability to make an affair seem vital and exciting, it is not in their nature to want to carry the frivolity on day after day. They prefer to put that energy into cementing a marriage or long-term relationship, as every minute of valuable time is precious to them in their climb up the ladder of social and financial success.

RÉGINE

I first met Régine when I visited her club in Paris with international society "playgirl" (as *Newsweek* dubbed her) Cappy Badrutt Hand, with whom I stayed when I visited France.

Régine is one of the most successful nightclub owners, with clubs in nearly every major city in the world, through which have passed nearly all of the world's most important leaders, entertainers, and business moguls.

She was born Régine Zylberberg, in Brussels, Belgium, on December 26, 1929, at 9:00 P.M., and during the war grew up in hiding in a Catholic convent when her father was taken to a detention camp.

Her Sun and Mercury are in the business sign of Capricorn, and she travels the world visiting her clubs. Her Moon is in the sensual sign Scorpio: "I love the glamour, the sophistication, and the sexiness. Remember I came from the streets," she says.

Mars, the god of war, is naturally in the fourth house of home and parents, and this determined Capricorn's childhood nightmare has driven her to succeed and create her own security.

Her Ascendant sign is Virgo, which rules service to others, food, and fashion, all of which are emphasized in her disco palaces.

The Sun highlights her fifth house of show business—Régine is also one of France's most loved recording stars—and what Régine delivers is entertainment, with her customers as the stars (many of them are), creating their own ambience. Jupiter, the planet of greater good fortune, located in the tenth house of achievement and fame, gives her success in all she touches.

JOHN DENVER

It is appropriate that John, born under the sign of Capricorn, the "mountain goat," would be so well known around the world for his megahit "Rocky Mountain High," which sold over a million records. Similarly, his compassion and concern for the welfare of others—a reason so many of his sign enter politics—is widely known, as he uses his concert tours as a platform to publicize his commitment to ending world hunger.

John was born Henry John Deutschendorf, Jr., on December 31, 1943, at 3:55 P.M. in Roswell, New Mexico. As well as his Sun, he also has the planet Mercury, the communicator, in Capricorn. His Moon is in the emotional, sensitive sign of Pisces, and his Ascendant is the mercurial Gemini.

Having Mars (energy), Uranus (recordings), and Saturn (rewards and work) also in Gemini in the twelfth house of producing behind the scenes indicates that a great deal of his talent is put into his recordings as well as his performances.

The Moon in Pisces is at the top of his chart in the house of fame, and in addition to his singing, John starred opposite George Burns (Capricorn, born January 20, 1896) in the movie *Oh, God!*

The restless spirit of his Gemini planets inspired his "Leaving on a Jet Plane" and "Fly Away" (which he did with Olivia Newton John, a Libra).

Changing his name to Denver "because of the connotation of the mountains," John's interests include forestry, hiking, the martial art of aikido, and skiing. He enjoys the wonders of nature and wide-open spaces. Knowledgeable about many areas of metaphysics, he is particularly involved with investigating pyramid power, he studied EST, and he is fascinated by space exploration.

He sings about the wonderful things of life, about loving one's mother, about sunshine, and happy tears. Describing his philosophy, he says, "Everybody else is talking about how hard life is, and here am I singing about how good it is to be alive."

MARY TYLER MOORE

Born: December 29, 1937, at 12:15 P.M. in Brooklyn, New York

I get a big thrill from watching Mary Richards, heroine of the "Mary Tyler Moore Show," knowing that Mary Tyler Moore has made herself a multimillionaire television tycoon. Her company grosses over $25 million a year.

It just seemed so unlikely that perky, pussycat comedienne Mary could also become the power behind her own empire. But that's one of the benefits of being born under the sign of Capricorn, and it demonstrates that there must be some aggression and determination under that vulnerable, girl-next-door, feminine veneer.

Mary is a hardworking Capricorn with Aries as her Ascendant (that explains her drive). Her Moon is in Sagittarius, the sign that rules legs and sense of humor. One of her first show business jobs was in the TV series "Richard Diamond, Private Detective," in which she played Sam, Diamond's sultry-voiced contact at the answering service. Her voice was heard, and she was filmed only from the waist down to show off her wonderful legs, but her identity was not revealed.

Uranus, the planet that rules television, is her rising planet in her first house, making her a natural for the medium, and giving her the comic instincts (Uranus) that combined with her amazing sense of timing (Capricorn rules clocks).

In her house of producing and organizing, Mary has Mars, the planet of action; Saturn, the planet of work and rewards; and her Part of Fortune all in Pisces. This twelfth-house influence on her life has made her a major force and power in the media, but it has also brought many difficulties and hardships as well as personal suffering through family tragedies.

Pisces is the sign of illusion, of the filmmaker. In her brilliant transition from comedienne to serious actress, Mary was able to win a Tony Award for her portrayal of a paraplegic in *Whose Life Is It Anyway*. She won an Emmy playing a cancer-ridden television reporter in "First, You Cry," and in 1980 she was nominated for an Oscar for her role as the mother in *Ordinary People*. The film won best picture, best director (Robert Redford), and best supporting actor (Timothy Hutton).

Ordinary People told the story of a family torn apart by the accidental death of a son. Tragically, the year the film came out, her own son accidentally shot and killed himself. (Pluto, the planet of drastic changes in her fourth house of family indicated a loss or separation from a family member under unusual circumstances.)

In her sixth house of work and health, Neptune, the god of the sea, ruler of liquids, and body fluids (as well as of the more creative filmmakers), while giving her success with her acting and movie career also brought her problems with diabetes.

As in so many successful people's charts, the pendulum seems to swing in equal proportion from suffering to joy and happiness.

In her tenth house of career, fame, and ambitions, Mary has the wonderful, jovial, beneficent planet Jupiter. Luck has been with her even during the worst times, and she has been able to regroup her team, pull herself together, and overcome the obstacles and emotional traumas. Success is always there for her whenever she chooses to go after it.

Her Sun in Capricorn is exactly located with Mercury, the planet of communication. She has been able to express herself through comedy and her astute characterizations in her various roles: "As a comedienne, I'm an observer of life and people."

Marriage is not easy for an ambitious Capricorn, especially when her Ascendant Aries and Moon sign Sagittarius both need a lot of independence and freedom. Her first marriage was to Richard Meeker, the father of the son who died. She then married a fellow Capricorn, NBC-TV chief Grant Tinker (born January 11, 1926), in 1963. They split up in 1980. She married Dr. Robert Levine in 1984, a happy relationship, ideal for her. He is fifteen years her junior.

"I am still a person who enjoys having control. But I know there are some things over which you have no control," she says philosophically (the "humble organizer"), "and you just have to accept that."

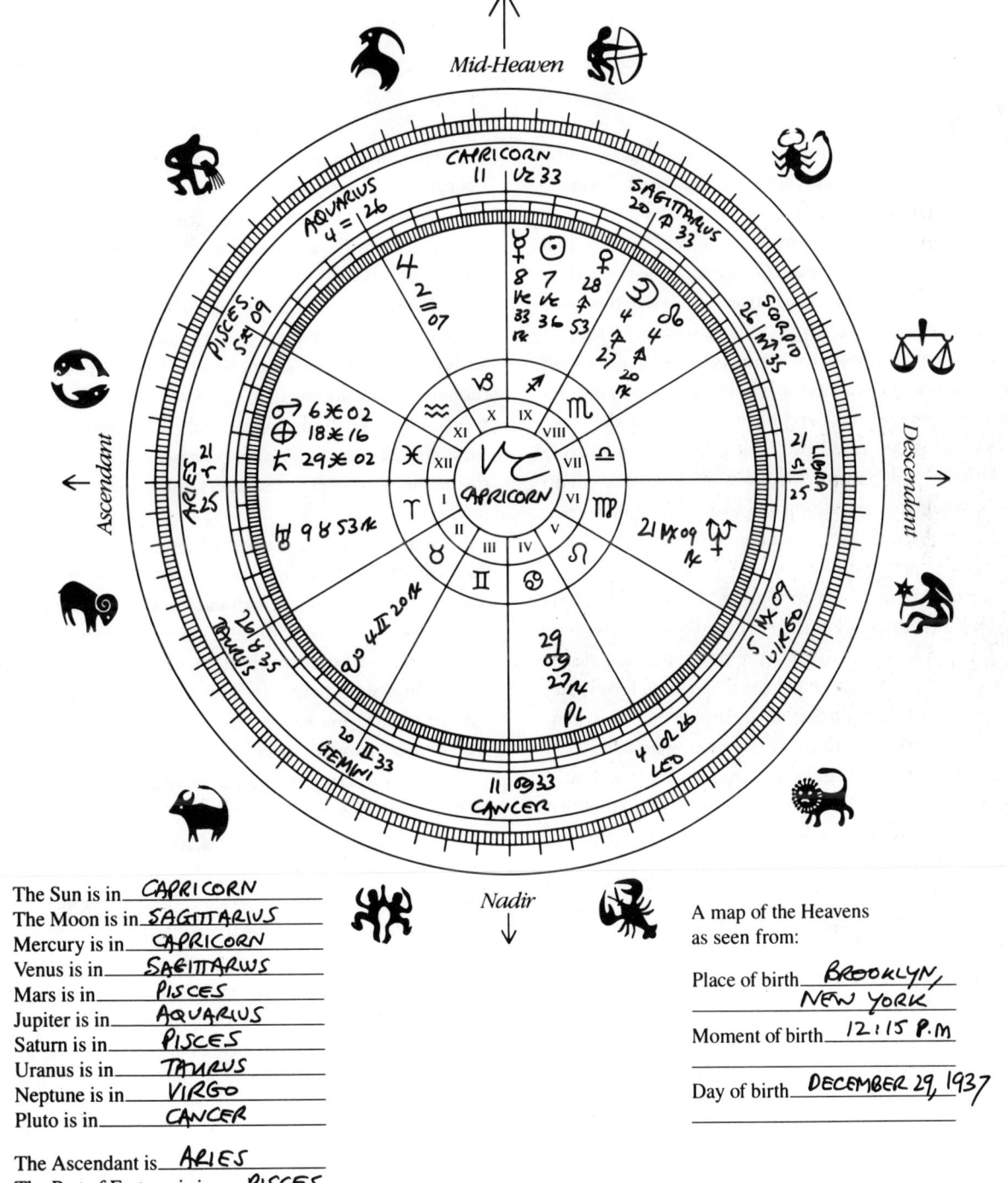

The Sun is in CAPRICORN
The Moon is in SAGITTARIUS
Mercury is in CAPRICORN
Venus is in SAGITTARIUS
Mars is in PISCES
Jupiter is in AQUARIUS
Saturn is in PISCES
Uranus is in TAURUS
Neptune is in VIRGO
Pluto is in CANCER

The Ascendant is ARIES
The Part of Fortune is in PISCES

A map of the Heavens as seen from:

Place of birth BROOKLYN, NEW YORK

Moment of birth 12:15 P.M

Day of birth DECEMBER 29, 1937

Stubborn Politicians

TAURUS DECANATE, RULED BY VENUS
January 2–January 10

Despite their outrageous public behavior, their gyrations and verbal battles, their heretical slogans and strange beliefs, they are led by what they think is the power of right over wrong and by faith that God—whoever or whatever God may be—is on their side. They tell themselves that it is love—whether love of their fellow human beings, love of justice, or love of revolutionary change—that compels them to make such drastic moves, that can get a whole nation rallying behind them one moment and burning them at the stake the next. They are ruled by Venus, the goddess of love and beauty, and Saturn, the strict disciplinarian who metes out rewards both good and bad. Actor Jose Ferrer, who works hard to create radiant characters, shows the best of this combination.

The rock star whose screaming fans tearing off his satin breeches, the yoga teacher whose flock follows him over thousands of miles and sits entranced by his words (which they only understand on a spiritual level), the revolutionary who murders all his opponents to set up a perfect world, and the world leader who is caught spying on his enemies, to be deserted by his friends and only exonerated by history—these are the "stubborn politicians." Whether pushing entertainment, religion, or street politics, each believes in the love and protection of God, each believes that they have the answer, and each is followed by thousands, if not millions, who confirm what they say.

They are never bored, yet they can feel lonely even in a crowd for they need a sense of affection and love around them. Very musical, they will get their groups singing boisterously to keep their spirits up. They are patriotic and devoted to their country and its flag and everything it represents. When low and sick at heart they call on their dearest and closest loved ones—their spouse, children, friends, and neighbors. As children they would be given leadership jobs at school and in their youth clubs. They were favorite monitors among schoolmates because they were always fair in designating authority and distributing chores. Their ability to make money would show early, and even in their teens they would come up with unique and clever ways to add to their pocket money, buying expensive bicycles and electronic gadgets or tape recorders and rock music instruments.

Their entrepreneuring abilities often carry on into their adult lives, when they become entertainment managers, theatrical agents, and producers of rock albums. Those with performing talents could easily handle an audience, and while making records would not appeal to their big-business minds, they will see the great potential for making money by making the occasional gold record with its million copies circulating the country.

These Capricorns need a marriage that will give them a sense of love and security. The love nest will be the center of entertaining and a welcome retreat when things become too pressured at the office. They like to share their friends and will regularly organize parties to introduce new and exciting acquaintances to each other, occasionally playing Cupid to the single, unattached individuals. As these Capricorns are such romantics, they appear to get along with all signs of the zodiac equally well. However, they prefer earth and water signs for a serious love affair.

JOEY ADAMS

It would be a happier world if comedian Joey Adams were elected president of the United States and his wife Cindy became first lady. After all, they have been supplying the elected presidential couple with material to deal with crises for years. Joey has been the official U.S. goodwill ambassador for six presidents (Democratic and Republican) and has helped many a "stubborn politician" become more relaxed and popular. Still, as a Capricorn, Joey has directly or indirectly been attracted to politics.

Born in Brooklyn, New York, on January 6, 1911, Joey has his Sun, Mercury (speaking and writing), and Uranus (talent and media) in the sign of Capricorn, which leans towards politics but also rules timing and clocks. Comedians depend on the timing of their one-liners or punch lines to get the right reaction.

His Mars (action and aggression) is in the humorous sign of Sagittarius, which helps him aim and score with his wicked sense of humor.

But it was his romantic Moon in the sign of Taurus that attracted him to his wife, Taurus Cindy Adams (née Heller), in 1951 when she was trying to become a comedienne. Cindy, whose own syndicated column appears every day in the *New York Post* along with Joey's daily column "Strictly for Laughs," was born in New York on April 24. Her Saturn, which represents her husband, is in Capricorn—a perfect match for Joey.

To quote from his new book *Roast of the Town* (Prentice Hall Press, 1986), Joey says, "This is the land of promise—especially before Election Day."

DAVID BOWIE

Planets are natural habitats to rocker David Bowie, who in his Ziggy Stardust incarnation ushered in the bisexual era.

His stage performances were so over-produced—with props, scenery, smoke bombs, fireworks, and sirens—that eventually he went bankrupt despite the fact that he had sold over two million records and had five gold albums.

Born in Brixton, London, on January 8, 1947, at 11:50 P.M., he changed his name from Jones to Bowie for the American hunting knife. He is a Capricorn with the Sun, Mercury, and Mars all in the sign.

His Moon, Pluto, and Saturn, all in the show business sign of Leo, attracted him to rock and roll, and later to acting in movies, including *The Man Who Fell to Earth* and *The Hunger,* and to Broadway, where he starred in *The Elephant Man.*

His Libra Ascendant gives him his tall, slim looks, and Neptune, the creative planet, also in Libra, first attracted him to commercial art, then advertising, and then music, with great emphasis on visual appearance and production. Neptune, god of the sea, also gives him his vivid, fertile, and colorful imagination. "I am an instant star," he says. "Just add water and stir."

JOSE FERRER

Born: January 8, 1912, at 10:15 P.M. in Santurce, Puerto Rico

Some of the most famous celebrities in London came to my house in Smith Terrace in Chelsea, either to consult me for an astrological reading or to see director Jack Clayton (Pisces) and his longtime associate Jeanie Sims, who used the basement as their production office for such films as *Room at the Top, The Bespoke Overcoat, The Innocents, The Pumpkin Eater, Our Mother's House,* and *The Great Gatsby.*

So it was that I first met Jose Ferrer. Jack Clayton had been associate producer of *Moulin Rouge.* Jose's great performance as Toulouse-Lautrec in that film remains in my memory forever.

Jose invited me to join him and his guests for dinner at the Thameside White Elephant restaurant. We discussed his horoscope and his amazingly versatile career.

Born to well-to-do parents, he moved to the U.S. mainland as a child. A Capricorn with his Moon and his Ascendant both Virgo, he was destined for a life of hard work, great achievement, and many rewards. And his Sun, located in the fifth house of show business, indicated where his success would lie.

In 1980 Jose was inducted into the Theater Hall of Fame. Only a Capricorn would be willing to devote his life to perfecting his craft, and it took the Virgo influence of his Moon and Ascendant to drive him to polish the fine details of his performances, characters, speech, and movement. Not only is Jose his own strongest disciplinarian, but he also encourages and brings out the best in other performers when he directs them.

Jose has never been put in a Hollywood or Broadway pigeonhole. His career has included memorable roles in *Cyrano de Bergerac, Richard III, Charley's Aunt, The Shrike, Joan of Arc, The Caine Mutiny, Lawrence of Arabia, Ship of Fools, A Midsummer Night's Sex Comedy,* and *Dune,* to name but a few. He won a Tony for *Cyrano de Bergerac* on Broadway, in 1947 and the Oscar for the movie version in 1952.

His Pluto in Gemini, in his tenth house of fame, gave him his resonant, multifaceted, and pleasing vocal quality, speaking skills, writing talents, and ability to create his bigger-than-life characters and still make them believable and vulnerable. He is always fine-tuning his instrument.

Love is very important in his life. Capricorns by nature appear more independent than other signs of the zodiac, yet they are the most sensitive, trying to hide this side of themselves from their loved ones, family, and public. His Sun, in the fifth house of love affairs, romance, and children, has brought him happiness, but the planet of sudden changes, Uranus, has created many emotional ups and downs. His first wife was actress Uta Hagen (Gemini); they had one child, Leticia. He then married Phyllis Hill. His third wife was singer Rosemary Clooney (Gemini), with whom he had five children—Miguel Jose, Maria, Gabriel, Monsita Teresa, and Rafael. He is now happily married to his fourth wife, Stella Daphne Magee.

His Venus and Jupiter, both planets of good luck, are in his third house of writing and communication in the sign of Sagittarius, the filmmaker. They give him the ability to take an idea or a role and recreate it on the screen as an actor, director, or writer. Mercury in his fourth house, also in Sagittarius, shows him working out of his home or place of residence. That is why New York City is such an ideal location for him, as he lives close to his beloved Broadway. He can walk to work.

CAPRICORN

Idealistic and a "stubborn politician," he took on the New York theater critics when he disagreed with their reviews of one of his plays on Broadway. He was vigorous in attacking them, as befits a man of great integrity—one who believes in what he is doing at all times and knows the right time to draw attention to his business.

It was important for Jose to go to college, as his Mars, the planet of energy, and his Part of Fortune are both in Taurus in the ninth house of higher education. It was while studying architecture at Princeton University that he discovered dramatics. That was the turning point in his life. In another setting, he might never have been attracted to show business.

He doesn't allow personal, financial, or emotional problems to slow down his progress. Nothing stands in his way, and he is a living example of mind over matter. After all, as he so astutely comments about life's frustrations, "I am more important than my problems."

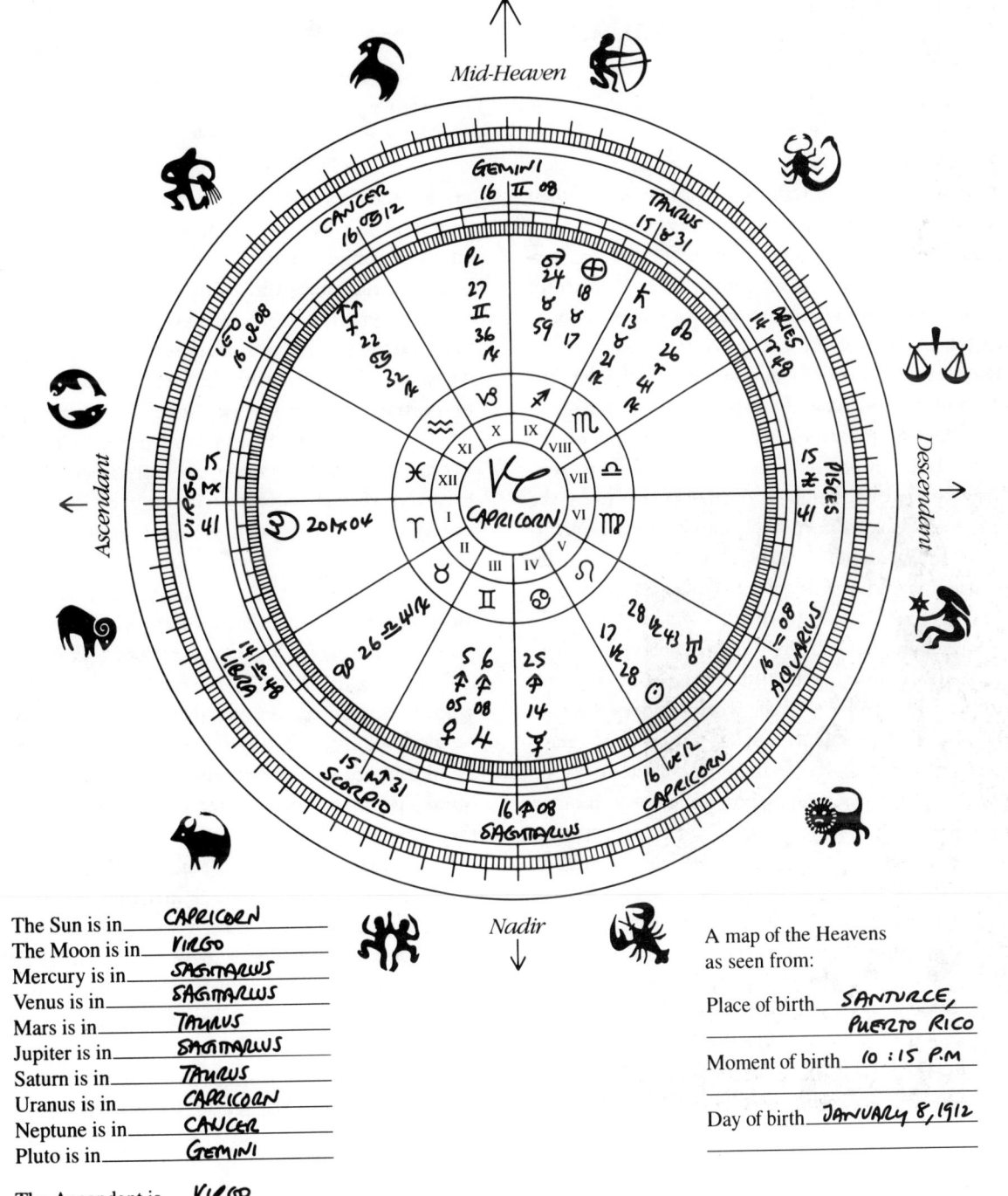

The Sun is in __CAPRICORN__
The Moon is in __VIRGO__
Mercury is in __SAGITTARIUS__
Venus is in __SAGITTARIUS__
Mars is in __TAURUS__
Jupiter is in __SAGITTARIUS__
Saturn is in __TAURUS__
Uranus is in __CAPRICORN__
Neptune is in __CANCER__
Pluto is in __GEMINI__

The Ascendant is __VIRGO__
The Part of Fortune is in __TAURUS__

A map of the Heavens as seen from:

Place of birth __SANTURCE, PUERTO RICO__

Moment of birth __10:15 P.M__

Day of birth __JANUARY 8, 1912__

Idealistic Revolutionaries

VIRGO DECANATE, RULED BY MERCURY
January 11–January 19

More than anything else they want their work, actions, and thoughts to be of service to mankind, for they are a mixture of the servant Mercury and the inspired worker Saturn. The influence of Virgo leads them into fields of endeavor that have social consciousness high on the list of priorities. They are so hardworking that they accomplish more than seems humanly possible and have the charisma to get masses to follow them to the crock of gold at the end of the rainbow. They are less subdued than other Capricorns, for they consistently think of others and try to be the symbol rather than the cause. Rambunctious Muhammad Ali, for example, is almost as well known for his charitable and diplomatic efforts as for his sensational fighting career.

Peace marchers and civil rights workers, foreign correspondents covering United Nations peacekeeping forces in strife-torn parts of the world, underprivileged youths fighting their way out of the ghettos, playwrights who express the feelings and passions of the times through their characters, pop singers who become heroes to their fans, singers and dancers who entertain the troops disregarding personal danger and discomfort, and those who bring joy and hope to little children through international organizations—all have elements of these discriminating and dignity-giving Capricorns.

Even as children they knew that "there had to be something better than this." They had the spirit to get themselves out of the gutter, the slums, the remote village, or the isolated island. With some innate belief that there was someone or something over the horizon that needed their special talent, they would pack their bags and run off while other children were still worrying about their high school homework. Not that they were not academic; many did go to a university, where their rebellious ways are still recalled with humor and admiration; others would pursue their studies later in life. Those who became writers or actors would write about or portray characters whose ideology matched theirs, whether head of the FBI or fairy-tale people with important messages to pass on. As entertainers they work hard and are perfectionists, wanting their skills to be an example to students who would follow, admire, and imitate them.

Always plotting and planning, they would have made wonderful revolutionary leaders had they not been pacifists at heart. Feeling that more can be done by love and kindness, they would build up an army of opponents who could not understand their selflessness and who would look for ulterior motives in their innocence. Physically strong and mentally resilient, they are capable of taking a great deal of abuse for the sake of any cause they believe in.

Romantically, they are much more involved with their careers or their goals for mankind, so many stay single for a long time or need a wife-husband-partner relationship, in which both strive for the same idealistic goals. Yet once they give their word or their love, they are loyal—if mainly from being too busy to look for someone else and having taken a long time to make up their minds in the first place! Sexually they are among the best; they have the physical drive and passions of

Capricorn and the desire to please and serve of Virgo. Should they have doubts about their partners' fidelity, they have the uncanny ability to become instantly cool and detached.

These Capricorns are men and women in search of romance through their work. They can miss the boat if they are not careful, remaining missionaries in faraway jungles, ministering to the sick, teaching the eager minds forgotten by nations whose technology has replaced the brains and leadership they once offered. They want love and they will give love; and once they have found their life partner, they will give all the love and romance that is necessary. All they want in return is approval of their goals, their methods, and their dreams for humanity.

ROBERT STACK

It seems as if Robert has always been an idealistic revolutionary, fighting crime in one form or another. First with his internationally famous role as Elliot Ness in the television series "The Untouchables," which ran for four years and is still playing reruns twenty-three years later, and which launched his superstar career and won him an Emmy. He followed with another series, "The Name of the Game," on which he portrayed the editor of a crime magazine, and two other police action series, "Most Wanted" and "Strike Force."

Born on January 13, 1919, at 4:30 P.M. in Los Angeles, he is a Capricorn with his Moon in Gemini, the communicator, and his Ascendant Cancer, the sign of the United States. The Ascendant shows where he would most excel, and there is nothing more American than the FBI, unless it is apple pie.

As his father was a millionaire advertising man, and his grandmother was the renowned singer Marina Perrini, Robert grew up surrounded by famous celebrities who were guests at his home. With his ruggedly handsome good looks, Robert was a flirtatious and flamboyant Hollywood playboy until he met starlet Rosemarie Bowe in 1956.

His Cancer ascending, together with Jupiter and Pluto in that domestic sign, really needed a secure domestic base, a family environment, with a wife and children to share it. Rosemarie, a Virgo born September 17, fulfilled his most romantic dreams, and they have been together now for thirty years. In Rosemarie's chart, Saturn is in Capricorn, thus her perfect choice for a husband was Robert.

Robert's Neptune (fragrance) and Rosemarie's Venus (fashion and beauty) are both in exactly the same degree of Leo, the showman, and they have formed their own fragrance and fashion company, Rosemarie Stack, Ltd. Their popular television show, on which they both appear, "It's a Great Life," adds another dimension to their busy lives.

Nominated for an Oscar for *Written on the Wind*, he has starred in many films since 1939, when he appeared in *First Love.* His other movies include *The High and the Mighty* (1941), *Is Paris Burning?, Airplane,* and many other favorites.

It was his Part of Fortune in Sagittarius, in the fifth house of show business and sports, that gave him first the skill to be a champion skeet shooter at age sixteen (Sagittarius is the man on a horse aiming an arrow) and then the love of horses that helped him major in polo at the University of Southern California. The influence of Sagittarius, then took him on to stardom.

PATRICIA NEAL

Winning an Oscar for her role in *Hud* in 1963, an Oscar nomination for *The Subject Was Roses* (her first film after recovering from a massive stroke), and a Tony for her Broadway debut in *Another Part of the Forest* in 1947, Patricia Neal is a winner in everything she does.

Unable to speak, read, write, or walk because of her stroke, after only three years of intensive therapy, Pat was acting again, with the typical drive and determination of this sign. Since then she has never stopped, and when she isn't performing, she is touring the country giving her autobiographical lecture, "An Unquiet Life."

Born in Packard, Kentucky, on January 20, 1926, at 4:00 A.M., Pat is a Capricorn with Aquarian influences, as her planets Jupiter and Venus are both in the sign of Aquarius, bringing her good luck with television.

I was invited to attend the surprise birthday party given in her honor by publicist Barry Landau (Gemini), who since law school has coordinated special events for various administrations. He invited many of his political and show business friends from Hollywood, New York, and Washington, D.C. It was held at the Watergate Hotel in Washington, D.C. the weekend of the presidential inauguration in which we had all participated. A throng of well-wishers was there to greet her including Tom Selleck (Aquarius) and his girlfriend Jilly Mack (Capricorn), Rich Little (Sagittarius, born November 26, 1938) and his wife Jean, Jamie Auchincloss (Jackie Onassis's half-brother, a Pisces, born March 4), Francis Humphrey-Howard, the late Senator Humphrey's sister, and Tyrone Power, Jr.

Bette Davis called to send her regrets at missing the party as she was snowbound in New York. Barry in a mood of mischief called Bette back and put Rich Little, impersonating Jimmy Stewart on the line. Before saying goodbye, however, Rich confessed who he was. The party guests couldn't wait to tell Jimmy Stewart and his former roommate President Reagan what had happened.

With Jimmy and the President laughing uproariously Jimmy, always the gentleman, thought he should call Bette back and clarify matters. The President humorously cautioned that Bette would probably think he was Rich Little and hang up.

Pat tantalized guests with Hollywood stories, one of which was her confession that while in High School she wrote love letters to Tyrone Jr.'s father, years before she co-starred with him in the movie *Diplomatic Courier* in 1952.

Idealistic in everything she does, she has the most amazing strength and fortitude, perhaps because of the location of her Moon in Aries, the warrior, the fighter, and the general. And her humanitarian Aquarius traits have helped her turn around the difficult experiences and tragedies in her life and to help others, less philosophical, to understand and to get over their crises, too.

"In everyone's life a lot of bad things happen," she says. "I just seem to have a larger dose of the bad things."

MUHAMMAD ALI

Born: January 17, 1942, at 6:35 P.M. in Louisville, Kentucky

For many reasons, being summoned by Muhammad Ali to visit his training camp in Deer Lake, Pennsylvania, was probably the most exciting moment of my life. Part of it was meeting with a great social hero, a champion, and feeling the aura of inspiration he gave to others, young and old, who were active at the camp. Second, being asked to work on his astrological chart, as well as those of his wife and all his children, seemed to me a very sincere and trusting gesture, particularly as I was going to indicate astrologically the results of his upcoming big fight in Kinshasa, Zaire, when he would attempt to regain his world heavyweight title from George Foreman.

In true Capricorn style, Ali had built the camp among the hills and thick trees of Pennsylvania. Made of logs, the cabins and the main gymnasium formed three sides of a square that blended nicely into the scenery and overlooked a spectacular view from this high point.

Ali is very sensitive and gentle in person and very considerate of other people's feelings and comfort. It is only when he is in front of the camera or in the public eye that the former Cassius Clay suddenly becomes Muhammad Ali, the celebrity, the actor, the "greatest."

It is his Leo rising that made him such a fine showman in his fighting career and later in his short-lived acting career. Even when he starred in *The Greatest*, in which he played himself, he received rave reviews, and I still remember his memorable performance in the NBC miniseries "Freedom Road," in which he played a slave, a Union soldier, and a U.S. senator.

His horoscope chart showed that he would win by a knockout. (Foreman was also born in this period of "idealistic revolutionaries;" his birthday is January 10, 1949), and in July, I publicly announced this. To make sure he would win, I drew a symbolic chart in which I moved his Ascendant back from 19:31 degrees to 7:35 degrees of Leo. That degree being known as a "pipeline to God," I felt that it would give him the added symbolic power of the planets.

As if by magic, the fight was postponed for a few weeks due to a cut over George Foreman's eye. The time period coincided exactly with the timing I had cheated on with Ali's chart. The chart became an important lucky token, and I redrew it on a piece of linen and sewed it into the lining of Ali's robe, behind one of the African blanket patches.

Forgetting the robe on the way to the fight, Ali drove back fifteen miles to his camp in Kinshasa to get it. George Plimpton, a Pisces, who was in the dressing room before the fight, tells how trainer Angelo Dundee wanted Ali to wear a robe with the map of Zaire sewn over the heart. Ali hit him and said, "I must wear my magic robe" (with his astrological chart in its lining).

Though I was invited to attend the fight in Zaire, the change of date conflicted with my other plans, so I listened to the fight on the radio. During the last minutes

of the fight, a Buddhist friend and I sat on the floor chanting from the Lotus Sutra, *nam myoho renge kyo* ("I believe in the mystic law of cause and effect"), hoping to give Ali some long-distance spiritual support. Chanting, like prayer, is believed to have a powerful sound vibration that can help make major and minor events take place.

In the sixth round Ali started to regain control of the fight, as I predicted. Eight minutes later, in the eighth round, Ali knocked out George Foreman. He was again world champion.

Ali's Ascendant (the place in which an individual will succeed) is Leo, and he won the fight in Kinshasa, originally called Leopoldville before Zaire—the former Belgian Congo—gained its independence.

The pride that he showed in his early years was a

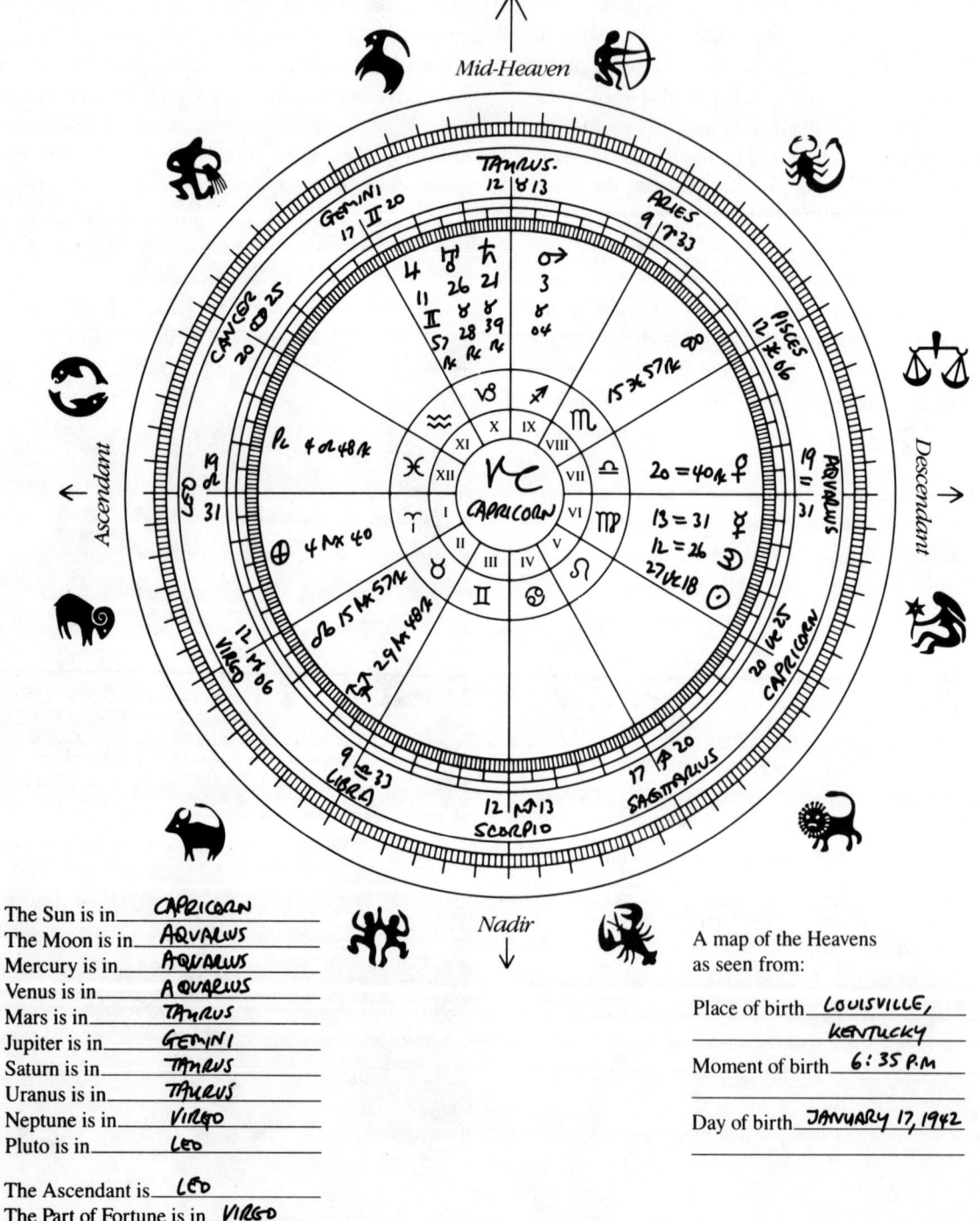

The Sun is in CAPRICORN
The Moon is in AQUARIUS
Mercury is in AQUARIUS
Venus is in AQUARIUS
Mars is in TAURUS
Jupiter is in GEMINI
Saturn is in TAURUS
Uranus is in TAURUS
Neptune is in VIRGO
Pluto is in LEO

The Ascendant is LEO
The Part of Fortune is in VIRGO

A map of the Heavens as seen from:

Place of birth LOUISVILLE, KENTUCKY

Moment of birth 6:35 P.M

Day of birth JANUARY 17, 1942

reflection in part of the Ascendant Leo, rising at the time of his birth. This gave him the traits of the king of the jungle, the flamboyant cat who stalks his prey in the ring, and of the actor who acts his way through television talk shows and press conferences. His dream of becoming a movie actor and his attainment of that goal in the film *The Greatest,* about his life, were followed by one success after another. He is as great on the screen as in the ring. His fans follow him from the stadium to the theater.

The Moon in Aquarius, the humanitarian sign that influences his religious and philosophical beliefs, blended with his Capricorn Sun sign, tends toward political and social changes more than the growth of faith. The driven idealism of Capricorn's "idealistic revolutionaries" led him to throw his Olympic Gold medal into the Ohio River, angered at the distinctions made between a hero and an ordinary black man in the South. His career has been marked by other courageous gestures—he was stripped of his boxing title when he refused military service on religious grounds. But perhaps that is one of the rights of religious leaders from the beginning of time—to be the conscience of the government and to inspire reforms or revolution. Aquarius is also the sign of intuition and predictive ability. Perhaps it is because Ali has Mercury and Venus in this sign as well that he was motivated to write poetry and to predict his victories in verse: "They all must fall, in the round I call."

The planets Saturn, Uranus, and Jupiter in the tenth house of government made him a major influence in political changes for blacks. Neptune, the planet of motion pictures, is in the area of financial prospects and well suited to Uranus, the planet that is said to rule television. Even though audiences around the world had already seen a lot of Ali the boxer on film and television, it was natural for him to move into the film and television industry after giving up his fighting career. Capricorn is the perfect sign for producing and organizing.

Ali always was, is, and always will be "the greatest" legend in our time.

AQUARIUS
Humanitarian of the Zodiac

SUN IN AQUARIUS, RULED BY URANUS
January 20–February 18

They can be the most aggravating sign of all the zodiac and still one of the greatest, for they use their intense curiosity and knowledge for the betterment of mankind. There is nothing an Aquarius doesn't know, from how to heal a cut foot to what rare wild leaf will counteract the poisons of an insect sting. They are au courant with the stock market, and they know which movie star is divorcing whom—and for which secret lover. They can give at least the surnames of most Third World leaders, and they know what books are out of print or out of stock at the library. These avid know-it-alls absorb and retain knowledge from reading newspapers and magazines, listening to the radio, watching television, or overhearing a conversation on the bus. Quite possibly they believe that they have a direct line to some celestial information bank that—for some privileged reason—feeds data only to Aquarians.

The musical *Hair,* and the hit song from the show, "The Age of Aquarius," associates them with the hippie movement of the sixties. They are radical and concerned about various causes, whether bank clerks, computer operators, or artists—they are all "plainclothes hippies."

Often very unconventional, they are full of energy and enthusiasm for life, with dynamic and outstanding personalities that sometimes appear false to more lethargic people. Their interest in other people's problems and welfare is genuine and from the heart. Charitable and humanitarian by nature, they rush to the side of friends in need and are always willing to help strangers, who rapidly become friends. But then, Aquarius is the eleventh sign of the zodiac—the house that rules friendships, social life, and personal hopes and wishes. Because of this they are great hosts and hostesses at parties or public events. Loud music and all the flashy metallic colors that are now part of our world have surrounded Aquarians over the centuries. They live in the future, all the time plotting and inventing and intuitively seeing clearly the direction in which the planet is evolving.

The ideals of friendship are the ideals of Aquarians, who need to be surrounded by kindred spirits and an entourage of faithful believers.

Romantically, they love everyone, and that can be the biggest problem they have to face in life. So emotionally involved in helping the deprived and the sick, and in solving the problems of the world and their neighbors, they have very little time to develop a good individual love relationship.

It is important for them to be free to love the world (in the spiritual sense) and be involved in their own work, hobbies, and outside interests. They have no need to share these activities with anyone, even those close to them, for each and every individual they meet becomes yet another "satellite" partner, at least for the duration of the relationship or project. This detachment, even in the strongest of marriages and love affairs, should never be thought of as a threat or sign of a rival interest, and it is important generally that their partners should not become too demanding emotionally or sexually and that they try to understand the unselfish, humanitarian needs of Aquarians.

There is no profession in which Aquarians cannot be found, but they prefer a career where they can put their charitable personalities to practical use, where they can be of most help to others. Once people can accept their outstretched hands with the same warmth and sincerity with which they are offered, there will be only peace, love, and happiness on this planet.

Universal Reformers

AQUARIUS DECANATE, RULED BY URANUS
January 20–January 29

The energy level of these double Uranian personalities is so powerful that they can make a resolution or put some great improvement into effect on one side of the planet and get immediate results on the other. The methods they employ to make life a little easier are usually so simple and utilitarian that governments and world leaders wonder why they didn't come up with the idea first. Their brilliance in applying their gigantic amount of knowledge in the simplest ways makes them latter-day saviors, angels, or knights on horseback.

No problem is too complicated for them to solve—whether a diplomatic stalemate between two stubborn world leaders, or the invention of a safety device for a vehicle that saves thousands of lives annually, or just a simple, everyday personality conflict between two neighbors who are radically opposed over a simple decision about some improvements for their street.

In battle they can predict what the enemy plans to do next; in peace uphold humanitarian causes by stalling or cleverly counteracting unscrupulous politicians' greedy plans. They are not physically strong but have the strength of a lion when their beliefs and philosophy are challenged.

Like ravishingly beautiful, feline Eartha Kitt, they light up a room as soon as they enter it. No matter how boring the conversation has been, their arrival raises the whole level of humor, wit, and chatter to such heights of intelligence that people refer to it years later with delight. They can save the day with games that other adults had left far behind them and revel in the fun of playing again. Their instant information service keeps them busy working as free agents, too, finding houses, jobs, and helpers for friends, usually with just one phone call.

Their phone bills are usually high from spending so much time tracking down information for friends and gossiping with family members. Impatient, they start the day early, often working many hours before really dressing, as their homes are usually their offices too.

Should they commit themselves politically to one side or another, they are the first to be criticized despite others' support of the same attitudes and beliefs. It seems that they can present an argument so strongly and convincingly that opponents cannot come up with sensible answers, and instead strike out physically or with sharp verbal abuse. Underneath Aquarians love it. It makes their statements more meaningful, as well as carrying publicity value in newspapers and magazines. They see the media as a great tool, to be exploited whenever necessary to preach, sell, or reform.

In romance these Aquarians prove devoted and loyal, sexually stimulating, and willing to serve the whims and needs of the loved one. These paragons of virtue seem too good to be true and make others suspicious even when there is no cause. Their visits to neighbors to help with family problems and their regular donations to local charities may become sources of irritation to their mates, who look for clues of some illicit romance or big love affair. Though they are quite innocent of all accusations—or even thoughts of misbehavior—their tendency to show too much interest in others, to show delight and affection openly, understandably appears to jealous spouses or companions as outright flirtation with others or rejection of true love.

Outside of marriage, love and romance no longer exist; their thoughts and concerns focus on greater matters. But the attention they give to their coworkers, their office furniture and new electronic equipment, and their favorite projects may represent the third corner of the triangle to a left-out lover. These Aquarians forget to involve their loved ones in their time-consuming activities and committee meetings. They cause others to become jealous of their time rather than their love.

MIKHAIL BARYSHNIKOV

This heroic dancer leaped across the world's political stage—a "white knight" of ballet—into the hearts and homes of American ballerinas and dance lovers. A "universal reformer," he brought with him from Russia the scrupulously taught and learned techniques of the Kiev Ballet and, in his role as artistic director of the American Ballet Theater, is passing them on to another generation of dancers.

Born in Riga, Latvia, on January 28, 1948, he has his Sun and Mercury, the communicator, in the sign of Aquarius, which rules the ankles; he has Venus, the artist, in Pisces, which rules the feet; and his Jupiter is in the athletic sign of Sagittarius, which rules the legs. No wonder he became obsessed with dancing as soon as he started to take ballet lessons!

Born under the sign of "freedom," he was too restricted in the Soviet Union, and as soon as he was able he defected. Though he says his home will always be Russia, he has happily become a U.S. citizen.

The Jupiter influence gave him success in the movies. His first movie, *The Turning Point,* was a hit, followed by *White Nights,* a film in which he starred opposite Gregory Hines (Pisces, February 14, 1946).

He has accomplished extraordinary feats since he left the Kiev Ballet in 1974 while performing in Toronto, Canada. In twelve years he has done it all.

TOM SELLECK

Speaking to Tom and his girlfriend Jilly Mack (Capricorn) at one of the presidential inaugural parties, I discussed the great compatibility in their horoscopes. Tom's Ascendant is Capricorn, so the two will have many similar personality traits, likes, and dislikes and be romantically in tune.

Tom Selleck is an Aquarius born on January 29, 1945, at 8:22 A.M., in Detroit, Michigan. His Moon is in Leo, the sign of the actor, next to the planet of big business, Pluto.

His series "Magnum, P.I." has turned him into television big business. He actually refused the lead in *Raiders of the Lost Ark* to do the show. Until then Tom had earned a good living working on various major shows and doing television commercials.

The location of his Venus in the watery sign of Pisces makes Hawaii, with its surf and beaches, an ideal place for him to work and to live. Being a "universal reformer," he has always kept away from the traditional Hollywood stereotyping and hype and has created his own star image.

The combined planetary influences of his Mars and Mercury in Capricorn have given him the handsomely chiseled features that making him both photogenic and trustworthy, whether fighting crime or selling a product.

Tom is a modern-day screen swashbuckler, jumping in where angels fear to tread in order to save a beautiful woman or to see that justice is done, and trying to help humanity through his personal appearances and charity in his private life.

EARTHA KITT

Born: January 26, 1928, at 12:10 A.M. in North, South Carolina

I was a surprise present "delivered" to Eartha when she appeared on a Baltimore television talk show on her birthday in 1978. We have been friends ever since, having appeared at many public events together and on nationwide television talking about her horoscope, her singing career, and her wonderful daughter Kitt. Eartha is a star and a mother.

She is hardworking and sensitive to the suffering of those around her, rich or poor. She is ready to speak out if the occasion warrants it, as she feels people have been too submissive for too long and are blind to the fact that what our governments are doing in world affairs may not be what it seems. She wants us to be ever vigilant and to keep those nervous "button-pushing" politicians on their toes.

A natural Aquarius, Eartha sees the world as one. The Third World is all part of the universe she has grown up in.

Her Aquarian sun sign makes her a natural humanitarian, but with the Moon in Pisces she is willing to sacrifice herself for what she believes.

Socially ostracized for ten years after telling President Lyndon Johnson and his wife what she thought of the Vietnam War, she was welcomed back to the White House as a heroine by President Jimmy Carter. She went on to star on Broadway in *Timbuktu* and appeared in guest spots on television and concert halls across America. She confided, "I don't think there is anything I have done that I wish I hadn't done. Because I learn from everything I do, I'm in school every day. My diploma will be my tombstone." She is a missionary wherever she goes. She brightens the lives of young and old, she takes time to teach underprivileged children to dance and act. Her public appearances give courage to blacks and whites who have been cruelly treated by "the system." It is her Libra Ascendant that gives her the ability to see both sides of a problem and act as a diplomat, professionally in her work with other performers and politically when faced with the realities of injustice within her own "democratic" government.

Eartha Kitt was born in the community of North, South Carolina, on January 26, 1928, at approximately 12:10 A.M. Orson Welles called her "the sexiest woman in the world." She has made triumphant personal appearances all over the world, hobnobbing with socialites and world leaders yet always concerned over the inhumanity and injustice in the world. She helped pay for a twelve-room school for South African blacks, and she spent many hours touring the run-down "colored" sections when she visited the country on a world tour. "I don't carry myself as a black person. I am a world person. I have tremendous curiosity, and I believe in firsthand knowledge. And I probably know more about South Africa than the politicians." And it is the Libra influence in her chart that gives her the grace and beauty that make her one of the most outstanding women of the century, if not in the history of the United States.

Jupiter in the area of show business and children has blessed her with success in both. Her talented and beautiful daughter Kitt MacDonald (Sagittarius, November 26, 1961), is fast following in her mother's

footsteps and is her constant companion and friend. Eartha's Uranus, located in the exact position as Jupiter, launched her into the recording market. Her recording of the bored vamp singing "Monotonous," from the Broadway show *New Faces of 1952* made her an instant international celebrity.

Venus and Mars in the house of writing, speech, singing, and general communications may have been responsible for her unique and beautiful voice quality as well as her success with her writings, books, and articles. She is a true reformer of the world she lives in—the world she happens to be in when she wakes up in the morning—and she is doing her part to change the inconsistencies of people's thoughts, behavior, and philosophy based on centuries of fear, cruelty, and injustice. She is a "universal reformer."

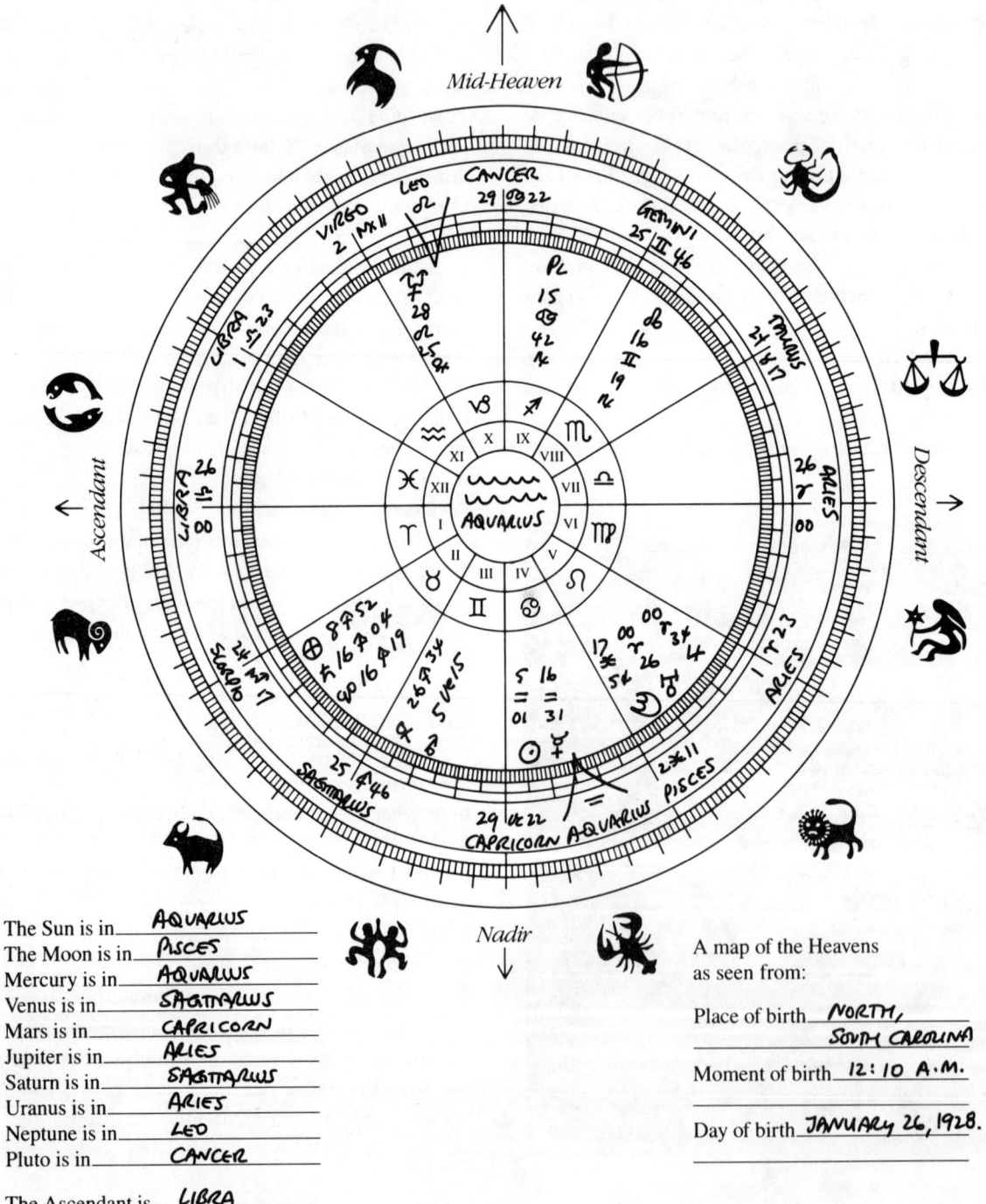

The Sun is in __AQUARIUS__
The Moon is in __PISCES__
Mercury is in __AQUARIUS__
Venus is in __SAGITTARIUS__
Mars is in __CAPRICORN__
Jupiter is in __ARIES__
Saturn is in __SAGITTARIUS__
Uranus is in __ARIES__
Neptune is in __LEO__
Pluto is in __CANCER__

The Ascendant is __LIBRA__
The Part of Fortune is in __SAGITTARIUS__

A map of the Heavens as seen from:

Place of birth __NORTH, SOUTH CAROLINA__
Moment of birth __12:10 A.M.__
Day of birth __JANUARY 26, 1928.__

Metaphysical Pioneers

GEMINI DECANATE, RULED BY MERCURY
January 30–February 9

These Aquarians are an interesting balance of the humanism and benevolence of Uranus together with the planet Mercury's area of worldwide communication. Aquarians' writings are published all over the world, and they are involved in teaching young students a new meaning to life that may hopefully be passed on to future generations. Others are involved in setting up relay stations for the telephone service, programming computers to service vast areas of the nation, debating and lecturing to colleges and trade union groups, as well as passing on the wisdom of astrology. Uranus rules computers, astrology, and flying—all three areas combine with mercurial words, speech, and travel to make these international Aquarians, who especially like to find new material, new audiences, and new conquests, true pioneers. Gentle yet strong actress Mia Farrow, long interested in spiritual exploration, is one of these astrophysical Aquarians.

A novelist expressing a philosophy that a whole generation will follow, an astrologer who wins a court action by accurately describing the character of the judge's three sons, a leader of the women's movement giving pride and meaning to the lives of millions of women, an artist who captures the feelings of a whole nation and moves governments into action, a filmmaker who bridges language barriers with his exciting new cinematography, a comedian who makes sorrow disappear with a lighthearted joke about a very serious matter, or the sports champion who is as popular in defeat as in victory—all have the attitude of the true pioneer, fighting nonviolently for what they know is best for the masses, yet wise enough to know that drastic changes will only bring pain, sorrow, and unnecessary suffering.

As children they would read so much that the school library could not keep up with them. They would read a book over and over again if they thought it mirrored their minds or their lives. They would escape as quickly as they could a television show or do their homework over the telephone with a school chum. While some may have had success with sports, most would have been more successful with the debating team, helping to publish the school newspaper, or running an after-school disco.

Their love of chatter makes them welcome guests, for they are filled with many stories and anecdotes and can report on all the latest gossip and scandal in the family or in the government office. Exaggeration is a minor vice, and lies—white ones of course—are all part of their charm, if and when they feel the situation can be highlighted by a touch of whimsy.

These Aquarians are not really looking for marriage. Many do marry, of course, and have long, happy lives with their spouses. But they most likely got married early, before they realized all the wonderful things life had to offer the single person—especially the one most important ingredient, freedom. Their visionary, pioneering spirit makes settling down a difficult matter.

Whoever is lucky enough to catch and marry one of these Aquarians will have a fun-filled life with wild and reckless adventures and never a dull moment. Much depends on what each is seeking from the other as well as from life itself. They try to make everyone around them happy, and generally create an atmosphere of jollity and love.

PRESIDENT RONALD REAGAN

Reagan is the first American president to come out publicly in the *Washington Post* and tell the nation that he does believe in astrology and that he reads Carroll Righter's horoscope column. It was through Carroll's advice in his early career that he took off to Las Vegas with his comedy routine, and reportedly Carroll has been a friend and adviser to him every since.

President Reagan was born in Tampico, Illinois, at 2:00 P.M. on February 6, 1911. He is an Aquarius with his Moon in Taurus—a very loyal, patriotic, yet stubborn sign—and his Ascendant is the strong, mysterious, aggressive, and warlike Scorpio.

The Taurus Moon gave him his pleasant voice, and he started his career as a radio announcer, before going into the movies. His Ascendant Scorpio puts the sign of Sagittarius in his first house, giving him a great love of horses, which, of course, made him a natural for Westerns.

As early as 1947 he was obsessed with politics, due in part to his position as president of the Screen Actor's Guild. His first wife, Jane Wyman (Capricorn, born January 4, 1914), cited this obsession as one of the reasons for their divorce. He later married Nancy Davis (Cancer, born July 6), his costar in the movie *Hellcats of the Navy*.

During his administration he has advocated religion, and the country has returned to old-fashioned, traditional spiritual values.

CARROLL RIGHTER

Doyen of the most famous Hollywood stars and dean of astrology to all the students who regularly attend his Institute of Astrology to reap the wisdom of his long experience and to absorb his wonderful ("the stars impel, they don't compel," he reminds listeners) philosophy, humor, and attitude to life, Carroll is the man who was most influential in my career in astrology, as well as being my teacher and friend. In true American style, Carroll Righter has been more responsible for the growth and acceptance of astrology in the United States today than any other person, encouraging, teaching, and wittily entertaining students and skeptics alike. A former lawyer, a protégé of the great astrologer Evangeline Adams, who was born February 8 (also Aquarius), Carroll moved to Los Angeles in his early thirties.

Born in Philadelphia, Pennsylvania, on February 2, 1900, at 9:36 A.M., and with Aries on his Ascendant it is no wonder that he became a leader in the field, a true pioneer, fighting against social attitudes toward astrology and winning. The Sun in Aquarius, ruled by the planet Uranus, which is traditionally the planet of astrology, is well placed close to Mars, god of action, war, and energy, and Mercury, the messenger of the gods, a combination that makes him read in nearly every country in the world. His syndicated columns, carried in hundreds of newspapers and magazines all over the United States and Europe—especially in West Germany and Finland—have encouraged the worldwide travel his Aquarian spirit loves so much.

"I always travel on a retrograde Mercury because I always know I will come back," he tells his students who worry about the effect of this traditionally malign planetary action on travel.

His Moon in Pisces in the area of religion in his chart, plus the pioneering aspects of his Ascendant Aries, have led him to be a hardworking leader of the Chirothesian Church in Los Angeles, California, of which he is chairman. He is a perfect example of a "metaphysical pioneer" in every way, from religion to astrology.

Pluto, the planet of big business is in Gemini, explaining the enormous success of his writings. This is especially true as the planet is located in his third house of communications, mail order, and studies. Close by is metaphysical Neptune, giving Carroll a great desire to preach his beliefs and give warmth, comfort, and support through his faith, which he readily shares with others—friends and strangers alike.

The Moon and Venus are within two degrees of each other, which—apart from giving him good luck with his public image—also gives him a youthful and slender appearance. A practical joker in public, he is also highly respected by the masses. Venus makes all who come into his company love him immediately and seek tidbits of the astrological trivia, gossip, and techniques that he has developed over the years.

His Part of Fortune is in the first house, which is the area of personality, disposition, and environment. He is his own best salesman. His personality is his fortune, and he welcomes all he loves into his home, where he conducts his school.

MIA FARROW

Born: February 9, 1945, at 11:27 A.M. in Los Angeles, California

One of the first major stars to fly off to India for a month of transcendental meditation with guru Maharishi Mahesh Yogi, she also became a "metaphysical pioneer"—a late-blooming flower child, whose interests include Zen, yoga, ESP, and TM. And it is interesting that her roles in *Rosemary's Baby, Secret Ceremony,* and *See No Evil* all had a mystical or diabolical involvement.

I met Mia in the plush setting of Pinewood Studios, where she was playing Daisy opposite Robert Redford in *The Great Gatsby.* We had lunch together and went over her horoscope chart. Mia, an Aquarius, was the natural choice to play opposite Redford, a Leo.

Originally Ali MacGraw (Aries, born April 1, 1939) was to play Daisy, while her husband Robert Evans (Cancer, born June 29, 1930) produced the film. But she ran off with Steve McQueen (Aries, born March 24, 1930), thus ending her role as Daisy.

Jack Clayton, the director, came up to have me look at his horoscope, to learn what his next move should be. He'd lost his star and his producer. I told Jack, a Pisces, that he should go to New York and within two weeks he would sort out the whole film. During the next two weeks he interviewed many young actresses in New York, finally deciding that Mia was perfect for the role.

It still took some time to get all the ingredients together to save "Gatsby." Jeanie Sims, Jack's associate, came and saw me and wrote out a small prayer to put in my Buddhist altar. It read, "Dear Gohonzon, please make 'The Great Gatsby' happen." David Merrick, a Sagittarius, took on the job of producing it, and it was soon on its way. My basement in Chelsea, their production office, was a hive of activity.

Mia grew up in California and abroad, daughter of actress Maureen O'Sullivan and movie director John Farrow.

An Aquarius with her Moon in Capricorn and her Ascendant Taurus, she was destined for fame in her career. Whatever she chose to do she would have success, as her Sun is located in the tenth house of ambitions and honors. Mercury in Aquarius, the sign of television, dictated that it would be show business, though her early ambition was to be a nun—the first childhood attraction to religion and metaphysics. It was actually her role as Allison MacKenzie in "Peyton Place," the first nighttime television soap opera, that propelled her into stardom. And Mars in Capricorn placed exactly on top of her chart gives her the energy, determination, and drive to succeed.

Jupiter in Virgo in her fifth house gave her success with show business and also the need for children. While she didn't have any with her first husband, Frank Sinatra (Sagittarius), she was only twenty when she married him; Frank was fifty. Mia has Sagittarius in her seventh house of marriage.

But it was her Venus and Part of Fortune in Aries that attracted her to conductor André Previn (Aries, born April 6, 1929). They married in 1970, had twin sons Matthew Phineas and Sascha Villiers Fletcher. They

adopted four Vietnamese children and, in 1985, she adopted another Vietnamese child.

Divorced from André since 1979, she is now the lover of Woody Allen, a Sagittarian.

Due to her Venus and Part of Fortune being in Aries, she was destined to triumph with her 1979 Broadway debut in *Romantic Comedy,* playing opposite Anthony Perkins (Aries, April 4, 1932).

The Taurus Ascendant gives Mia a love of music, and so it was natural for her to fall in love with a conductor. But Venus in Aries, in the twelfth house of self-undoing, makes her very impulsive and compulsive when falling in love, often ending a good relationship on a passionate whim.

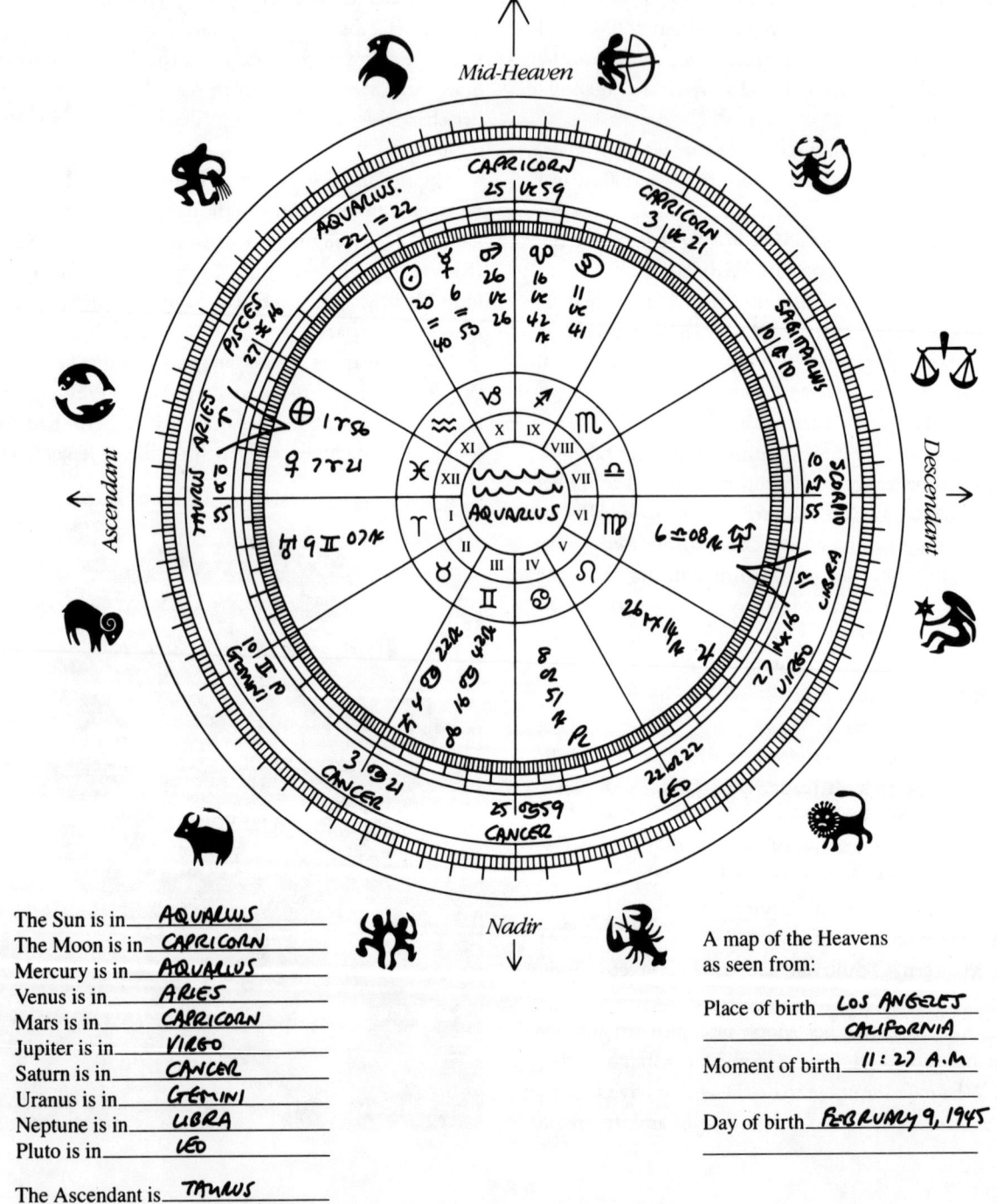

The Sun is in AQUARIUS
The Moon is in CAPRICORN
Mercury is in AQUARIUS
Venus is in ARIES
Mars is in CAPRICORN
Jupiter is in VIRGO
Saturn is in CANCER
Uranus is in GEMINI
Neptune is in LIBRA
Pluto is in LEO

The Ascendant is TAURUS
The Part of Fortune is in ARIES

A map of the Heavens as seen from:

Place of birth LOS ANGELES CALIFORNIA

Moment of birth 11:27 A.M

Day of birth FEBRUARY 9, 1945

Neptune in Libra in her sixth house of work obviously highlights her moviemaking career; Neptune is the planet of illusion. Yet she has great creative talents—she paints and draws, makes patchwork quilts, and enjoys sewing. And it was the same mysterious planet Neptune, in this sixth house of health, that made her a victim of polio when she was nine years old, followed by many childhood illnesses. Though physically fragile, she is mentally and spiritually strong.

On the last day of shooting *Gatsby,* Betty Field, who had played Daisy in the 1949 movie version, died of a cerebral hemorrhage. I discovered that Betty's birthday (February 8, 1918) was the day before Mia's, another mystical link. Betty also played in the 1957 movie *Peyton Place.*

Mia is given to long bouts of silence. It was her guru who said, "Mind is like an ocean. The surface layers of the mind function actively while the deeper levels remain silent." And he added, "The purpose of life is the expansion of happiness." She seems finally to have found happiness, and through her acting, her interest in child psychology, and her love for Woody and her children, she continues to be a "metaphysical pioneer."

Radiant Humanitarians and Trendsetters
LIBRA DECANATE, RULED BY VENUS
February 10–February 18

These lively and attractive Aquarians are a beautiful mixture of the Venutian qualities of Libra combined with the Uranian disposition of Aquarius, giving us flashes of what to expect from the future. Dynamic John Travolta, whose *Saturday Night Fever* ushered in the disco era, is a good example. These Aquarians uplift mankind in such a way that the destitute can smile at the incongruities of life, and flood victims can wave farewell to their homes knowing that with the support of these Aquarians, all is well with the world, it is just the people in it who are topsy-turvy.

These Aquarians are courageous speakers and organizers of the masses. Without realizing it they can start a fad, a craze, or a revolution. Their great foresight, their visions of what life will be in five years, five decades, or five centuries make them verbal battlers rather than generals and dictators.

As children they would lie at night looking out of their bedroom window watching their beloved planets and stars float across the sky. Even without a telescope they could point out Venus and the Milky Way, Orion and the constellation of Sagittarius. They could dance before they could do algebra and read all their parents' library long before they started school.

Their voracious appetite and aptitude for knowledge make it easy for them to get ahead even without a formal education, and their confidence in themselves and their ideals give them a drive and enthusiasm that are very contagious.

Their love of music, especially disco and modern psychedelic sounds, makes them great socialites, always seen at the best parties, at the newest night spots, and with the "in" crowd, though they will protest that they prefer a quiet evening chatting with friends around the fire.

In romance they are great fun but not too willing to play a heavy emotional role, and they tend to run away or find excuses for their single status. Nearly all Aquarians like their precious freedom, and protect this natural birthright. But with the Venus-Libra effect, they do like the idea of marriage, a permanent relationship, and a home environment full of beautiful and artistic objects including themselves, as long as they have sufficient freedom to bring the world in. They have always been told that they have good looks, photogenic qualities, and a charisma that makes them stand out at parties. Even when they don't say anything or react, their stillness communicates their true deep feelings.

MARISA BERENSON

It was early in January and very chilly in London, when I received a call from Marisa from Ireland.

"It's beautiful here; even the rain is warm and gentle. Do come."

With costar Ryan O'Neal (Taurus), Marisa was filming the movie *Barry Lyndon,* which was being directed by Stanley Kubrick (Leo, born July 28, 1928). She had leased a whole wing of Carlton House in Maynooth, County Kildare, a short drive from Dublin.

I had flown to Paris to meet with Marisa on many occasions, but this particular journey did feel rather clandestine.

"Oh, Fredrick dear, what's happening to me?" she asked.

We sat in front of the huge, blazing log fire in the manor house; the Christmas decorations were still up. Ryan lived in another residence several miles away. Burning candles and leaving a few tarot cards out overnight to conjure up good vibrations, we looked carefully at Marisa's horoscope chart.

Marisa was born in New York City on February 15, at 1:45 P.M., an Aquarius with her Moon in Sagittarius and her Ascendant Cancer.

Marisa is one of this century's greatest beauties, and the planet Venus, goddess of beauty, is in her tenth house of fame. Her photographs have graced the covers and inside pages of the most stylish magazines in the world.

Her Sagittarian Moon attracted her to acting and the movie industry and also to her long-term, much-publicized love affair with wealthy heir David Rothschild (Sagittarius).

Marisa and I had a pre-Christmas lunch at Orsini's restaurant in New York. Next to my plate she placed a little gift box.

"I was walking past this jewelry shop when I was pulled into it; this little object caught my eye, and I knew it was just for you. Open it."

I opened the box, which contained a little gold orb.

"Now open that up!" Marisa exclaimed excitedly, looking at my bewildered expression. I fumbled and found a tiny catch. The hinged sections opened up into a beautiful crucifix, with each section like small pyramids with various masonic signs engraved on each facing.

"You'll have fun trying to find out what they all mean."

Marisa had opened up a new and most important door. In the search for the meanings, I was led into joining a Masonic lodge in New York; the spiritual, metaphysical, and charitable works of the organization attracted me. Not too long after, I became a master Mason of my lodge, a 32nd Degree, and a Patron of the Order of the Eastern Star. Thanks to Marisa, masonry is now a vital part of my life.

YOKO ONO

She said, "All my concerts had no sounds in them: they were completely silent. . . . People had to make their own music in their minds."

Widow of John Lennon (Libra, born October 9, 1940), she is reportedly one of the richest women in the world and one of the most spiritually creative in the United States. An avant-garde artist, she has made her own solo albums to critical acclaim and was famous in her early career for staging special creative "events" of new art forms. She is a trendsetter.

Born on February 18, 1933, at 8:30 P.M. in Tokyo, Japan, she is an Aquarius with her Moon in the philosophical sign of Sagittarius and with Libra as her Ascendant, the sign of fine arts, music, and singing.

Using metaphysics, astrology, tarot cards, and numerology, Yoko has been able to handle the many major crises that life has brought her, those first shared with John while he was alive and now her own ups and downs. She even uses these disciplines in helping to produce her albums, and for other important career decisions.

A philanthropist (she has helped scores of artists and musicians), a humanitarian interested in easing the suffering of the world, and a marcher (with John) for peace, she has set her own goals, which, finding others whose hearts beat to the same drum, have become trends.

MATT DILLON

Fate stepped in when Matt Dillon cut a class and was signed up by talent scout Vic Ramos (Virgo) who was looking for new faces and bodies for the film *Over the Edge.*

Matt was born February 18, 1964, at 6:00 A.M. in New Rochelle, New York. With the Sun and three planets, Mars, Mercury, and Saturn as well as his Ascendant in Aquarius, he was destined to be a star. He has all the looks, charm, and charisma of a major star and is one of the new brand of heartthrobs on the screen.

Praised for his dramatic as well as his comic roles, he is one of the major box office draws in the United States, capturing the new, young market. His *Flamingo Kid, Target,* and his two Francis Ford Coppola–directed movies, *The Outsiders* and *Rumble Fish,* have established his career.

Naturally, with all those planets in Aquarius, he is a student of astrology. And he needs that Aquarius "freedom." Though he has many girls pursuing him, he is not ready to settle down. "My work has to be first." he says.

JOHN TRAVOLTA

Born: February 18, 1954, at 2:53 P.M. in Englewood, New Jersey

John Travolta started the whole world dancing again. There hadn't been an overnight success like *Saturday Night Fever* in years, tantalizing the mind, spirit, and feet of the disco generation.

I felt like the fairy godmother of the film, having been responsible for coproducer Kevin McCormick's decision to stay with Robert Stigwood to produce the movie, and I was invited to the opening night party at London's most popular disco.

John is an Aquarius with Cancer as his Ascendant and his Moon in Virgo. Young people identified with his Age of Aquarius attitude and with the sensitive vulnerability of his Ascendant. Within twenty-four hours of the New York premiere, eligible young men all over the country rushed after work on Friday to the stores so they could step out on Saturday.

Girls melted again at the sight of their super macho

companions boogying across the dance floor, putting Fred Astaire and Ginger Rogers to shame. Discos opened up all over the world. The fever had started.

The Moon, which rules romance and marriage, in Virgo the sign of bachelors and spinsters, makes it very difficult for him to find the perfect lover. His Cancer ascendant attracted him to Diana Hyland, an established actress who was eighteen years his senior (also an Aquarius, she was born January 25, 1936). They fell in love while making a TV film together, "The Boy in the Plastic Bubble," in which she played his mother. Their affair attracted much publicity. She died the following year in John's arms, having lost her battle with breast cancer.

Like the crab, John's Cancer influences make him a recluse who loves his home surroundings and also his rather solitary hobby of flying, another Aquarian activity. His dark, sad eyes are due to Venus and Mercury being in Pisces, and these planets help him to express his feelings, which seem to come from his entire body.

As a trendsetter John had just the right amount of charisma and, fortunately, more than enough talent to carry it off. An actor with many successful years behind him on Broadway, in a minor role in *Grease,* and on television in "Welcome Back, Kotter," he was a popular favorite with the viewers, but this sudden career leap with *Fever* made him the biggest box office attraction in a long time. His next big film, *Grease,* was the biggest money-maker in 1978, with box office receipts of over $125 million.

It was natural, astrologically, to star him with Lily Tomlin (Virgo) in a romantic movie, *Moment by Moment,* as his Moon is in her sign. And it was Sylvester Stallone, Cancer, who took over the job of creating a new body for John when he took on the directing of the *Fever* sequel, *Staying Alive.* The first house, which is ruled by his Ascendant, Cancer, has a major effect on appearance as well as personality.

Mars, the planet of action, in Sagittarius (thighs and

legs) in the fifth house of show business, certainly must be responsible for all the gyrations, dances, and physical activity in his movies. Jupiter in Gemini also affects dancing prowess and gives him a witty sense of humor that comes out in his performances more than in his quiet personal life.

All Aquarians love to travel, and John is no different, except that now he owns his own jet. John is a pilot, and there is nothing that he feels he cannot do that he'd like to do. As with other trendsetters, the magic is there already; all that is needed is a magician like John—plus a few spells.

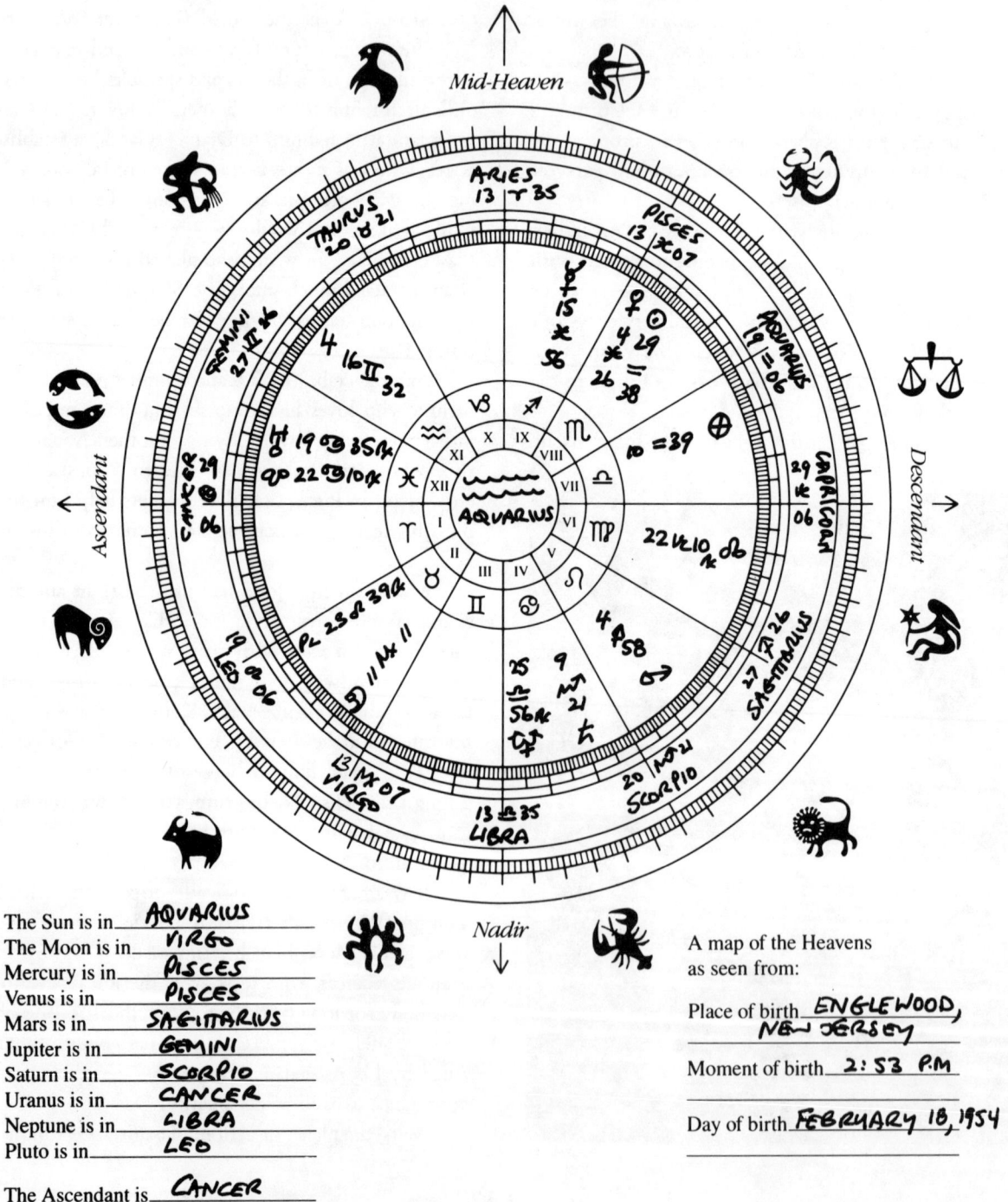

The Sun is in _AQUARIUS_
The Moon is in _VIRGO_
Mercury is in _PISCES_
Venus is in _PISCES_
Mars is in _SAGITTARIUS_
Jupiter is in _GEMINI_
Saturn is in _SCORPIO_
Uranus is in _CANCER_
Neptune is in _LIBRA_
Pluto is in _LEO_

The Ascendant is _CANCER_
The Part of Fortune is in _AQUARIUS_

A map of the Heavens as seen from:

Place of birth _ENGLEWOOD, NEW JERSEY_

Moment of birth _2:53 P.M_

Day of birth _FEBRUARY 18, 1954_

PISCES
Conscience of the Zodiac

SUN IN PISCES, RULED BY NEPTUNE
February 19–March 20

Pisces love to cry. They will sob and suffer at the injustices of the world; they will weep with joy as an astronaut sets foot on the moon for the first time. Tear-faced, they will glow with pride as the national anthem plays at some sporting event. They choke as they try to hold back their happiness while the organ plays at a friend's wedding. Ruled by the watery planet, the god of the sea, Neptune, it is no wonder that they are not content shedding a few tears from joy as well as sadness. They love living on islands, by the sea, river, or stream. They prefer an illusionary dream life as an escape from harsh realities, but generally rise to the call of battle (in the medical corps, of course) or to the screams for help from a wounded stranger.

The Good Samaritan was a Pisces, if not by birthdate, certainly by disposition. A Pisces is an island. An island of refuge welcoming the shipwrecked and the oppressed and offering a paradise of tropical fruits, warm, balmy days, shelter from the storms, and romance in the misty twilight.

They are very sympathetic, kind, always ready to help the sick and suffering of the world. Many are found working long hours in hospitals, convalescent homes, public institutions, and in the last outposts of missionary stations in riot-torn African nations. They take on the role of dedicated martyrs, and the more they personally have to endure poor living conditions, the more they can accomplish in raising the level of morality in the modern world, so lost to materialism, profit, and greed.

The emotions and devotion of Pisces make for a wonderful love life, yet their own suffering and self-inflicted anxieties make their loved ones question the success of the relationship. They create many sorrows and unhappy situations for themselves, because they feel it is very important to have misery and heartbreak around them. Some even contrive it or make an interpersonal relationship difficult in order to achieve this anguish. Their loved ones know they love to cry. However, that is not the real problem; they have seen them cry on happy occasions and at funny movies. Somehow, while they are attracted to this sweet, cute, and lovable behavior, they cannot divorce themselves from the idea that somewhere deep down inside they are to blame. Happiness seems to come from imaginary things, from their fantasies. The illusion has many assets, though, especially when it comes to escaping from life's realities, problems, and lessons.

Once they stop trying to be the traditional martyr for some personal cause they can attain anything in their world through their faith.

Pisces is the twelfth sign of the zodiac—the one that rules religion, the secret and hidden side of life, the deep-seated conscience, the solitude and loneliness that all people feel at some moment of their lives, and obstacles as well as actions of self-undoing. Spiritually they have traveled through all the other signs and are about to begin again on a very high level from having learned all the lessons of life. They are great storytellers from having experienced all of life's mysteries and adventures in other lives, on the ladder of reincarnation. What they relate they know or they feel, and what makes their listeners attentive and full of awe is the most important ingredient from the Pisces' own personal attitudes. They *believe* in what they do. They would rather be tortured than do something against their idealism—and many *are* tortured.

It is not by sheer coincidence that the symbol of christianity is the fish. Outside the tombs of the Christian martyrs in the catacombs in Rome is drawn the symbol of the fish. They willingly accepted their death through torment, at the hands of fools, the jaws of the lions, and the fires of the soldiers after their leaders were crucified. This they could put up with, for their executioners were all disbelievers.

Idealistic and mentally agile, they prefer jobs that combine both a challenge and a service. Their talents are unlimited, for they have faith in themselves equaled only by their faith in their fellow human beings. Writing stories and poems has always been a natural creative outlet for them. Many great actresses and actors have suffered brilliantly on and off the screen. And, as indicated earlier in this chapter, there are probably more

Pisces working in hospitals and institutions than any other sign.

Those less service-minded but idealistic in wanting to improve the world or to explore its great potentials will become sea captains and sailors, work on cruise ships, and make excellent bartenders, life guards, and gasoline station owners in resort areas. Many become astrologers and psychics; others, faith healers and religious workers. Their religious interests often get them working voluntarily, and their knowledge of after-life states makes them sincere and devoted morticians.

Dedicated, determined to improve the lot of everyone they come in contact with, they can if they are not careful miss their own glory in this life. They will happily bypass the rewards this time around, knowing so well that next time they can catch up on ambitions left unfulfilled. Their glory is waiting for them and they know it.

Romantic Martyrs and Inspirational Poets

PISCES DECANATE, RULED BY NEPTUNE
February 19–February 29

Everything in the lives of these Pisces is romantic. They see the best in every situation, whether recovering from an emotional separation, the loss of a job, an operation that would have another less philosophical person complaining and grumbling, racial intolerance, and the loss of brothers gunned down by assassins' bullets. When they cry the world cries with them; when they laugh the world laughs too. Neptune is twice as powerful with these Pisces but can also be twice as deceptive.

They are willing to give up their entire fortune, their career, reputation, and fame for the one they love; Elizabeth Taylor is as renowned for the drama in her personal life as for her acting. No journey is too long, no obstacle too great to reach those most dear to them. They are willing to stand in front of the verbal firing squad and receive wound after wound and still never give in. Their selflessness in times of famine, drought, pestilence, and disease is legendary.

Yet most are easily deceived, often by those they love most of all, making them an easy mark for con artists in all parts of the world. They are innocents, children in the hands of rough, tough, business associates and rivals. Having been caught many times in traps that offend their own basic nature, they retaliate by becoming deceivers, no longer the victims but the culprits. Having very little faith in the honesty of others, they themselves become elusive, indecisive, cautious, and withdrawn, against their own heart's desires. They resort to fabricating the truth, vacillating, and lying in order to protect themselves and their beliefs.

As soon as you meet these Pisces, it is love at first sight. They need protection and love, and willing victims rush in from every nook and cranny. Communication is easy with them: they love to talk, are curious about everyone they encounter both intellectually and sexually, and they are happy to walk up the aisle with one they feel sorry for as well as love, for they want to help, be of service, and be worshipped.

Never really believing the worst of people, they are silly when it comes to handing out donations, for they see the need in all charities, all mass organizations and religions, and every beggar on the street. Still, there would be a lot more anguish and misery in the world if it weren't for these soft-hearted Pisces, who with a sincere and heartfelt gesture lift the spirits of the blind, the lame, and the crippled as well as the drunk, downtrodden, and depressed who grab at life on every downtown corner.

Their talents are unlimited, for they have great imaginations that will help them take on the cloak of any character, and to play any role both at work and at home. Writers, poets, and musicians are found in abundance in this Pisces, for they shun the riches and material blessings of the world in order to promote their ideals and those of their loved ones. They eventually have glory, wealth, and riches showered upon them by their grateful followers.

Their leadership qualities come to the fore in times of idealistic revolution, and they have the qualities to raise banners in civil war and to free the oppressed in peacetime. In their climb up the political ladder, sorrow and regrets surround them—miscalculations and misdemeanors that would not affect a less sympathetic and gentle sign. There is always a place in the religious hierachy for them, and they make the most plausible and exciting metaphysicians, for they know just how to capture the spirit and imagination of their followers and to illustrate with great clarity the meanings of life's wonderful treasures and mysteries. Very often developing a small group of worshippers and disciples who, after their death, pass on the message, the philosophy, and by so doing write their name into the annals of spiritual history.

These Pisces can have everything possible for a romantic marriage, but they can also weave a web of intrigue and emotionalism. Sexually they have tremendous versatility and imagination, being dreamy, romantic, and adventurous.

PRINCE ANDREW, DUKE OF YORK

Royal weddings are inspiring and romantic especially when between two highly suitable young lovers who have captured the hearts of a nation.

Prince Andrew, in true Pisces fashion, had been a martyr for love, dashing off around the world with various beauties, and had also been actively engaged in the Battle of the Falklands against Argentina. Perhaps he had decided to sow his wild oats, just in case he were killed in action.

However, once he fell in love with Sarah Ferguson, a friend of his sister-in-law, Diana, he gave up his former life and settled for marriage.

It was a perfect match. Sarah, too, had had former sweethearts, so overcoming any potential complications regarding ex-lovers.

Prince Andrew was born on February 19, 1960, at 3:30 P.M. in London and is officially a Pisces, with his Mercury in that sign too. It is the sign of the fishes, and he took to the navy as quickly as fish take to water. His Ascendant is Leo, the show-off, and his Moon is in the sensual, mischievous sign of Scorpio. He always loved to shock the royal family and the public by romping around Buckingham Palace with his latest girlfriend while his parents were out of town.

Sarah was born October 15, 1959, at 9:03 A.M. in London, a Libra with Scorpio ascending, which attracted the Prince's Moon. Her Moon is in the aggressive, independent sign of Aries.

During an interview on "Good Morning, America" on ABC-TV, the happy couple discussed their future wedding date. Andrew, with the royal family's true chauvinistic attitude, answered one of the questions put to them about how they chose the wedding date.

"Well, *I* just thought that date would be ideal for everyone."

To which Sarah remarked, smiling, *"We, dear, we."*

"Oh, yes," responded Andrew. "I have to remember it's *we.*"

GLORIA VANDERBILT

One of today's most romantic designers, as well as something of a martyr due to her "poor little rich girl" childhood, Gloria Vanderbilt is also a poet, an actress, a painter, and a business entrepreneur, as well as having been a wife and mother.

She has inspired women to add magic to their lives, and to add glamour to their wardrobes.

Gloria was born in New York on February 20, 1924, a Pisces with her Moon in the show business sign Leo, which took her into the theater and added the sparkle to her line of jeans, which sells over 10 million pairs a year.

Jupiter and Mars close together in Sagittarius have made her take wild gambles in life that have paid off, and she has been able to add enormously to her Vanderbilt inheritance.

Gloria's choice of a swan insignia for her fashions reflects her favorite role as an actress, in her favorite play, *The Swan.*

Quoting Byron, her third husband, writer Wyatt Cooper, said of Gloria, "She walks in beauty like the night."

ELIZABETH TAYLOR
Born: February 27, 1932, at 7:56 P.M. in London, England

A true "romantic martyr," Elizabeth suffers through one big love affair or marriage after another, devoting herself both to her current husband and his career at the same time as she works at her own star-studded and glittering occupation.

Her first marriage was to Nicky Hilton (Cancer, born July 7, 1926); then actor Michael Wilding (Leo, born July 23, 1912); followed by the great movie producer Michael Todd (Cancer, born June 22, 1909); after his tragic accident she married Eddie Fisher (Leo, born August 8, 1928); then Richard Burton (Scorpio, born November 10, 1925), who played opposite her in the movie *Cleopatra* and whom she actually married twice; and went on to marry John Warner (Aquarius, born February 18, 1927), who became senator from Virginia.

It is the sign of Libra rising in her chart that gave her her beauty and glamorous looks. Traditionally ruled by the planet Venus, the goddess of love and beauty, this Libran influence blesses people with a youthful appearance. It also gave her her indecisiveness when it came to leaving Richard Burton; after their first divorce, they remarried quite quickly only to divorce again. Richard, being a Scorpio, was very strong in her horoscope chart; she was very attracted to him because her Moon was in Scorpio at the time of her birth, indicating a strong powerful attraction.

Venus, the planet of love, is well placed in the house of marriage, giving her love in marriage, yet it is unfortunately conjunct with Uranus, planet of unexpected happenings and changes, within one degree of each other, creating many sudden changes, losses, and separations from loved ones.

Most of the activity in Elizabeth's chart focuses around show business as well as love affairs and speculation. In the house of theater, film, and television, she has the Sun and Mercury, the planet of speech and communication, exactly in the same degree of Pisces, which would account for her success through her distinct vocal quality and through the cinema in particular, which is ruled by the sign of Pisces. Mars is also close by, which may have created some of the upsets and frictions in romance as well as added some of the great energy and power needed to perform some of her many exacting roles. Pisces also have a tendency to hold onto body water, making it hard to lose excess weight in middle years.

Pluto, the planet of big business, is high in her chart in the area of career, fame, and government, which is what has attracted her to men of power, like Warner, as well as to other stars.

Jupiter helps her attain many of her life's personal desires, dreams, and wishes, protecting her from some deceptive associates and friends whose thoughts and ambitions may not be as pure and well defined as hers.

Interestingly, her Part of Fortune is located in Gemini in the ninth house, indicating that her fortune would be made in places far from birth, with international

business and travels. Born in England, she has spent most of her life away from her birthplace, even though she still holds a British passport.

Deeply religious, she converted to Judaism when she married Michael Todd and has been a great champion of Israel, a role that would give her much soul searching and anguish at times, but, true to her Pisces martyr nature, an "inspirational poet" to us all.

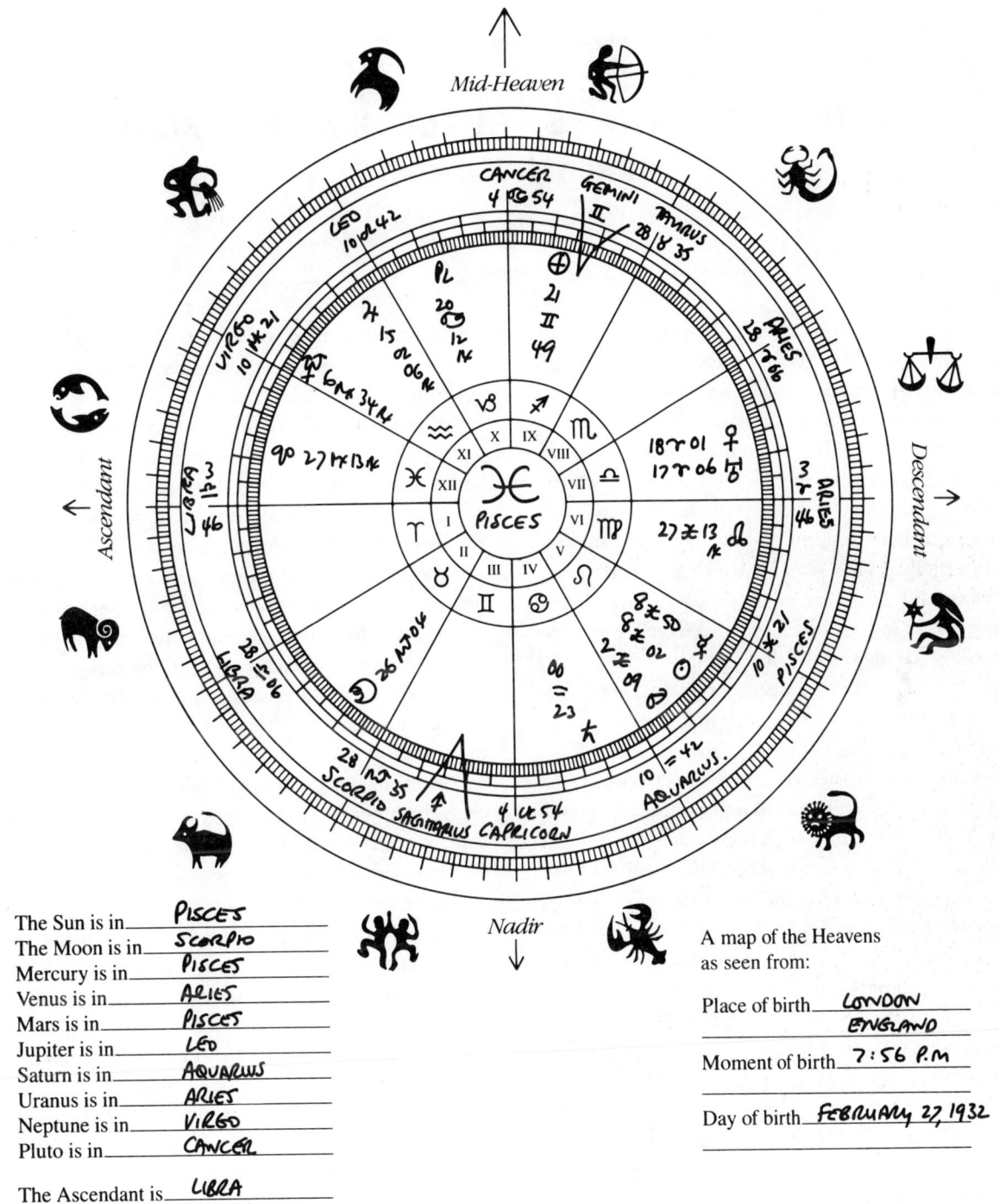

The Sun is in _PISCES_
The Moon is in _SCORPIO_
Mercury is in _PISCES_
Venus is in _ARIES_
Mars is in _PISCES_
Jupiter is in _LEO_
Saturn is in _AQUARIUS_
Uranus is in _ARIES_
Neptune is in _VIRGO_
Pluto is in _CANCER_

The Ascendant is _LIBRA_
The Part of Fortune is in _GEMINI_

A map of the Heavens as seen from:

Place of birth _LONDON ENGLAND_

Moment of birth _7:56 P.M_

Day of birth _FEBRUARY 27, 1932_

Home Entertainers

CANCER DECANATE, RULED BY THE MOON
March 1–March 10

There is much pleasure to be gained from just knowing these Pisces, for they are home entertainers at heart. Gracious, buoyant Lynn Redgrave, who rocketed to stardom as poignant homebody *Georgie Girl,* is one of these Pisces. The Neptunian influence attracts them to all that is pleasurable—eating, drinking, watching movies, painting, and other artistic pursuits—and the Cancerian lunar influence makes them want to do it around the home. They were the true home entertainers, long before the discovery of television and the stereo, for they could invent games and make their homes so welcoming that they could lift the spirits of all who entered and keep them amused for hours, until, exhausted, the guests would return home to bed.

Caterers who come to your home and take off all the pressures and worries; the maid who volunteers to help with the party on her usual night off; the neighbor whose wizardlike magic with lights and sounds can transfer a basement or living room into a disco—these Pisces all have this ability and talent to get people to entertain themselves at home. Many television technicians, producers, and directors have this combination, as they want to keep their audiences at home glued to the tube, watching the latest soap opera episode, the news, or a musical special. It's their job and they have failed if you turn off the set, put on your coat, and leave the house on an errand or for a chat with the neighbors.

They have the knack of inventing reasons for parties. No need for a birthday or an anniversary—they will think up a reason, a cause, and will come up with a memorable evening at home.

As children they were always having dolls' parties, inviting their friends in to share the miniature cakes and sip imaginary tea from the dolls' tea set. As teenagers, when their parents would leave them at home, they would invite all their friends, pick up some soft drinks and potato chips, and have an informal party.

The arts were more attractive to them than the rougher outdoor activities and sports, but they could become the local champions at indoor games like table tennis, cards, and Monopoly. And they could cheat, with an innocent look on their faces, for they would take great pleasure in cheating just for the fun of seeing if anyone noticed! Oil painting and chess make an excellent combination for these Pisces—one creative, the other strategic. They don't have to be commissioned to do the ceiling of the Sistine Chapel or enter the world chess championship to be happy. They could just as well paint a mural on the living room wall or play a game of chess with the delivery man.

Romantic and loving to a fault, they usually end up loving more than one person at a time (but usually their spouses know about that already). Strangely devoted to the home and family, they have a capacity for loving so many people that it usually ends up showing through a maternal or paternal gesture rather than a love affair, for they wish to preserve the status quo and just let their unrequited love be a dream for the future. Wanting to keep love in the home, they will pour their excess love and affection onto their children and their children's friends, creating just as much jealousy in their marriage partners as if a big romance were going on.

HARRY BELAFONTE

A "home entertainer" whose home is the world, Harry was a major force behind the making of the record "We are the World," which raised millions of dollars for African famine relief. Harry Belafonte has always been a leader, respected and followed for his great wisdom. He brought a higher consciousness of the civil rights movement into our homes and an awareness of the hungry to our dining tables.

Born in Harlem, New York, on March 1, 1927, at 10:30 A.M., he moved to Jamaica when he was eight. Returning to New York to study, he became hooked on show business when given two tickets to see the American Negro Theater. He discovered folk songs and became the calypso king.

He has his Sun, Mercury, Jupiter, and Uranus all in the sign of Pisces—sensitive, sentimental, and concerned about humanity. This combination of planets also gave him the good luck and talent that took him into the movies, including *The World, the Flesh, and the Devil*, which he produced himself. Committed to creating more opportunities for blacks, he joined with Sidney Poitier (Pisces, born February 20, 1924) and made the *Uptown Saturday Night* trilogy and *Buck and the Preacher*.

He says, "I felt that if we could just turn the nation around, things would actually fall into place. And it is actually happening."

GLENDA JACKSON

She loves her home, professes a love of gardening, and knows exactly what is meant by the saying, "You're closest to God in a garden." She enjoys cooking, reading, and, naturally, art and music. Most of her own entertainment is in the home, and through the magic of television she can bring her old movies and new television shows right into the front parlor.

Born on March 9, 1936, in Birkenhead, England, Glenda is a wonderfully romantic Pisces, with her Moon in the practical, earthy sign of Virgo.

Saturn, the planet of hard work and rewards, was also in Pisces in exactly the same position as her Sun, thus bringing her great success in her career. She won two Oscars for *Women in Love* and *A Touch of Class*

Her Mars in the aggressive sign of Aries may explain her very powerful on-camera image, usually playing forceful roles. On Broadway she used floor-length hair as a whip, as Charlotte Corday, in *Marat/Sade*.

She won an Emmy for her portrayal of Elizabeth I and another for her part as Yeléna Bonner in *Sakharov*. Both her Mercury and Venus are in Aquarius, bringing her more and more onto the television screen.

Very independent and discriminating, due to her Virgo Moon, Glenda says, "When the work isn't interesting, I won't do it."

LYNN REDGRAVE

Born: March 8, 1943, at 8:00 A.M. in London, England

Lynn and I were billed together for a special home furnishings promotion, at one of New York's top department stores, to attract lunch-hour shoppers. Several hundred people packed the ninth floor area. A makeshift stage had been built, with a wonderful zodiac design motif, from which I was to give the customers some heavenly advice from the celestial stars and then bring on more earthly "heavenly bodies." This particular day it was Lynn Redgrave, the star of *Saint Joan* on Broadway.

She arrived with her hair almost in a crew cut for the role, looking very slender and glamorous. We had met before at a mutual friend's home for a small dinner party, after which I had done her horoscope, so I was already familiar with her chart. Publicly I announced a few predictions that I knew would please her and afterward privately gave more personal news.

It wasn't long after that that I appeared on the TV game show "To Tell the Truth," and she was a panelist, so she had to disqualify herself from guessing the right person.

Lynn has become one of the most admired, loved, and compassionate actresses on television today on both sides of the Atlantic. A Pisces with her Moon in Aries and her Ascendant Pisces, this double helping of the "fishes" in her chart has given an extra emotional strength to her talents and a sensitive quality to her performances.

It may have been her height (she is now a slim five foot ten), or her late physical development, or the overshadowing fame of her late father, Sir Michael Redgrave (Pisces, born March 20, 1908), one of Britain's greatest actors, or her older sister, actress Vanessa Redgrave (Aquarius, born January 30, 1937), that encouraged Lynn's first ambitions of being an equestrienne or a cook.

But "father knows best," and her most respected father persuaded her to follow in the family tradition. Her first movie, *Georgie Girl*, was a hit, and Lynn and fellow Piscean actress Elizabeth Taylor shared the New York Critics best actress award in 1966—Lynn for *Georgie Girl*, and Liz for *Who's Afraid of Virginia Woolf*.

She has one brother, actor Corin Redgrave. The mother of all three is British actress Rachel Kempson. Though Lynn is unlike her brother and sister politically (she claims to be a confirmed capitalist), their father was once banned by the BBC in the early 1930s for his outspoken leftist views.

Lynn is a household name in Britain and in the United States. As well as appearing in many television shows and movies, she was the cohost of NBC's syndicated show, *Not For Women Only*, and hardly a day goes by that she doesn't give good eating advice in her commercials for Weight Watchers prepared meals.

Like all Pisces, love and marriage are very important for Lynn, and she married her former manager, producer, and director, John Clarke. They have three children, Benjamin, Kelly, and Annabel.

She recently starred on Broadway with Rex Harrison (Pisces, born March 5, 1908) and Claudette Colbert (Virgo, born September 18, 1905) in the play *Aren't We All*.

PISCES

Her Moon and Venus in Aries in her first house of personality have given her the verve and joy for living that she brings to her performances. Her moods are contagious and her wit is disarming.

Jupiter in her fourth house of home and family gave her the good fortune of being born into the Redgrave clan and later to create her own happy family with John and the children.

Lynn is a true "home entertainer," visiting her many fans through the magic of the media, whether in a drama, a game show, in one of her movie reruns, or as a spokeswoman for a special TV event. Wherever she goes on tour with a hit show, she is recognized and loved. The audiences line up to see her whether in California, Nebraska, or Iowa. They just want to reach out, touch her hand, and say "Hey, there, Georgie Girl."

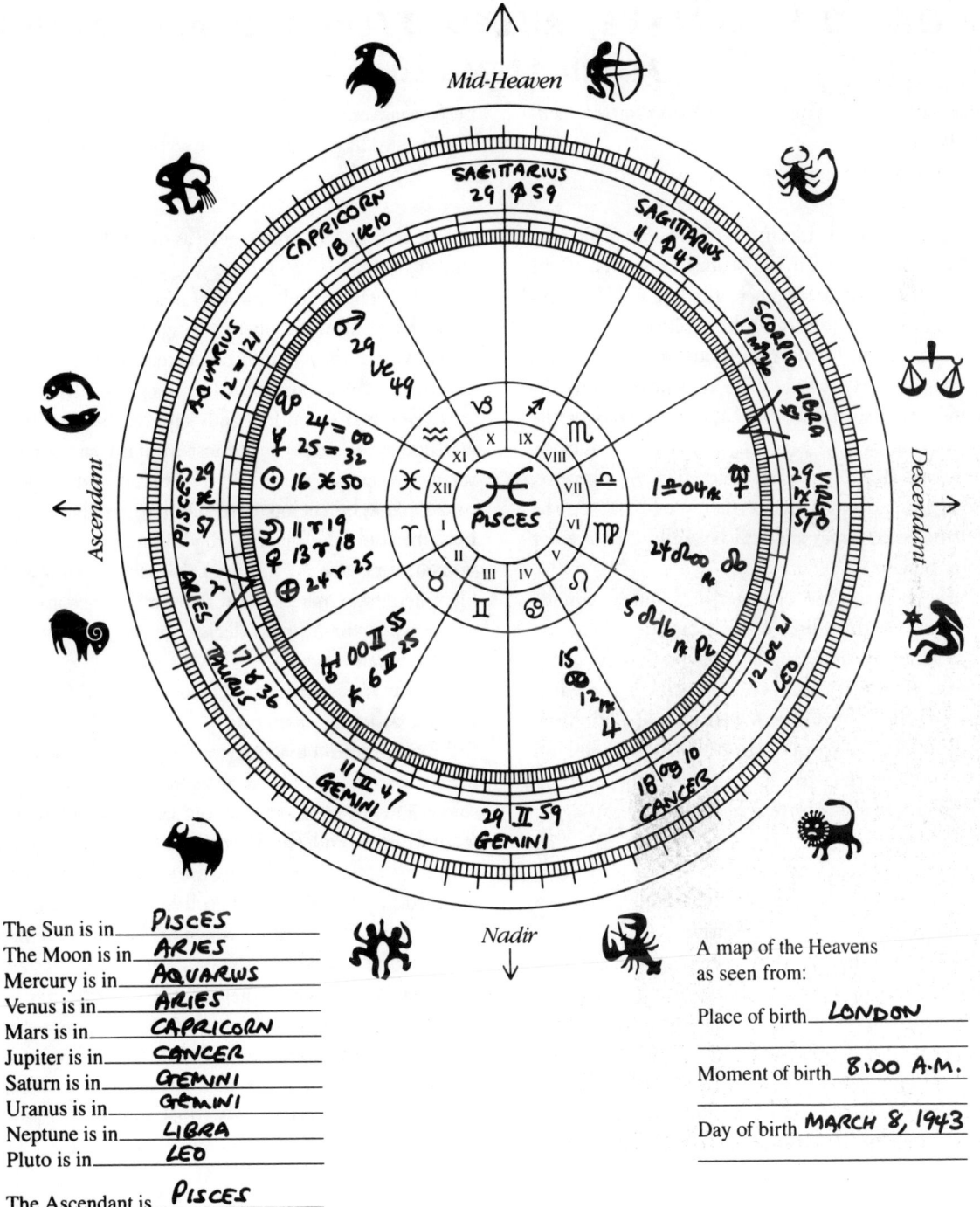

The Sun is in **PISCES**
The Moon is in **ARIES**
Mercury is in **AQUARIUS**
Venus is in **ARIES**
Mars is in **CAPRICORN**
Jupiter is in **CANCER**
Saturn is in **GEMINI**
Uranus is in **GEMINI**
Neptune is in **LIBRA**
Pluto is in **LEO**

The Ascendant is **PISCES**
The Part of Fortune is in **ARIES**

A map of the Heavens as seen from:

Place of birth **LONDON**

Moment of birth **8:00 A.M.**

Day of birth **MARCH 8, 1943**

Born-Again Mystics

SCORPIO DECANATE, RULED BY PLUTO AND MARS
March 11–March 20

Inspired, creative, idealistic, and highly spiritual, these Pisces have all the wonderful traits of the watery planet Neptune, together with the wild and exotic tendencies of Scorpio's ruling planet Pluto and coruler Mars. Gamin, feral, impetuous, tragicomic Liza Minnelli has enacted many of these tendencies. Pluto, the god of the underworld, joins Neptune, the god of the sea, and with the help of Mars, the god of war, has made an intense and devout human, who, like the phoenix, will rise again and again out of the ashes. They can be reborn a thousand times and still be willing to die for what they believe.

Whether a pinup girl or singer back home reminding soldiers in the front lines of their families and loved ones, a scientist or writer, bandleader who lifts the spirits of the senior citizens at the weekly social, a comedian who raises millions of dollars for handicapped children on television, or a stubborn religious fanatic standing on the corner in all weather passing out leaflets and warning people of their "sins"—all are at heart these "born-again mystics."

They are mystical in appearance; they seem to transcend this world. Even in school they stood out from other children, mainly by their sensitivity and interest in the arts rather than their schoolwork and sports and their seriousness in religious pursuits. Many of these children were groomed for the priesthood or life in a convent. Others kept their thoughts secret, especially from adults and older children. They feared for their security as well as their treasures. They could see well into the minds and attitudes of their peers and superiors and would always see the selfishness of man, even as small children growing up.

This childhood insight made them very self-protective, and this tendency to withdraw into a private world where they would be protected from the opportunists and rapists (mental as well as physical) made them invisible (as their ruling gods suggest, below the water and under the earth) or almost militant in their beliefs, trying to spread them all over the world—and often to people who, being quite content in their own beliefs, become the enemy, the villains, and the devil-worshippers. The purifying of their souls, while admirable when done in a peaceful fashion, can become frightening when these Pisces decide to wage a holy war or hold a witch hunt.

They are so creative that many spend a few years in the arts, acting or singing, painting or dancing. Others follow the natural tendency of Pisces and write beautiful poetry and prose. The more socially minded organize singles clubs, cruises, and other forms of adult entertainment or are wonderful hosts and hostesses at nightclubs, yet many give up their first desires to satisfy the Piscean martyrdom role and give their lives to religion, or to the needy and the suffering. When in hospital or medical work, these Pisces usually end up in the surgery or mortician's unit, where their highly spiritual and philosophical attitudes help them to handle patients, relatives, and other members of the staff with a soothing manner.

When it comes to romance they can be the most dramatic and overpowering or they can be the most cool and mysterious, but it is easy to see the two sides of these highly emotional and volatile characters. In love they worship, as in their faith, and in their sexual lives they follow the rituals working to the climax as in the religious ceremonies of old, offering and sacrificing their whole body and soul, and enjoying the frenzy and head-spinning emotion of it all.

GEORGE PLIMPTON

All his life George keeps being reborn; he has so many hats, titles, and talents that he uses a computer to keep track of all his knowledge and contacts.

He played quarterback for the Detroit Lions in the movie *Paper Lion,* pitched for the New York Yankees in *Out of My League,* played hockey with the Boston Bruins, flew on a trapeze, played percussion with the New York Philharmonic, writes books and articles, and is an accomplished professional photographer.

It isn't at all surprising to find that George, born in New York on March 18, 1927, at 2:00 A.M., is a Pisces with his Saturn in the sporty sign of Sagittarius, also the traveler and filmmaker.

Having his Pluto in the same degree of Cancer as the birthday of the United States (July 4, 1776), he is an all-American hero, if only of his own making. He was made Honorary Fireworks Commissioner for New York City when his book *Fireworks* came out in 1984.

Perhaps his main platform or pulpit, continues to be the *Paris Review,* which he publishes quarterly. We are all awaiting George's next big adventure to appear in print or on the big screen. We can experience the thrills and excitement, through the eyes of this born-again (and again and again) mystic, of whatever else he may want to be.

RUPERT MURDOCH

Today's mystics are the newspaper writers and the anchorpersons on the television news. What Rupert Murdoch has done is add a new excitement to the way newspapers are designed, printed, and published in order to recapture the millions of readers lost to the television, as evidenced by the demise of so many vital newspapers across the country. In this way Rupert has become a crusader and a savior.

Born March 11, 1931, in Melbourne, Australia, he is a Pisces with his Moon in the sign of the hunter and traveler, Sagittarius, and his impact has been felt in all parts of the world.

His papers and magazines range from the *Times* in London and *New York* magazine, to the more popular tabloids like the *New York Post,* and London's *News of the World* and *The Sun.*

Jupiter, the planet of good fortune, is in Cancer along with Mars, and though he has had luck and success in the United States, he has not been free of fights, battles, and heated negotiations with his writers, editors, and unions.

Mercury is also in Pisces, and he believes in everything he says and does 100 percent. His Sagittarian emotional Moon makes him outspoken, honest, blunt, and frank; there is no hiding his views—people know where they stand.

Now that he has finally taken over the Fox Television network, he will, by law, have to sell his New York and Chicago newspapers. He is now the "born-again mystic" of television, the Barnum of the media.

LIZA MINNELLI

Born: March 12, 1946, at 7:58 A.M. in Los Angeles, California

If anyone has the ability to bring back emotional memories from a generation when her mother enthralled and captured the hearts of the whole world, this bundle of Piscean love and joy can do it, and with such magic and charisma that we may think that Judy Garland is speaking and singing through Liza.

Yet Liza is independent, has her own style and pizzazz, and will become a legend in her own right. She has always been trendy, encouraging her groupies who follow and worship her, while she has worked desperately to develop a good relationship with her husbands, and lovers, as they were pursuing their independent careers. Finally, with her new husband Mark Gero, her producer, she has much more in common, and her national tours and foreign bookings don't keep them apart.

Liza visited me in London during her romance with Peter Sellers. On the BBC-TV "Nationwide News," I had predicted that she would not marry Peter, although all headlines predicted she would. Three days later the street doorbell rang. I answered it and there was Liza standing on the doorstep.

"Hi. I'm Liza."

I was suddenly speechless. All I could think of to say was, "Liza with a Z?" but stopped myself. I invited her in and while I made tea (always soothing), I could hardly speak. My heart was pounding. Here was my favorite star sitting in my living room! I pulled myself together and started the reading.

A Pisces with her Moon in Cancer and her Ascendant Taurus, Liza is exceptionally sensitive, emotional, and affectionate with lovers, friends, and business associates.

The Taurus Ascendant gave her her beautiful singing voice (Taurus rules the throat), while Pisces gave her the great dramatic talents that won her an Oscar for *Cabaret,* a Tony for *Flora, the Red Menace,* and an Emmy for her album, *Liza with a Z.*

I actually saw her in *Flora.* Mark Gero's father, Frank, was the production manager.

Liza is a great star with an incredible horoscope to support her many talents.

While Taurus gives her her musical and creative talents, her Venus and Mercury in Aries give her the power to belt out a song—wearing out her audiences as they watch one of her energetic and physical dance routines—and to meet a few of her most intimate friends after the show to dance till three at a local disco.

But at heart Liza, with her Sun in Pisces and the homeloving Moon in Cancer, wanted to settle down in marriage, with a family, but her career always stood in the way until now.

She also has Mars, the planet of energy, and Saturn, the planet of discipline, in Cancer, next to the Moon. This has given her the additional sensitivity to put over her emotions and to communicate with the audience in a unique way. It may also explain the early loss of her mother and the closeness to her father, director Vincent Minnelli, a Pisces like Liza, born February 28, 1903. She is the fulfillment of the Garland-Minnelli legacy.

These three planetary influences in the third house of travel and studies gave Liza a very erratic education. She attended over sixteen different schools on both sides

PISCES

of the Atlantic before she was in her mid-teens. Liza made her first public appearance at the age of seven at the Palace in New York City, where her mother was starring. Judy would call her onstage to dance.

With so many ups and downs and a feeling of insecurity, especially with Pluto, the planet of drastic changes, in her fourth house of home and family, Liza left home at sixteen. But she had learned how to handle herself and her talent in the world of show business by seeing the mistakes of her mother.

Like fellow Pisces Liz Taylor, who has also had many ups and downs emotionally and who has similar health problems, Liza will have to share her life with her fans and with the world. They will love with her, cry with her, and most of all understand her by empathizing with her. Her mystical quality attracts more and more audiences and perhaps frightens away the demons that pursued her. She has been "born again."

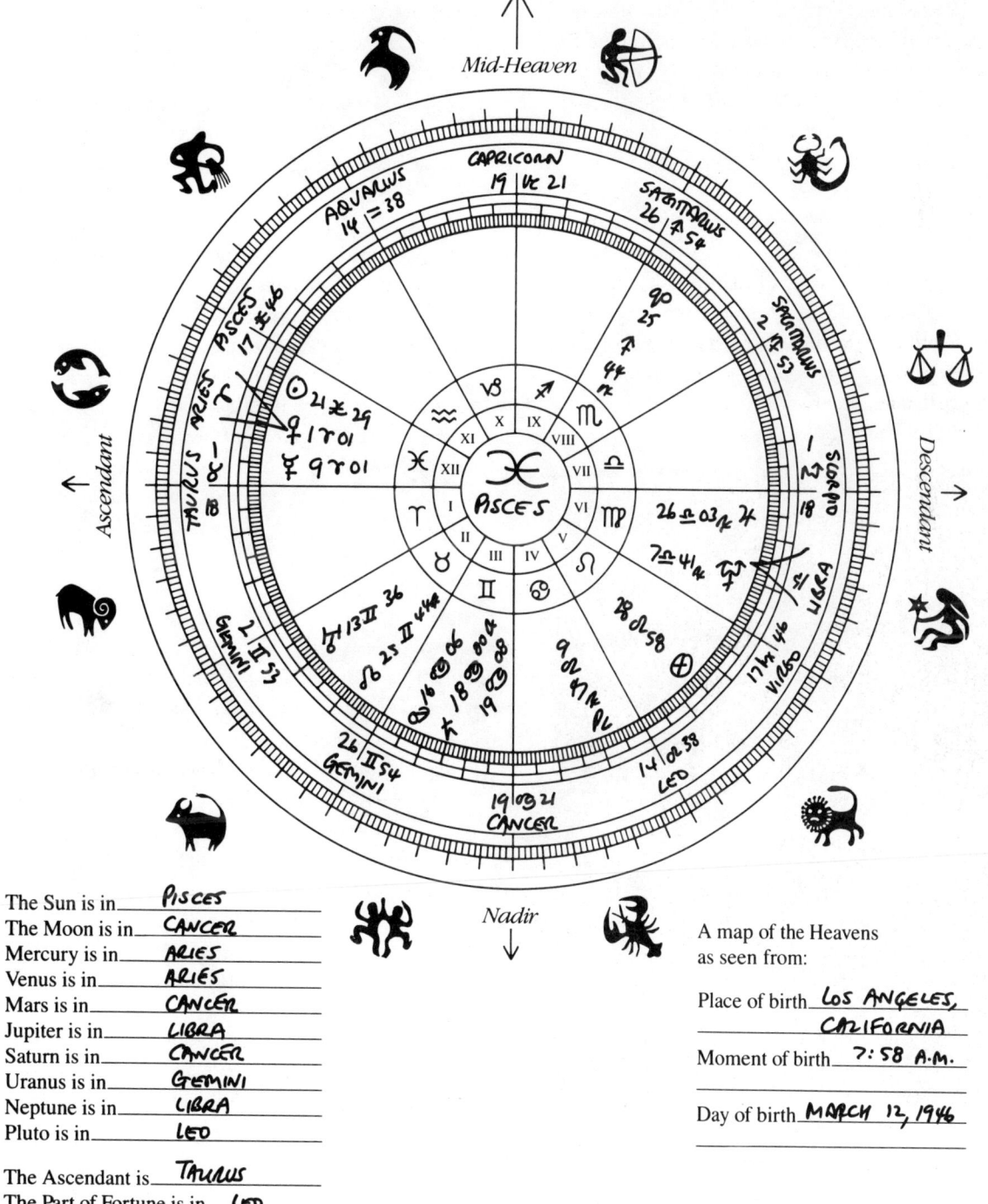

The Sun is in _PISCES_
The Moon is in _CANCER_
Mercury is in _ARIES_
Venus is in _ARIES_
Mars is in _CANCER_
Jupiter is in _LIBRA_
Saturn is in _CANCER_
Uranus is in _GEMINI_
Neptune is in _LIBRA_
Pluto is in _LEO_

The Ascendant is _TAURUS_
The Part of Fortune is in _LEO_

A map of the Heavens as seen from:

Place of birth _LOS ANGELES, CALIFORNIA_
Moment of birth _7:58 A.M._

Day of birth _MARCH 12, 1946_

Interpreting a Horoscope Chart

The familiar horoscope wheel of the zodiac is like another language, with each segment, planet, sign, and degree helping the astrologer or student interpret the "message" from the stars. Understanding the symbols of the zodiac is the key to decoding the message and gleaning the knowledge and wisdom that it imparts.

To quote from the New English Bible (Gen. 1:14), "God said, 'Let there be lights in the vault of heaven to separate day from night, and let them serve as signs both for festivals and for seasons and years.'"

THE HOROSCOPE WHEEL

The horoscope chart or wheel is very easy to understand. It is a map of the heavens as seen from an individual's place of birth at the exact moment (hour, minute, second) of the date of their birth (month, day, year).

The wheel turns in a clockwise direction as the Sun rises in the sky. The left-hand side of the chart, known as the Ascendant, represents the eastern horizon, where the Sun would be seen at approximately 6:00 A.M. every day (depending on sunrise and the latitude of the birthplace). The top of the chart, called the Midheaven, is where the Sun would be at noon, and is the southern position of the chart. The right side opposite the Ascendant is called the Descendant. It is where the Sun sinks in the west at approximately 6:00 P.M. (it varies at different times of the year and according to the latitude of the birthplace). The northern position at the bottom of the chart, called the Nadir, is where the Sun would have traveled at approximately midnight.

If a person was born at 2:00 A.M. the Sun would be rising from the Nadir (midnight) toward the Ascendant (6:00 A.M.). If a person was born at 8:15 A.M. then the Sun would be somewhere between the Ascendant (6:00 A.M.) and the Midheaven (noon). If a person is born at 4 P.M. then the Sun would be between the Midheaven (noon) and the Descendant (6:00 P.M.).

HOUSES

There are twelve segments (called houses) in each day, and it takes the Sun approximately 2 hours to travel across a house before moving into the next. Therefore the Ascendant changes signs every two hours.

It is important to know the time of birth in order to determine where the Sun was located, and from that information, to calculate the position of all the other planets and the degrees and signs of the various astrological positions, such as the Ascendant, Midheaven, and the spokes of the wheel (which are called angles).

The twelve houses are numbered counterclockwise starting at the Ascendant, which would be the first house. Each house represents a different part of an individual's life.

First House. This represents the individual's personality, appearance, disposition, public image, attitudes, and environment.

Second House. This shows financial prospects, possessions, and ways that the individual will make money.

Third House. This is the house of communication, the way the individual travels, talks, writes, and studies. It is also concerned with their close relatives and neighbors.

Fourth House. This represents the home, family, parents, and place of birth, and shows opportunities for real estate and property matters.

Fifth House. This house is concerned with love affairs and romances, children, recreation and resorts, show-business activities, television, movies, performing arts, and also gambling.

Sixth House. This is the house of service and work. It represents an individual's livelihood, service to others, and business ventures. The health areas that may need checking, plus employees that may be hired are also included.

Seventh House. This is the house of partnerships, marriage (romantic or business), contracts and documents, and in some cases rivals.

Eighth House. This is a money house that encompasses income from work, inheritances, legacies and gifts, other people's money as investments or loans, and antiques and valuable items belonging to the dead.

Ninth House. This is the house of higher education, religious, spiritual and metaphysical pursuits, long journeys, travel and business abroad, foreign affairs, universities, institutes, legal and publishing matters, and places far from birthplace.

Tenth House. This is concerned with the individual's goals, ambitions, careers, fame, honors, achievement, and connections with the government.

Eleventh House. This house is concerned with the individual's true desires in life, their hopes, wishes, and dreams, their friendships and influential acquaintances, and their social life and clubs.

Twelfth House. This house shows the obstacles, difficulties, and lessons the individual may have to overcome. It indicates the enemies, and warns of self undoing, solitude, seclusion, but shows the benefits of working and producing behind the scenes.

THE PLANETS

There are 10 heavenly bodies: the Sun, Moon and eight planets (Mercury, Venus, Mars, Jupiter, Saturn, Uranus, Neptune, and Pluto). Each travels at a different speed through the zodiac. The Moon travels once through the zodiac every 28½ days; the Sun once every 365 days; Mercury and Venus, once every year; Mars once, every 2 years; Jupiter, once every 12 years; Saturn, once every 29½ years; Uranus, once every 84 years; Neptune, once every 165 years; and Pluto, once every 248 years.

While these are approximate travel periods, you can see that there is little chance of any two people having the same horoscope chart. It is unlikely for two people to be born at the exact moment in the same place on the same day. There will be many similarities among individuals' horoscopes and their lives but no two charts are exactly alike. Every horoscope chart is unique.

CHARACTERISTICS ASSOCIATED WITH EACH PLANET

Sun is the person's own individuality, their real personality, the person they are deep down—the "true" self.

Moon defines one's emotional personality, sensitivity, and instincts, and plays a great part in the choice of partners in love and marriage.

Mercury (Messenger of the Gods) is the planet of communication, speech, writing, thinking, studying, and traveling.

Venus (Goddess of Love and Beauty) is the planet of good luck, beauty, love, the arts, fashion, music, and money.

Mars (God of War) is the planet of action, energy, enthusiasm, and drive, as well as friction, anxiety, and war.

Jupiter (God of Greater Good Fortune) is the planet of wealth, good fortune, expansion, success, and philosophy.

Saturn (God of Time) is the planet of discipline, work, limitations, restrictions, and consequences (good and bad), and can be the husband or the father.

Uranus (God of the Universe) is the planet of new inventions, space-age discoveries, electronics, television, video, computers, talents, and sudden changes and events.

Neptune (God of the Sea) is the planet of

creativity, intuition, clairvoyance, mystery, illusion, art, photography, movies, the visual arts, and activities connected with liquids, water, and the sea.

Pluto (God of the Underworld) is the planet of big business, the masses, gangs, radicals, and large ventures.

OTHER ASTROLOGICAL POSITIONS

The Ascendant is the Zodiac sign that is ascending, or rising, over the horizon at the exact moment of birth. This illuminates another dimension of the personality. It defines the environment in which the individual should excel, has a strong influence on the individual's physical appearance, and offers clues about their health. It represents the personality and the image that they show to the public.

The North Node shows the karmic rewards to be gained in this life.

The South Node shows the karmic lessons to be learned in this life.

The Midheaven is the highest point of the horoscope chart and describes the type of goals, ambitions, and career that would have the greatest success.

In analyzing the planetary location in a chart, one would look at three important ingredients: planet, sign, and house. For example, *Venus in Pisces in the ninth house,* could be interpreted as "the lover (Venus) would be a Pisces (or have strong Piscean characteristics) in places far from birth (ninth house)." Likewise, *Venus in Virgo in the seventh house* may mean that the individual's "love nature (Venus) looks for perfection (Virgo) when considering marriage (seventh house)."

The location of the house is important in determining what area of life is being influenced by that planet. The signs help to describe the effect or situation. For example, the location of Jupiter in the second house would have a totally different meaning from Jupiter located in the seventh or tenth house.

SIGNS

We are all familiar with our own sign of the zodiac, which is determined by date of birth. But all the planets travel through the twelve signs of the zodiac, and depending on the time and day of birth, everyone will have a different configuration of planetary signs. One may have Mars in Scorpio, another may have Mars in Aries.

The twelve signs and their respective dates are listed below, however, each year there are slight variations in the first and last dates, that is, when the Sun moves from one sign into the next. By referring to an ephemeris (a book of tables listing the exact scientific position of the Sun, Moon, and all the planets for every day of every year), the astrologer can chart this movement.

Each sign is also ruled by one of the planets, which gives the sign its nature and determines personality. The characteristics attributed to each sign and planet are explained later in this section.

Another important consideration is the planet's location in a sign: Venus in Taurus, or Venus in Aquarius, for example.

Aries (The Ram) born March 21–April 19, ruled by Mars.
Taurus (The Bull) born April 20–May 21, ruled by Venus.
Gemini (The Twins) born May 22–June 21, ruled by Mercury.
Cancer (The Crab) born June 22–July 22, ruled by the Moon.
Leo (The Lion) born July 23–August 22, ruled by the Sun.
Virgo (The Virgin) born August 23–September 22, ruled by Mercury.
Libra (The Scales) born September 23–October 22, ruled by Venus.
Scorpio (The Scorpion) born October 23–November 22, ruled by Pluto.
Sagittarius (The Archer) born November 23–December 22, ruled by Jupiter.
Capricorn (The Mountain Goat) born December 23–January 19, ruled by Saturn.
Aquarius (The Water-bearer) born January 20–February 18, ruled by Uranus.
Pisces (The Fishes) born February 19–March 20, ruled by Neptune.

An individual may be born with one or more planets in a sign. An individual may have one planet in Aries, two in Taurus, three in Leo, two in Sagittarius, and one in Pisces. This person would be a mixture of all these planetary positions taking into careful consideration the nature and the personality of the planet and sign.

BASIC CHARACTERISTICS OF THE ZODIAC SIGNS

Aries: Agressive, optimistic, confident, egotistical, impatient, impulsive, pioneering, leader, temperamental.

Taurus: Determined, stubborn, thrifty, possessive, industrious, affectionate, artistic, financial-minded, loyal, devoted.

Gemini: Talkative, witty, changeable, worrisome, versatile, open-minded, superficial, impatient, jack-of-all-trades.

Cancer: Moody, sensitive, emotional, protective, sympathetic, self-indulgent, unselfish, maternal, reclusive, home-loving.

Leo: Flamboyant, pretentious, philanthropic, vain, domineering, magnanimous, dignified, snobbish, leader, dynamic.

Virgo: Practical, hard-working, critical, worrisome, inquisitive, dependable, sanitary, precise, literary.

Libra: Indecisive, charming, diplomatic, tactful, extravagant, impartial, creative, musical, just, fashionable, artistic.

Scorpio: Secretive, suspicious, jealous, sexual, rebellious, determined, supportive, inspiring, romantic, magnetic.

Sagittarius: Idealistic, outspoken, devout, humorous, athletic, spendthrift, gambler, generous, impractical, visionary.

Capricorn: Hardworking, honorable, trustworthy, unsympathetic, conservative, materialistic, sensitive, efficient.

Aquarius: Humane, generous, friendly, eccentric, impetuous, inventive, freedom-loving, unconventional, trendy.

Pisces: Inspirational, sensitive, visionary, mystical, helpful, healer, self-sacrificing, creative, compassionate, writer.

Frequently, a person has only their Sun sign in their zodiac sign, and all the other planets are located in other signs of the zodiac. This does not minimize the importance of their Sun sign, but the particular traits and characteristics associated with that sign may be hidden by the traits of the sign or signs in which the other planets or located.

INTERPRETING BROOKE SHIELDS'S HOROSCOPE CHART

Brooke was born at 1:45 P.M., just after noon. The Sun had passed across the Midheaven and was beginning to sink in the West (Descendant), and was located in her ninth house. The following is an Analysis of the planetary positions at the time of Brooke's birth.

The Sun was in Gemini in the ninth house. Brooke (Sun) was destined to excel in the communication field (Gemini) internationally and at the university (ninth house).

The Moon was in Gemini in the ninth house. Her sensitivity and emotions (Moon) are expressed through her speaking, acting, and writing (Gemini), and in publishing, traveling, and doing things internationally (ninth house).

Her Mercury was in Taurus in the ninth house. Once she has set her mind (Mercury) on something, she will loyaly and devotedly stick to it (Taurus), especially where spiritual, legal, and educational matters are concerned (ninth house).

Her Venus was in Gemini in the tenth house. Her good luck and beauty (Venus), through the communication fields, television, acting and speaking (Gemini), will attract great success, honors, and fame (tenth house).

Her Mars was in Virgo in the twelfth house. There will be lots of action and energy (Mars) connected with her work (Virgo), including rehearsing, studying, and producing behind the scenes (twelfth house).

Her Jupiter was in Gemini in the ninth house. Brooke will have a lot of good fortune and wealth (Jupiter) in connection with traveling, speaking, and writing (Gemini), either at the university or in connection with long distance business.

Her Saturn was in Pisces in the sixth house. She will work hard, have much self-discipline, and receive many rewards (Saturn) through helping others, as well as through the motion picture industry (Pisces), fashionable clothing advertisements, and health spa commercials (sixth house).

INTERPRETING A HOROSCOPE CHART

Her Uranus was in Virgo in the twelfth house. Using her talents on television (Uranus) she will help others and work hard (Virgo), rehearsing and producing behind the scenes (twelfth house).

Her Neptune was in Scorpio in the second house. Making movies, being photographed, and other creative enterprises (Neptune) focus on her sensuality (Scorpio) and make money for her (second house).

Her Pluto was in Virgo in the twelfth house. She has the ability to be involved with many large business ventures (Pluto) in connection with work, clothing, and health (Virgo), filming or televising behind the scenes (twelfth house).

Her Ascendant was in Virgo. Her public image (Ascendant) has been made to represent purity, with a sensual virginal quality (Virgo).

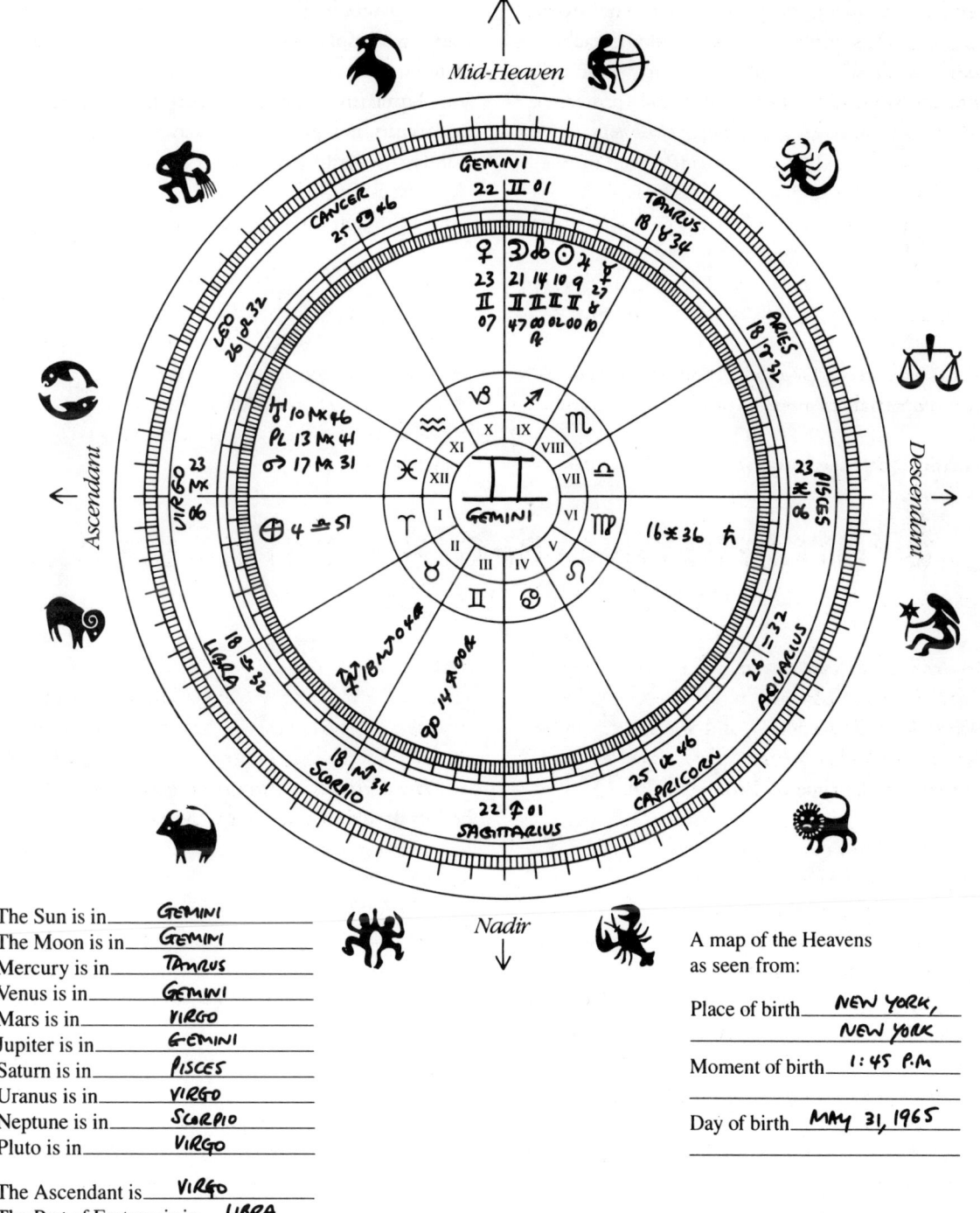

The Sun is in _GEMINI_
The Moon is in _GEMINI_
Mercury is in _TAURUS_
Venus is in _GEMINI_
Mars is in _VIRGO_
Jupiter is in _GEMINI_
Saturn is in _PISCES_
Uranus is in _VIRGO_
Neptune is in _SCORPIO_
Pluto is in _VIRGO_

The Ascendant is _VIRGO_
The Part of Fortune is in _LIBRA_

A map of the Heavens as seen from:

Place of birth _NEW YORK, NEW YORK_

Moment of birth _1:45 P.M_

Day of birth _MAY 31, 1965_

Her Midheaven was in Gemini. Her ambitions and goals (Midheaven) will achieve greatest success if connected with the field of communication, especially writing and speaking.

Her North Node was in Gemini in the ninth house. Big rewards in this life (North Node) will come through study and communications (Gemini), especially with university life and her motion picture career (ninth house).

Her South Node was in Sagittarius in the third house. Her lessons in life (South Node) come from her desire for freedom, her early travels, and her movie making (Sagittarius) while studying during her early education (third house).

Her Part of Fortune was in Libra in the first house. Her great success, wealth, and good fortune (Part of Fortune) will be due to her good looks, beauty, youth, and charm (Libra) which is a natural part of her personality (first house).

It was easy to see why Brooke with four planets (as well as her North Node) in the ninth house was to have "success at a young age," as those planets would gradually move over her Midheaven into the tenth house of fame and success. "International fame" was also indicated by so much astrological activity in the ninth house, which also influenced her to go to college, and gave her several legal battles to fight as well. Together with her Part of Fortune being in her first house of appearance and personality, she was blessed with the looks that would make her fortune.